Judeochristianity: The Meaning and Discovery of Faith

Judeochristianity

The Meaning and Discovery of Faith

"For my house shall be called a house of prayer for all peoples"
(Isaiah 56:7).

Charles "Carlos" Gourgey

Parson's Porch Books   Cleveland, Tennessee

Parson's Porch Books
121 Holly Trail Road, NW
Cleveland, Tennessee 37311

Judeochristianity: The Meaning and Discovery of Faith
© 2011 by Charles "Carlos" Gourgey. All rights reserved.
Published 2011.
Printed in the United States of America.
ISBN 978-1-936912-18-6

No part of this book may be reproduced or transmitted in any form or by any means, electronic or mechanical, including photocopying, recording, or by information storage and retrieval system, without permission in writing from the publisher.

To order additional copies of this book, contact:

Parson's Porch Books
1-423-475-7308
www.parsonsporchbooks.com

For Karen,

*My wife and soul mate
And companion throughout this journey*

CONTENTS

PREFACE	ix
INTRODUCTION	xv
PRINCIPLES OF JUDEOCHRISTIANITY	xxv

PART I — THE PATH

CHAPTER I: DOES GOD EXIST?	3
CHAPTER II: WHO WAS JESUS?	13
CHAPTER III: OUR TWO NATURES	23
CHAPTER IV: ETERNAL LIFE	41
CHAPTER V: LOVE AND AWARENESS	63
CHAPTER VI: COMPASSIONATE SEEING	87
CHAPTER VII: SELF-ESTEEM	95
CHAPTER VIII: PRAYER	103
CHAPTER IX: THOUGHTS ABOUT AN AFTERLIFE	121

PART 2 — OBSTACLES ON THE PATH

CHAPTER X: SELF-HATRED	137
CHAPTER XI: OVERCOMING ANGER	155
CHAPTER XII: A SPIRITUAL RESPONSE TO FEAR	167
CHAPTER XIII: THE TRANSCENDENCE OF GRIEF	177
CHAPTER XIV: THE PROBLEM OF SUFFERING	195
CHAPTER XV: FACING THE FEAR OF DEATH	253

PART 3 — APPROACHING THE DESTINATION

CHAPTER XVI: SELF-ACCEPTANCE	267
CHAPTER XVII: THE MESSAGE OF THE CROSS	285
CHAPTER XVIII: FAITH	311
CHAPTER XIX: A NEW CREATION	337
CHAPTER XX: A HINT OF A GREATER LOVE	351
CHAPTER XXI: THE HOPE OF RESURRECTION	357
ABOUT THE AUTHOR	375

PREFACE

This book is about faith, what it is and how we find it.

"*La fe es número uno*": "Faith is Number One." This is what one of my hospice patients told me when I asked her how she is able to maintain her confidence in spite of having to face illness and death.

For over two decades I have had the privilege of working at Cabrini Hospice in New York City and at similar hospice and nursing home settings using my skills as a musician and music therapist. What has impressed me most of all is how faith, for those blessed to have it, helps people meet just about any tragedy with confidence and a strong spirit. Of course even the spiritually strongest have their fearful moments, but are not defeated by them. Faith is the dominant force in their lives.

I believe we were all meant to have faith, though for many of us acquiring it is difficult. For some of us it may take a lifetime. But there is much we can learn along the way. I have certainly learned a great deal from my patients who have had this faith, and I continue to learn from their example.

This book is not a scholarly exposition of the history or writings of either Judaism or Christianity. The relationship between the two as it has evolved over the centuries is complex and could be the subject of an extensive separate study. Rather this book asks the question: "If we consider looking at Jewish and Christian tradition as a continuous whole linked through the prophetic proclamation of the Covenant, rather than as two sets of competing beliefs and practices, what kind of approach to faith would evolve?" In this book I explore what faith is, what it means to find it, and the obstacles we struggle with along the way. I have discovered that the most effective and genuine faith is not what we often tend to think. Often we confuse faith with belief. This is not the Bible's understanding of faith, and it should not be ours. Faith is much more than belief. It is a complete inner transformation opening the heart to goodness. I believe this is what the Bible means by faith, and also that this understanding of faith is the most spiritually healing for us.

This inquiry into faith is set against the background of the connection between Judaism and Christianity. So often religion has become a force dividing people. That was never the intention of the founders of these great traditions. From the Prophets to Paul we find a vision of walls between people breaking down, of people uniting under faith in a universal God.

Jesus crystallized this message in a unique way. He took the relationship with God that his own people had discovered, combined it with the Hebrew Bible's injunction to love the stranger, and found a faith that includes all people without distinction under God's love and promise. This too is an important theme in this book.

It is my hope that this book will help bring people together in a faith that is both comforting and challenging, as we search for the strength that only faith can give.

Thanksgiving 2008

ACKNOWLEDGMENTS

I would like to mention a number of people who deserve my deep gratitude:

My late father, who possessed the kindest heart I have ever known.

My mother, who has been a steadfast and always reliable friend.

My sister Annette, who has always supported me and helped me with her willingness to challenge me when she thinks differently.

My wife Karen, of whom I can never say enough—more than a companion, a loyal soul mate and the greatest blessing in my life. Karen "gets it" about Judeochristianity. If you want to see its values in action, just witness the respect and love with which students with disabilities are treated in her computer center.

The late Julie Swanson, my Christian/American Indian (her preferred designation) spiritual director, who predicted that my destiny would be to build a bridge between Christianity and Judaism. (You will meet this remarkable woman in chapter 14.)

Dr. John Killinger, who gave me great encouragement by believing in this project.

Dr. Eric Killinger, my editor, who also provided needed support as well as a keen aesthetic sense for the visual presentation of the text.

And finally all the patients with whom I have worked, who taught me things about love I could have learned from nobody else: My hospice patients, many of whom still provide an example to which I aspire by the deep faith they discovered while facing death. And now the nursing home residents whose rights I work to defend, who possess hardly anything of status or material value but who touch my heart with their honesty and lack of pretense. More than anyone else they teach me the true meaning of the respect that our Prophets, from Isaiah to Jesus, had for the worth and dignity of those whom our society holds of little account. Never in all our history has there been a more urgent need in this country to learn what this means, now that the "financial crisis" has so greatly widened the chasm between the rich and the poor. What Isaiah and Jesus both taught—that all the trappings of religion mean nothing, and indeed are blasphemous if we fail to care for "the least of these"—applies as much to us now, and perhaps even more, than it did to the people of their own time.

INTRODUCTION

Judeochristianity: The Bridge Between Judaism and Christianity

When the planes struck the Twin Towers on September 11, 2001, we entered a new period of history. Many Americans were forced to face the ramifications of conflicts originating thousands of miles from home. We could not afford to remain ignorant of history, of geography, of problems in places some of us could hardly even pronounce. And most especially, many of us became aware of the role religion plays in these conflicts, often fueling and intensifying them.

More of us started reading books and taking courses in Islam. I took those courses and I read the Qur'an. And I was struck by something that startled me.

In the Qur'an I found a heavy emphasis on belief—so strong that God even condemns nonbelievers to hell. What most impressed me was the similarity to what many religious fundamentalists believe in my own country. So many people think God judges us—absolutely and everlastingly—based on what we believe. But the question is, which God? Do I follow the God who condemns me if I'm not a Muslim, or do I follow the God who condemns me if I'm not a Christian? And are the two really very different?

If religion, which is supposed to express and guide our deepest spiritual aspirations, leads to such intolerance, then it's gone off the track. The loving God we profess is not consistent with a God who permanently cuts off so many people with no hope of forgiveness or redemption, including sincere and kindhearted people who have simply failed to discover the right thing to believe. We need to reexamine our religious traditions to find the truly compassionate God underneath all the obscuring doctrines and theologies. For us in the West this means reexamining the roots of both Jewish and Christian tradition and how they are connected.

On 9/11/01 America was attacked by an uncompromisingly intolerant religious ideology. How we should respond to that is beyond our present scope. Our concern here is what we need to do to make sure our own house is clean. Now that we ourselves have experienced the destruction to which religious intolerance can lead, we need to make sure that our own religion is free of such prejudice. When joined together, Judaism and Christianity give us the message of a God who is truly universal, good, and loving, who holds us to ethical standards and also gives us faith to meet life's challenges.

Religious hatred has become an increasingly divisive force in the world. We can make our own society stronger by building our resistance to it. We need to look at our values, uprooting any vestiges of intolerance that would make us in any way similar to anyone who would use religion to divide people or to set one group over another. We can do this, because in spite of our own very often brutal and intolerant religious history, the roots of Western religion grow from the soil of tolerance, justice, and love.

To be sure, these core values were not present from the beginning. The Bible is an honest record of human conflict, including religious conflict. It took a long time for truly God-centered values to evolve. When we look beyond the history, we find the Hebrew Bible (commonly known as the "Old Testament") teaching love of the stranger, and its prophetic tradition reaching toward a vision of universalism. In the New Testament we find Jesus teaching that God's love extends to everyone, regardless of religion or ethnic group, and that we are called to reach beyond our own borders to embrace those who are different.

We have drifted far from these roots. Our spiritual traditions have become fragmented. Our religions have many denominations and speak with many voices. This diversity can be a strength. Nevertheless the truths of our great religious traditions, specifically Jewish and Christian tradition, need to be reconnected in order to present the full power of the vision that inspired them.

America has been called a "Judeo-Christian" society. What exactly does this mean? Simply that we have both Jews and Christians here (not to mention members of other religious groups)? Then why the hyphenation? There is some common bond between Judaism and Christianity, between Jews and Christians, that today we can identify more clearly than in any previous historical period. There is something common to both Jewish and Christian tradition that has the potential to create an affinity in spite of our differences, and that underlies the values upon which this country was established.

We do have separation between church and state, which has helped prevent religious excesses, preserve religious tolerance, and keep our society strong. That must never change. But I still wonder: what if we took the "Judeo-Christian" aspect of our cultural history more seriously? What hidden connections might we discover? What kind of spirituality might evolve?

Let's make this more specific. First of all, Jesus was a Jew and must be understood within his original Jewish context. He had no intention of founding a new religion. In fact, much of what he taught falls squarely in the tradition of the Hebrew prophets, and especially the prophet Isaiah, his spiritual mentor. The following themes are central in both:

- The reaffirmation of the divine Covenant, the relationship between God and the people of God.
- The call for the restoration of justice and for attention to the needs of the weakest in society.
- The demand that religious leaders lead with integrity.
- The condemnation of empty rituals, religious ceremonies performed just for show with no effect on the conduct of ordinary life.
- Confidence in the redeeming power of God.

Without an Isaiah, there would not have been a Jesus.

Of course this is not all Jesus taught, and we'll consider other implications of his teachings in future chapters. If Jesus had only repeated what came before him, his own prophetic vocation would not have been necessary. However, so much of what he taught is in direct line with the teachings of the prophets who preceded him that it may prompt one to wonder:

What might have happened had Jesus been accepted as a Jewish prophet?

This is not the same as asking, What if Jews had accepted Jesus as Christians do? I am not presenting a choice between Judaism and Christianity, but asking how we might understand the Bible if we could see Jesus as continuing and perhaps even completing the tradition of Hebrew prophecy. Can we see Jesus transforming his own religion rather than establishing a new one? The question poses a challenge both to Judaism and to Christianity.

It also suggests an idea that might seem strange: the possibility of seeing the entire Bible (what is commonly called the "Old Testament" or "Hebrew Bible" together with the "New Testament") as a continuous whole. This would differ from the traditional Jewish view, which accepts only the Hebrew Bible, and also the Christian view, which sees the "Old Testament" as basically an introduction to the "New," which supersedes it. This biblical continuity is really an extension of the idea that Jesus's prophecy can be seen as continuous with Isaiah's. There may be deeper reasons why the two "Testaments" are commonly juxtaposed than are apparent at first glance. Prophetic continuity—the link between Isaiah and Jesus—exemplifies biblical continuity—the spiritual link between the two "Testaments" themselves.

"Continuity" does not imply repetition. Jesus's teachings are continuous with Hebrew prophecy, but they also carry it further. Here are some of Jesus's key teachings that bring this tradition forward:

- The Covenant is reaffirmed and extended to all people, Jew and non-Jew alike.
- The law is reaffirmed and is most deeply fulfilled through

an inner transformation leading to the capacity for genuine love.
- The love that fulfills the requirements of the law is not the love most familiar to us but "non-self-interested" love, which calls upon us to transcend ourselves.
- This particular love (which does not negate other forms of love) therefore applies equally to friend and to stranger, to those inside and outside one's family, one's religion, or one's ethnic group.

"Non-self-interested" love actually has its roots in the Hebrew Scriptures, but Jesus called explicit attention to it and made it the center of his teaching. It is the path toward covenantal partnership with God. Those who seek to realize it, from whatever group they may come, will know they are included in the Covenant and will "inherit the Kingdom of God."

This requires some explanation. It is difficult to grasp Jesus's message fully without understanding the structure of the Bible itself.

And here a difficulty arises. Bible scholarship has radically changed the way we view sacred texts. While fundamentalists stick to what they believe is a strictly literal interpretation of the Bible, many others, just as deeply religious, do not. We are more conscious now that words, concepts, customs, and events had different meanings at different times, and that the historical setting plays a large role in understanding the intention of a particular text.

The problem is that Bible scholars often disagree. Even the most modern scholarship often cannot tell us with certainty what the text "really" means. Struggling with questions like "Which events narrated in the Bible actually took place?" or "Which sayings attributed to Jesus actually go back to him?" has its place in our efforts to discern the meaning of the biblical text. But it is fraught with controversy, since any significant position taken by one biblical scholar may be contradicted by the position of another. Bible scholarship therefore cannot be a path to certain knowledge, nor can it be a path to faith.

Nevertheless, we cannot afford to ignore what Bible scholars have to say. Bible scholars provide indispensable information about the historical and cultural context of these sacred writings. They give us guidelines for judging the plausibility of our interpretations, and their work helps protect us from substituting our own inventions for the actual intent of scripture.

We therefore need to live with the tension between accepting the Bible as it was given to us and tempering our own understanding with the insights of biblical scholars. I have found it helpful to accept the Bible just as we have it, as an organic whole. However, this does not make me a literalist. For while the Bible may not be one hundred percent historically true, it is nevertheless symbolically true. The Bible endures because it expresses profound truths in symbolic form.

One of the Bible's most powerful symbols is the history it records, which has significance far beyond any reference to actual events. The Bible is an inspired work that took shape over many years in the collectivity of the spiritually receptive human consciousness. The pieces of biblical history—the loves, the hates, the wars, the politics—are human experiences akin to our own, but the way the Bible puts them together points toward higher truths. A wisdom beyond any individual human being guided its formation. It is therefore not by chance that certain books are included in the Bible and others are not. Virtually every part of the Bible contributes, in some small or large way, to its meaning as a whole. This is true even though the Bible comprises works by different authors who could not have known each other, since they were separated by large spans of time and space.

The teachings of Jesus do not represent a break with Hebrew prophetic tradition; they carry it to its logical conclusion. Seeing the prophetic tradition this way transforms our understanding of faith. Often faith is identified with belief: belief in the occurrence of "miracles," belief in the "historicity" of certain events, belief in doctrines such as the divinity of Jesus or the virgin birth. For many these beliefs are sacred and must be treated with respect.

But as the Bible itself amply demonstrates, faith is much more than belief. There is a vast difference between the mind's assent to a given proposition, which we usually mean by "belief," and the deep inner transformation that is the essence of biblical faith. If faith is equated with belief, then by defending our faith we are defending beliefs. And that always means defending our own beliefs against someone else's beliefs. This has made religion a divisive and destructive force throughout much of our history.

Instead of basing faith on belief, we can base faith on a principle. We have already spoken of the "covenantal" relationship between God and the people of God. The basic principle of faith implicit in the Bible is this:

> *The one sure way to enter the Covenant with God is to commit to the pursuit of the ideal of non-self-interested love. Those who make this commitment will know they have been included in this relationship and that God's presence plays a special role in their lives.*

This is the Bible's core message reduced to a single paragraph. Once we understand it, there will be no need to defend any one particular belief against any other. God does not care if you are a Jew or a Christian or a Muslim or a Buddhist or a Hindu or an atheist. Membership in the Covenant is open to all. God looks to the heart, and what is in one's heart is not defined by one's religious affiliation.

I do not ask Christians to give up their Christianity, Jews to give up their Judaism, or anyone else to adopt either. Anyone can appreciate this approach to the Bible and to the prophetic teachings, regardless of religious background. Anyone can enter the covenantal relationship by devoting one's life to the realization of non-self-interested love—a greater challenge than one might think. No one is asked to take anything "on faith"; that is, to accept anything without question. If this approach to faith has any validity it will demonstrate itself in the life of each individual who makes the commitment that is the basis of faith.

The name for this approach to faith is "Judeochristianity." It is not a new religion but simply a way of identifying the point where Jewish and Christian tradition meet, and what that can teach us about faith. Jesus's purpose was not to establish a new and separate faith but to expand Judaism to a universal faith based on love, justice, and tolerance.

The times we are living in can easily challenge anyone's faith. Faith based upon belief can falter if those beliefs clash too strongly with one's experience. A faith is needed that can take into itself even our worst experiences. Such faith can help us withstand fear and despair. This approach to faith is existential; that is, it can be tested in our actual existence, in life as we live it, with all its uncertainties. It does not require any specific belief. But it does ask for commitment.

We will have many difficult questions to consider: What is faith? What is God? What is prayer? Why do we need faith? Is it ever too late to acquire faith? Why do we suffer, and what meaning can God have in a suffering world?

The most difficult questions are precisely the ones we need to ask. Our urge to ask them indicates the need for faith is greater than ever.

PRINCIPLES OF JUDEOCHRISTIANITY

1. The basic text of Judeochristianity is the Bible as preserved in Jewish and Christian tradition. It consists of two parts: the Hebrew Bible and the New Testament.

2. The Bible is the divinely inspired word transmitted through human understanding over many times and places. The Bible must be understood as a whole, without picking and choosing only those parts that serve one's interests. Nevertheless, the human process of transcription and transmission is fallible. Therefore the Bible cannot always be taken literally, and must be understood within the context of its original time and place.

3. Biblical scholarship and criticism are invaluable, and can provide needed insights concerning the Bible's historical context and the meaning of the text itself. However, they cannot be an exclusive guide since many of these insights rely upon educated speculation. One must struggle with

scripture, sifting its eternal truths from their time-bound expressions, trying to understand these truths through faith and with the heart.

4. The Hebrew Bible must be understood as a complete entity. Its books are to be presented in their original order, which reflects the way its shapers conceived its story: It is the story of the discovery of God's intimate relationship with human beings through the history and experience of the Hebrew People. It tells how these people searched for God, found God, became estranged from God, and found God again. That is where the original order ends (2 Chronicles), not with the announcement of the Prophet Elijah's coming (Malachi) that concludes the Old Testament in Christian Bibles. The Hebrew Bible contains its own message and is not simply an introduction to the New Testament. Its message is the relationship between God and people, which is called "covenant."

5. The New Testament represents the continuation and culmination of Hebrew prophecy. Through Jesus's life and teachings we learn that God's intimate relationship with human beings extends to every individual member of every nation on earth. It was Jesus's prophetic vocation to bring this message to the world. The New Testament extends the Hebrew covenant to all of humanity.

6. Judeochristianity is a way of seeing both Judaism and Christianity that emphasizes the continuity between these two traditions. It makes no commitment to either Jewish or Christian religious doctrine or practice. It does not ask people to give up their religious practice or to adopt a new one. All are invited, whether they believe Jesus to be the Son of God, the Messiah, the last of the Hebrew prophets, or are perhaps wondering just who Jesus was and what makes him

important. Christians need not suspend their belief in Jesus's divinity, nor need Jews accept this belief, in order to appreciate and benefit from this approach. Judeochristianity is a unifying approach that accepts Jews, Christians, and others exactly where they are.

7. The central idea in Judeochristianity is non-self-interested love. Non-self-interested love is defined as the awareness of others' individuality. Jesus's task was to teach this love, which he saw as the ultimate destination of Hebrew prophecy. By his complete willingness to embrace his suffering and by his faith in redemption in spite of it, Jesus became a representative of all human suffering, and his suffering became a prophetic demonstration of his message of God's transforming love.

8. God can neither be defined nor grasped with the intellect, but may be described as Absolute Goodness. Created in God's image, we are endowed with a sense of goodness, which enables us to distinguish good from evil. This sense is limited, is not infallible, and may encounter difficulty evaluating competing goods. We must therefore exercise it with caution and self-awareness; nevertheless, it is our most reliable path to knowledge and guide to action. We may try to ignore or suppress this sense of goodness, or dismiss it from fear of facing ambiguity; nevertheless, we are responsible for cultivating it to the best of our ability. "The Spirit helps us in our weakness" (Romans 8:26): if we are genuinely devoted to understanding goodness, we will receive aid from beyond ourselves.

9. We cannot comprehend the whole of goodness but we can discern its many specific expressions, such as love, beauty, honesty, integrity, generosity, patience, compassion, truth, and justice. The highest good of all is non-self-interested

love, and is the standard by which other goods are judged. We can develop our sense of goodness. Self-examination is important, lest we substitute our own prejudices or desires for what is truly good. We have the capacity to tell the difference between desire and true goodness, and when we are honest with ourselves, we know. A well-developed sense of goodness is the soundest basis for faith, especially for those who have not learned faith when very young. Internalizing a sense of what goodness really is, we acquire hope in a saving Presence beyond ourselves, which is the source of the good that we perceive.

10. Keeping all this in mind, it is possible to speak of the reason for which we were created. We were created to reveal the goodness of God. We do this by expressing goodness directly in all its different forms, and by choosing goodness over its alternatives. Our highest purpose and the greatest good we can manifest is learning to love without self-interest. Therefore this principle can serve as a guide to action in difficult situations. We can ask ourselves: of all the choices available, which most enables God's nature to be known?

11. We can even speak of a specific reason for the creation of each one of us. This individualized reason is called our destiny. It is the unique way in which we each are called to express goodness in our own lives. It may involve the talents we were given, the jobs we must perform, or entirely different things, including our network of relationships and the ways we express love through them. We may think of the spiritual journey that orders our lives as the search to find and fulfill our destiny. We cannot know it in advance. We discover it by devoting ourselves to God's will, which is the expression of goodness. To practice this we search for and

follow the cues that point us toward ways of expressing goodness that best fit our individual constitution and life circumstances.

These principles lead to the following article of faith:

The purpose of our lives is to realize non-self-interested love. If we cherish it and are working toward it, God helps us. If we ignore it, then we are left to our own devices.

THE TEST OF TRUE RELIGION

The foregoing principles lead us to a criterion through which religions may be judged. Much religion, especially theistic religion, is characterized by intolerance based upon belief. The message is: Believe what I believe, or God will reject you and throw you out of the kingdom.

Such religion is contrary to love, and therefore denies the goodness that is God's essence.

There is one simple criterion by which any religion may be judged: Does it lead its adherents in the direction of non-self-interested love? If it does, then it should be respected. If it does not, then there is a better way. Doctrinal distinctions are secondary, and of no importance when the time comes for us to account for how we have stewarded the resources with which God has entrusted and blessed us.

Any religion that encourages intolerance, that sets itself up as the only way to salvation, that preaches God's rejection of those who believe differently regardless of their hearts and deeds, does not have the true spirit of love and cannot be a true path.

A NOTE ON LANGUAGE

While the language of this book is strictly gender neutral, some of the biblical quotations may seem not to reflect this. No translation of the Bible is perfect. I have looked at many. In my opinion, the New Revised Standard Version exhibits the best balance between comprehensibility and faithfulness to the original Hebrew and Greek languages. It is also far more gender neutral than its predecessor, the Revised Standard Version, as well as many other versions. Even so, some references to God are phrased in masculine terms. This is difficult to avoid, considering the original text and the time and place from which it came. The understanding of God presented here is nevertheless genderless, and these biblical quotations should so be understood.

Unless otherwise indicated, quotations from the Bible are taken from the New Revised Standard Version. For the Gospel of Thomas I use the translation by Stevan Davies, *The Gospel of Thomas Annotated and Explained* (Woodstock, Vermont: SkyLight Paths, 2002).

A NOTE OF CAUTION

To prevent any possible misunderstanding, this approach has nothing in common with Jews for Jesus or "Messianic Judaism." Those are actually forms of Christianity pretending to be Judaism: they demand belief in the basic tenets of evangelical Christianity and are intolerant of those who do not believe. Their intolerance and condemnation of nonbelievers, according to the criterion stated above, make their legitimacy questionable.

Judeochristianity is neither Judaism nor Christianity but a bridge between the two. Its mission is to explore the implications of Jewish and Christian teaching when Jesus is seen as continuing the line of Hebrew prophecy and moving it forward. It does not ask people to believe anything but only to consider what Judaism and Christianity have to teach each other and to teach us as well. Specific beliefs are the domain of each individual's relationship with God. Both Jewish and Christian beliefs are respected here.

ADDITIONAL READING

At the related web site (www.judeochristianity.org) the reader can find additional articles, including several on spirituality and disability, proper attitudes toward nonbelievers, the meaning of forgiveness, and the doctrine of vicarious atonement. There is also an introduction to the Bible showing how it is to be understood from the perspective of Judeochristianity and the continuity between prophetic tradition in the Hebrew Bible and New Testament.

PART 1

The Path

I

DOES GOD EXIST?

Give thanks to the Lord, who is goodness.
 (Psalm 118:1, original translation)

Does God exist? This is the fundamental question of religion. People have tried to prove it, and people have tried to disprove it. All those efforts are meaningless, because the word "God" has no clear definition. So people argue for or against the existence of God, with no agreement about what God actually means. No wonder the usual result is confusion.

When referring to God, people can mean very different things. Many people think of God as a being, with a will and feelings like humans have, though not necessarily with a human body. So for them the question "Does God exist?" means, "Is there a Supreme Being with these human-like characteristics, but without a body and with unlimited power?"

This understanding of God, however, is not universal. For many people this kind of God is too human and takes too literally certain biblical references, describing God for example as a "man of war" (Exodus 15:3, KJV), a "jealous God" (Exodus 20:5), or repenting his actions (Genesis 6:7, KJV; note that this God has a gender, usually masculine, sometimes feminine). A person like us, even without a body, does seem limited, as long as such a person experiences human emotions and regrets. Yet many find such a God comforting, a God with whom one can have a personal relationship.

My intention is not to tell people how they must think of God, but to ask that we consider more carefully what we mean when talking about God, and to define the question of God's existence in a way that can speak to everyone. When we ask, "Does God exist," it seems we are really asking: Are we alone? Or is there a reality beyond the sensible world that is essentially good, that gives meaning to our lives, and that might even have redemptive power?

The existence of God is not a proposition that can be proven true or false. In fact, God cannot even be defined, but only approached through faith. God is too great for anyone to say exactly what God is. But we can consider descriptions of God that aid our understanding. We cannot capture the whole of God in words, but the right description can help us approach spiritual reality.

In our search for this description, let's start with a tale from ancient philosophy. In a famous dialogue by Plato a young man, Euthyphro, for whom the dialogue is named, encounters the philosopher Socrates at the entrance to the Athens courthouse. Socrates is waiting for his hearing on a charge of impiety—corrupting the youth by undermining their faith in the accepted religion—a charge that eventually led to his execution. He learns to his astonishment that Euthyphro has come to court to prosecute his father on a charge of murder. A field laborer died on the family farm, and Euthyphro claims it was due to his father's negligence.

Socrates, understandably concerned about matters of piety because of his own predicament, wonders whether taking such action against one's own father is an impious act. To have committed such a serious act, surely Euthyphro must know what is pious and what is not. Would Euthyphro be willing to teach Socrates the meaning of piety?

Euthyphro takes the bait. Sure of himself, he tells Socrates that piety means that which the gods love. Socrates replies that this cannot possibly be true, because the gods disagree and fight among themselves, so what one god loves another god may hate. This would make the same act both pious and impious, a clear contradiction.

Euthyphro admits his definition must be wrong, so with Socrates's guidance he changes it to say that piety means that which all the gods love. Socrates responds by turning the conversation around and asking the critical question: Is an act pious because the gods love it, or do they love it because it is pious?

Euthyphro is forced to admit that a pious act is loved because in itself it is pious. It is not pious because it is loved. In fact, it would still be pious even if it were not loved.

Socrates now takes the discussion in a new direction. He notes that a pious act is a just act, so piety must be a part of justice. He wants to know what distinguishes pious acts from other just acts. Euthyphro responds that piety is special because it means doing service to the gods. It is what the gods love. Socrates catches him: saying that piety is what the gods love is the very same definition of piety with which the discussion began, and which they had rejected! So poor Euthyphro and Socrates find themselves back where they started, wondering what piety is really all about.

Let us focus on the key idea in this dialogue: that piety has its own value, which is independent even of what the gods like or don't like. Now let's translate it into our own context. Socrates observes that piety is a part of something greater, which is justice. We can go even further, to say that justice is a part of something greater, which is goodness.

So instead of talking about piety and the gods, let's talk about goodness and God. Does goodness have its own value, independent even of what God likes?

This question seems strange. It is generally understood that the God of Judaism and Christianity is good by nature, and cannot will anything but good. But is the good that God wills good because God wills it—or does God will it because it is good?

The question is not as trivial as it may sound. For centuries people have believed, and many still believe, that whatever God wills must be good simply because God wills it. Our limited notions of what is or isn't good simply do not apply. There is some truth to this—we cannot always reliably tell what is good. Often what seems good to us may turn out bad later, and vice versa. But this truth is not absolute, as the Bible itself makes abundantly clear.

Just as we cannot always reliably tell what is good, so we also cannot reliably know what God's will is. We often identify God's will with what we have been taught as children. We can feel certain about God's will, and closed to any questioning. This was the attitude of the friends of Job. They knew the answer to Job's questions: it is God's will that Job suffer as punishment for his sins. Job's limited notions of what is or isn't good simply do not apply. This is the response of traditional religion—and in the end (Job 42:7), God condemns it.

Job's understanding is limited, but his quest was just and good—that is God's final response. We have not only the right but the duty to search and inquire and exercise our human sense of goodness—as long as we remain cognizant of our limitations.

There is a standard of goodness over and above any human understanding of God's will. This standard cannot be known with certainty—and that should keep us humble—but it does exist. Religion has often fallen into demonic realms because of our failure to investigate and apply this standard to the best of our limited ability. If we have been taught that the crudest thing imaginable is God's will, then that often is sufficient for us: it is God's will, it must be right, and human notions of goodness do not apply. And so many fundamentalist Christians and Muslims are convinced that people who do not believe as they do are forever condemned to suffer at God's hands—and this must be right, because it is God's will, or so we have been taught. But how can a good God endlessly torture people who have lived good lives and practiced kindness to others, just because their beliefs are different? It is a mystery, we are told, and it is not questioned because it is God's will.

Because God's supposed punishment of the righteous nonbeliever is eternal, there is no conceivable good that could come from it. In precisely this type of situation we cannot afford to ignore our human sense of goodness. What we learn from Plato is that if God's will clashes fundamentally with goodness, then it is the former that must be questioned. If there is no possible way to find goodness in what we think is God's will, then either God's will is not good, or it is not really God's will. This means there must be a standard of value that is above our understanding of God's will—and that standard is goodness itself.

Of course, a good God can will only what is good. But that is not what makes it good. And we human beings are not completely helpless. We cannot always have certainty about knowing what is good, but we do possess a limited sense of goodness that guides us if we choose to attend to it.

This finite sense of goodness has been implanted in us by something beyond ourselves and greater than ourselves. We cannot totally encompass what this is, but our sense of goodness is witness to its existence. Whatever it is, we can call it God. We cannot define God or capture God's essence completely in words, images, or ideas. But we can offer a description of God that may provide a hint of understanding. And since, as we have seen, goodness is good even prior to what God wills, perhaps goodness itself is where we should be looking for God. And so we can refer to God as Absolute Goodness.

While goodness cannot be completely defined, it can be extensively described. It is not an empty abstraction, nor is its content arbitrary. We will have a lot to say about the specific attributes of goodness in succeeding chapters. But we can begin with this fundamental statement about goodness:

> *He has told you, O mortal, what is good;*
> *and what does the Lord require of you*
> *but to do justice, and to love kindness,*
> *and to walk humbly with your God?* (Micah 6:8)

Something inside us must resonate—justice and kindness are good, we know they are good, God has told us they are good, and even if God had not told us, they would still be good. Goodness is not arbitrary.

Goodness also inspires love. We are commanded to love God (Deuteronomy 6:5). Loving God means more than loving an unseen person. God is Absolute Goodness. Those who love goodness for its own sake, goodness itself and not just what is good for them, love God. The pursuit of goodness can be a passionate undertaking, infusing one's whole life with meaning. Sifting true goodness from personal desire is a formidable challenge that perhaps no one can accomplish perfectly—but striving to do so is what it means to search for God.

There is also power in goodness—this is the Bible's message. As our hearts fill with goodness going beyond self-interest, we more closely conform to God's image, and God responds as though recognizing God's own image within us. And so even in the most extreme circumstances we may still find ourselves supported by God's presence—we have many testimonies to this from survivors of the world's worst tragedies. God is not merely a remote, sympathetic but powerless observer, even though portraying God that way has become somewhat popular. God plays an active role in our lives, guiding us and influencing the course our lives take. This is what is meant, even in the Bible, by divine power. It cannot be proven. But we can try to discover it and test it and live it.

God's power cannot be proven and so is a matter of faith. Faith is more than simply belief. Faith is the growing awareness of God's power in our lives. We never get a complete answer—some things must remain hidden (Deuteronomy 29:29, Hebrews 11:1)—but we get little clues and inklings of this power, which help us gradually learn to trust it.

The path of faith is indirect, and full of obstacles. There is so much in our experience to make us think that indeed we are alone, and that there is no power beyond human power and the mindless power of nature. Jewish and Christian tradition unite to tell us there is more to the story. As we find the place where these two traditions meet, the mystery of faith begins to open to us.

II

WHO WAS JESUS?

Amy was a patient of mine at the hospice where I was the music therapist. She did not know how much time she had left, only that her days of mental clarity were severely numbered. Amy was Jewish, but had been searching for the meaning of Jesus, since she felt his message speaking to her but did not understand why. The different teachings she received from different churches confused her, especially the demand that she must believe certain things in a certain way or God would reject her.

One day Amy asked me simply, "Who was Jesus?" and did I have anything I could give her to read? I thought about her question, about the fear as well as the spiritual yearning that prompted it, and wondered how to make the answer simple, as Jesus would have liked, since he told us to be simple too. That night I wrote the following article, and gave it to Amy the next day. I saw her reading it every day since.

JESUS, ONE OF THE most influential figures in history, goes by many names to different people: prophet, priest, King of the Jews, Son of Man, Son of God, even God Himself. But who really was Jesus, and what was his real significance?

Jesus was a simple man with a simple message, but unfortunately theology has made him very complicated. One cannot really find Jesus through theology, so save yourself the trouble and don't even try. One can understand Jesus only through the heart, because that is where he directed his message. What you believe about Jesus is not important, so please don't worry about that. Jesus would certainly recognize those who, like him, cherish goodness, regardless of what they believe. He was not interested in personal recognition. "Why do you call me good?" said Jesus to a man who asked him how to inherit eternal life, "No one is good but God alone" (Mark 10:18). Jesus did not want attention focused on himself, but only on God.

To understand Jesus's message we must go back to the beginning. In the beginning, people did not know God. They looked for God in all the wrong places. They made up gods and worshiped them, because it made them feel secure. Each nation had its own god, and these gods often made war against each other.

Then one man, Abraham, said that all this was wrong. He had a conviction that the real God must go beyond all these man-made gods. He spent his life searching for the real God, and experienced God through a promise that today we call the "Covenant."

This "Covenant" is a relationship between God and human beings. Basically, it says that those who seek to understand God's will and who honor it will discover the presence of God in their lives. It does not say they will be free from suffering, but rather that in spite of their suffering they will sense God present with them. "When you pass through the waters, I will be with you; and through the rivers, they shall not overwhelm you; when you walk through fire you shall not be burned, and the flame shall not consume you" (Isaiah 43:2).

But what does it mean to do God's will? The one who explained it best to all of us was Jesus. Jesus was the last and greatest of the Hebrew prophets. His task was twofold: to explain the true meaning of the Covenant, and to bring its message to the entire world. Before Jesus the Covenant became known and was recorded in the experience of the Jewish people, and that is why they were called "chosen." Jesus's task was to let all the people of the world know that they too are chosen and just as much loved by God.

How did Jesus explain the meaning of the Covenant? One day someone asked Jesus, "Which commandment is the greatest?" To which Jesus replied: "'You shall love the Lord your God with all your heart, and with all your soul, and with all your mind.' This is the greatest and first commandment. And a second is like it: You shall love your neighbor as yourself" (Matthew 22:37–39).

Thus the greatest commandment and the heart of the message is love.

And so Jesus also says, speaking in the name of God: "This is my commandment, that you love one another as I have loved you" (John 15:12).

The answer is to love, but not just ordinary love. It is to love as God loves, without limit, the stranger as well as the members of one's family or inner circle of friends.

Now do not be discouraged if you cannot realize this love perfectly. Nobody can. And we are not required to. All we are asked is to seek it with all our heart: "Seek first the kingdom of God, and all these things will be given to you as well" (Luke 12:31).

We may call this special love "non-self-interested love" because it goes beyond all self-gratification and truly recognizes the other. As this love enters our hearts, it will build our faith, because those who know love will also know a loving presence that is beyond them and greater than they are. This loving presence will accompany us on our journey, up to the very end. "God is love, and those who abide in love abide in God, and God abides in them" (1 John 4:16).

If we want to know more about this love, we cannot do better than the famous words of Paul:

> *Love is patient; love is kind; love is not envious or boastful or arrogant or rude.*
> *Love does not insist on its own way; it is not irritable or resentful; it does not rejoice in wrongdoing, but rejoices in the truth.*
> *Love bears all things, believes all things, hopes all things, endures all things.*

> *Love never ends. But as for prophecies, they will come to an end; as for tongues, they will cease; as for knowledge, it will come to an end....*
>
> *And now faith, hope, and love abide, these three; and the greatest of these is love.* (1 Corinthians 13:4–8, 13)

Love is the root of our faith. On our journey we will know many moments of anxiety and fear. But fear is not the last word. Every experience of fear is finite and will come to an end, but as Paul says, "love never ends." And love is the antidote to fear: "There is no fear in love, but perfect love casts out fear" (1 John 4:18). Now love might not get rid of our fears right away, especially if we have lived with fear for a very long time. But love is something we can practice, until little by little the love in our hearts displaces the fear. Whenever you are afraid, just allow your breathing to relax and remember a moment when you either gave or received love. Keep remembering those moments until they become an actual presence of love inside you.

And never forget that no matter how weak or sick you are, you can always give love. We can practice love simply by becoming aware of others, aware of their needs and desires. When you smile at the strangers who come to care for you, or when you offer them a kind word, you make them feel that their work is worthwhile and you are giving them love.

Of course you will not always feel like smiling. Maybe sometimes you will feel like crying, or like screaming. Do not judge that. Even Jesus felt fear up until the day he died, as he prayed in the Garden of Gethsemane that he might be spared. But any fears that still arise will not keep you from God's love. You can always return to those moments of love when the episode of fear passes.

And when the time finally came for Jesus to meet his suffering, he was saved by the presence of God. He said on the cross, "Father, into your hands I commend my spirit" (Luke 23:46), and finally, at the very end, in a last moment of acceptance, he said: "It is finished" (John 19:30).

And so it will be for you too, and for all of us who are seeking to know God and to be conformed to God's image, which is love. The more we love, the more we are like God. And God will always recognize that sacred image within us and respond to that love. As we gradually come to know this response, we will know we are not alone

THE DEVELOPMENT OF JESUS'S MINISTRY

To these words I wrote for Amy we can add a biblical perspective, to flesh out the picture of Jesus as seen through Judeochristianity. Jesus was indeed given a very special task, but just like the rest of us he did not begin life conscious of his destiny. He had to discover it through the actual process of living it. One article of faith, which we can test in our lives through practice, is that if we commit ourselves to follow God's will to the best of our ability and to know our God-given destiny, then over the course of time it will be revealed to us.

Early in his ministry, in the Sermon on the Mount, Jesus delivered the following teaching:

> *You have heard that it was said, "You shall love your neighbor and hate your enemy." But I say to you, Love your enemies and pray for those who persecute you, so that you may be children of your Father in heaven; for he makes his sun rise on the evil and on the good, and sends rain on the righteous and on the unrighteous. For if you love those who love you, what reward do you have? Do not even the tax collectors do the same? And if you greet only your brothers and sisters, what more are you doing than others? Do not even the Gentiles do the same? Be perfect, therefore, as your heavenly Father is perfect.* (Matthew 5:43-48)

Jesus took a teaching from the Hebrew Bible and expanded it. The teaching is Deuteronomy 10:19: "You shall also love the stranger, for you were strangers in the land of Egypt." According to Jesus this means: Don't just love the people who love you. Don't love only the members of your own family, your own ethnic group, or your private circle of friends. Everybody does that, and it's no accomplishment. Rather, extend yourselves to love those who are strangers, to love those who are different, and who may not even share your interests. That is loving the way God loves, and God recognizes it and responds to it.

If there is one truly central teaching in all of Jesus's ministry, this is it. It is the basis of what we are calling "non-self-interested love," and is what makes the biblical message transformative.

Next, we encounter an irony. Jesus so beautifully articulated this teaching, yet he still had to learn it for himself. I believe many spiritually gifted teachers experience this: they teach what inspired them so that they may learn it themselves. Here is how Jesus learned it: Jesus's original understanding of his mission was limited. When he first sent out his disciples to teach, to help, and to heal, he told them to minister only to their own people:

> *These twelve Jesus sent out with the following instructions: "Go nowhere among the Gentiles, and enter no town of the Samaritans, but go rather to the lost sheep of the house of Israel. As you go, proclaim the good news, 'The kingdom of heaven has come near.' Cure the sick, raise the dead, cleanse the lepers, cast out demons. You received without payment; give without payment."* (Matthew 10:5–8)

Here Jesus instructs his disciples in non-self-interested love, but it is not yet universal.

Then one day Jesus meets someone who is able to teach him. It was a non-Jewish woman from the surrounding country, of the people whom Jesus instructed his disciples to avoid.

> *Jesus left that place and went away to the district of Tyre and Sidon. Just then a Canaanite woman from that region came out and started shouting, "Have mercy on me, Lord, Son of David; my daughter is tormented by a demon." But he did not answer her at all. And his disciples came and urged him, saying, "Send her away, for she keeps shouting after us." He answered, "I was sent only to the lost sheep of the house of Israel." But she came and knelt before him, saying, "Lord, help me." He answered, "It is not fair to take the children's food and throw it to the dogs." She said, "Yes, Lord, yet even the dogs eat the crumbs that fall from their masters' table." Then Jesus answered her, "Woman, great is your faith! Let it be done for you as you wish." And her daughter was healed instantly.* (Matthew 15:21–28)

How fascinating that not long after Jesus preached "if you greet only your brothers and sisters, what more are you doing than others?" his disciples tell him to cast away this strange foreign woman, and he acquiesces! No, he tells her, my ministry is only intended for Jews. Is it possible that even Jesus falls into an old ethnic prejudice when he tells her, "It is not fair to take the children's food and throw it to the dogs"? One might have expected the Canaanite woman to react with indignation at the offense. Instead, she shows disarming humility: "Yes, Lord, yet even the dogs eat the crumbs that fall from their masters' table." Her faith makes a deep impression on Jesus, and his attitude changes. Very likely Jesus remembered the Roman centurion he encountered before he organized his ministry, whose faith had also impressed him (Matthew 8). God's love ignores the distinctions we make between people that can seem so important to us.

We have been told: "You shall love your neighbor as yourself" (Leviticus 19:18). Jesus repeats this teaching to a young lawyer who asked him what one must do to inherit eternal life. The clever lawyer tests Jesus with the question: "And who is my neighbor?" (Luke 10:29). Jesus responds with the story of a Samaritan who showed kindness to a man who had been robbed and beaten, after some Jewish religious officials ignored him. The Samaritan bandaged the man's wounds, gave him shelter, and paid for his care. That is the meaning of "neighbor." That Samaritans and Jews had been long-time enemies did not matter at all. The people of God are defined not by ethnicity or by religion but by their love of goodness.

And so when Jesus gives his final declaration he no longer speaks exclusively of the "house of Israel" but says instead: "Go therefore and make disciples of all nations" (Matthew 28:19). The divine Covenant, revealed in the history of the Jewish people, has become a blessing to all. By bringing this message to the world Jesus completed and fulfilled Hebrew prophecy.

III

OUR TWO NATURES

To set the mind on the flesh is death, but to set the mind on the Spirit is life and peace. For this reason the mind that is set on the flesh is hostile to God; it does not submit to God's law—indeed it cannot, and those who are in the flesh cannot please God. But you are not in the flesh; you are in the Spirit, since the Spirit of God dwells in you.

Romans 8:6–9

THE "MIND-BODY" PROBLEM

How are the mind and the body related? This is a very old problem in philosophy. The body exists in physical space; the mind does not. How can they both be part of the same being, and how do they interact?

Today many dismiss this question for its apparent assumption of dualism, a point of view no longer in fashion. Some say the mind and body are not really different. Some say the mind is simply a property of our complex brain, and has no independent existence. Others say the body is a product of the mind's imagining.

The Bible appears to take the view that mind and body are distinct. Paul in particular opposes the "spirit" and the "flesh." Paul is often misunderstood and accused of disparaging the body. However, these terms do not refer to mind and body in the usual sense. They refer to two distinct natures we possess as human beings. Understanding these two natures gives us insights into ourselves that can greatly deepen our relationships with others.

A Jewish mystical tradition describes this symbolically. Why did Adam and Eve sew themselves garments (Genesis 3:7)? God created them as pure souls and placed them in a beautiful garden. God also clothed and protected the soul by creating for it a garment, the body. Comfortable in the garden, Adam and Eve forgot their identity as pure souls. They thought their bodies were their true identities, and that they were still naked. To cover and protect their bodies they constructed new garments from fig leaves.

The "body," or our physical nature, is a symbol of what we might call the psychological self. This is what Paul means by "flesh": not the literal, physical body, but the human self with its desires, its appetites, and its passions. It is our human sense of identity. And it is very fragile. Some of us identify with our work. If we lose our work, then we lose our self. Some of us identify with our relationships. If we lose our relationships, then we lose our self. Some of us identify with our talents. If we become incapacitated and cannot use them, we no longer know who we are. The result is profound anxiety. In his book *The Meaning of Anxiety*, psychologist Rollo May called anxiety the "fear of the dissolution of the self." When that with which we identify is lost or threatened, we feel we are disintegrating, and we start to panic.

A VIEW OF THE SELF

This may lead us to wonder: Can we find a sense of identity that is firm, and that can withstand these threats against our being?

In Plato's *Phaedrus* Socrates presents an intriguing metaphor for the workings of the soul (or perhaps we should call it the "total self"):

> *In every one of us there are two guiding and ruling principles which lead us whither they will; one is the natural desire of pleasure, the other is an acquired opinion which aspires after the best; and these two are sometimes in harmony and then again at war, and sometimes the one, sometimes the other conquers.* (Plato, *Phaedrus*, translated by Benjamin Jowett)

We try to manage these two sometimes conflicting natures like a charioteer driving two horses heading in two different directions:

> *As I said at the beginning of this tale, I divided each soul into three—two horses and a charioteer; and one of the horses was good and the other bad: the division may remain, but I have not yet explained in what the goodness or badness of either consists, and to that I will proceed.*
>
> *The right-hand horse is upright and cleanly made; he has a lofty neck and an aquiline nose; his color is white, and his eyes dark; he is a lover of honor and modesty and temperance, and the follower of true glory; he needs no touch of the whip, but is guided by word and admonition only. The other is a crooked lumbering animal, put together anyhow; he has a short thick neck; he is flat-faced and of a dark color, with grey eyes and blood-red complexion; the mate of insolence and pride, shag-eared and deaf, hardly yielding to whip and spur.*

One part of us is driven by emotions and appetites, while another aspires toward higher values. Meanwhile a third part, the conscious part, feels caught in between, sometimes not knowing which one to follow, or wanting to follow the higher but finding difficulty escaping the lower.

This tripartite division of the self sounds temptingly like Freud's id and superego (the two horses) and ego (the charioteer). There are similarities, but in borrowing this metaphor of the charioteer we are following neither Freud nor Plato exactly. It is simply a good image to describe the tension between our spiritual and animal natures.

Now the "dark horse" is not really "bad," at least not all the time. That horse is a part of our human nature and not to be rejected. Nevertheless, conflicts do often arise, in which negative emotions cause us much stress and suffering. These stressful feelings tell us we are out of contact with our spiritual nature (the "soul" rather than the "self").

We can describe these two sometimes conflicting natures as follows: One is the spiritual nature, the pure soul (much different from Freud's superego), and the other is the animal nature, which often acts like a mask over the soul.

Both Jewish and Christian tradition recognize the purity of the soul as God created it. The traditional Jewish daily morning prayer opens with these words:

> My God, the soul you have given me is pure. You created it, you formed it, you breathed it into me, you guard it within me, and you are destined to claim it from me and return it to me in the ultimate future.

Like Adam and Eve we may have forgotten our soul-nature, but we can find it again:

> *Do not lie to one another, seeing that you have put off the old nature with its practices and have put on the new nature, which is being renewed in knowledge after the image of its creator. Here there cannot be Greek and Jew, circumcised and uncircumcised,*

barbarian, Scythian, slave, free man, but Christ is all, and in all. (Colossians 8:6–9)

The pure soul does not belong to any of the temporal categories that separate people from each other. Each soul possesses a natural attraction to other souls, which we experience as the good will we are inclined to show even toward strangers who may be our guests, who may require our assistance, or whom we may simply chance to meet along the way. But we are separated by the fear and suspicion that human limitations impose on us, which include scarcity, competition, the desire for power, and the urge toward self-aggrandizement. Healing comes on the level of the pure soul, where "there cannot be Greek and Jew" in the sense of specific identifications that become walls of division.

Genesis (1:27) describes the creation of the pure soul, through God's image, living in harmony with the rest of God's creatures. The first chapter of Genesis does not describe our physical world. It describes a purely spiritual world, an organic whole, in which every creature has its place. The human has dominion over the animal, but the two are in cooperative relationship. People do not eat animals for food, but are in fact vegetarian (Genesis 1:29). Even animals are vegetarians (1:30), implying that in the original pure creation (the spiritual world itself) even the animals do not attack each other. (See also Isaiah 11:6–9, which describes our restoration to the spiritual world in the Messianic age.)

This harmonious world is not the world we experience. The world we live in now is grounded in conflict. Animals must attack other animals if they are to survive. And we human beings also possess an animal nature—the "dark horse" of the charioteer.

The Bible describes this dark element by introducing the serpent in Genesis 3. The serpent is the part of human nature capable of resisting God's will—and thus capable of throwing the human being out of consciousness of the spiritual world. And this is indeed what happens, when due to the serpent's machinations Adam and Eve find themselves thrown out of the garden and barred from returning.

The relationship between body and soul is paradoxical. The body is the soul's visible expression while we live on this earth. We experience spiritual energy—"enthusiasm" (being "possessed by God")—as physical vitality. Through the body we perceive the beauty of music, of great art, and of other human beings through their kind words and deeds. Spiritualists who denigrate the body fail to realize that on this physical plane the body enables us to perceive all that is spiritual.

Nevertheless, the body and soul are also in tension. The body derives from the animal nature. It is governed by physical impulses, drives, and appetites that are not evil in themselves but that do not always serve spiritual purposes. Consider the animal kingdom, where predatory behavior is the norm. Animals must attack and tear and wound and eat other animals simply in order to live. Even violence within a single species is not uncommon, as when two animals fight over a desired mate, or a scarce piece of food. This is not evil. It is the way animals are; it is their nature.

It is our nature too. We have the same impulses, and these impulses are mediated through the body. Bodily existence is inconceivable without physical urges—to eat, to copulate, to dominate, to claim pieces of territory, to compete for scarce resources. This is the norm within the animal kingdom, to which we also belong.

But unlike the animals, unrestrained predatory behavior in humans is evil. Why? Because it violates our spiritual nature. It is healthy for an animal to act exclusively like an animal. It is not healthy for human beings, and those who do bring great damage to their souls.

A male animal who mounts a female without asking, simply because she strikes his fancy, is acting according to his—and her—nature. But when this happens with human beings, we call it rape, one of the most horrifying violent crimes imaginable. Why? Because invasion of another person's body without her consent is a violation of her individuality. Individuality is a property of the soul. If we treat another person's body like a thing, made only for our own pleasure, we discard the person's individuality, and people who are sensitive to the presence of their own souls react to this with horror.

People vary greatly in the degree to which they are awake to the presence of their own souls and those of others. The psychopath, most unfortunate of human beings, has no awareness of the soul. Awareness of the soul, or of a person's individuality, is what we experience as love, and is in fact the definition of love. Quite possibly the purpose of our bodily existence is to enable us to discover and increase our capacity for love.

SPIRITUAL EXISTENCE IN AN ANIMAL WORLD

I always used to wonder, Why did God create the dinosaurs? Dinosaurs had no spiritual awareness that we know of; they neither worshiped God nor produced great art or literature. Yet God must have considered them important, because the length of time humans have existed is but a drop compared to the millions of years that dinosaurs dominated the earth. Nevertheless, we no longer hear from the dinosaurs.

Perhaps God created the dinosaurs, and all pre-human creatures, to establish that this is an animal world. This is not our home. We were temporarily transplanted here, to learn what a spiritual entity can learn only in an animal world. It is actually quite ingenious. Imagine God wondering how the greatest value of all, love, could be learned and revealed. Love means little in a world of only God and angels. Neither God nor angels need anything. They do not suffer.

So it is reported that after having created the animals God told the angels, "Let us make man in our image" (Genesis 1:26). Let us add to the animal kingdom a spiritual being, the human being, so that through this creature's struggle with this difficult animal nature love will emerge. Love can be learned only where there is need. In the physical world there is need, there is want, there is pain and suffering. Compassion is love responding to suffering; it cannot exist in a world without suffering. Suffering shakes people out of their sleeping comfort. In a world free of suffering, the awareness that is love's essence could never develop. And only in an animal world can suffering exist.

So we all face a challenge. We have many choices. Do we conform to our nature as soul, or to our nature as animal?

Sometimes the two go well together. We say grace over a hearty meal. Great music exhilarates the senses. We rejoice in physical love. In all these activities our two natures are joined. The Psalmist knows this too: "You cause the grass to grow for the cattle, and plants for people to use, to bring forth food from the earth, and wine to gladden the human heart, oil to make the face shine, and bread to strengthen the human heart" (Psalm 104:14-15). "You open your hand, satisfying the desire of every living thing" (Psalm 145:16). Body and soul are not dualistically separated. What is good for the body is often good for the soul.

But not always. The drives that motivate greedy, aggressive, predatory behavior in animals operate in human beings as well. In the animal kingdom this is inevitable: animals must eat each other to survive. However, they do not experience any conflict about it. Even the prey experiences no conflict: it just tries to flee. But human beings experience conflict. Many of us don't like to eat animals, so we become vegetarians. But this is not for everyone: our physical constitution makes it difficult to achieve a complete and balanced diet that way. So we compromise. We may eat animals (Genesis 9:3), but we must make sure to slaughter them in a way that minimizes their pain.

We must also make other choices. Human beings are not wired to be monogamous. Animals are promiscuous, and so are human beings if they follow their animal nature. But some are blessed to experience the rewards of marriage, the depth of one relationship that lasts over many years. We choose to give up something for it: the intensity of many lovers in favor of committing to a single one. The one deep connection brings spiritual fulfillment far beyond the pleasures afforded by the many. Still, this particular conflict between our animal and spiritual natures has caused much heartbreak and ruined many lives.

We are more fulfilled, more whole and more healed, when the spiritual nature is ascendant. The animal nature does not disappear. Sensual pleasure is very much part of a healthy marriage, and of aesthetic enjoyment. We can savor a delicious meal with joy and gratitude. To lead a spiritual life we need not suppress or reject the animal side, but instead of dominating, the animal serves the spiritual. That is health. When the animal dominates the spiritual, that is the preparation for evil. The lustful or predatory impulses that turn a person into only a body, a thing without an individuality, are the negation of love itself.

FINDING OUR IDENTITY

Earlier we asked the question of finding a firm sense of identity that can withstand the doubts that hostile people or traumatic experiences may plant in our minds. We were each created with such an identity, which we may call our individuality.

Our individuality coincides with our spiritual nature. The animal nature is present as a catalyst, to help us learn, and to help us express that individuality. But the individuality itself is the soul, the spiritual nature we possess even before entering human form, and the only nature that survives into eternity.

It is easy to lose track of our identity. We are not conscious of it at first. We grow up with a false sense of identity, which to a large extent is formed by the thoughts of people around us. We inherit many of these thoughts from our parents, and adopt many self-defining thoughts from others whose impressions of us seem to matter. Such an identity is inherently unstable, which often makes us unduly sensitive to the praise or criticism of others. If we don't like the identity these impressions have given us, we may try to find an identity in work, or in relationships, or in anything that gives us a sense of ourselves we find easier to live with.

None of these efforts will lead to happiness. We might even fear someone else will steal our identity. This "identity theft" can occur if we see someone more talented, or who makes more money, or has a prettier wife, or a better job—that is, if we find anyone who appears to excel at something in which we have invested our sense of identity. If pangs of jealousy make us "feel like nothing," it is a sign that our false sense of identity has been shaken and that we are afraid of losing it.

The way to find our true, unshakable identity is to learn to perceive the soul. We need to acquire the ability to perceive both our own individuality and that of others. This is necessary for love, since genuine love is the awareness of another's individuality. The recognition of another's individuality is the greatest gift we can give. It is healing and liberating. Seeing the true individuality of another can help free that person from the limitations and even the torments of a false acquired identity. It can help reveal others to themselves. In the presence of such an understanding vision, people feel loved.

It is difficult, however, to give what we do not have. We need to develop our own spiritual perception, and to become aware of our own individuality. We can take as a goal the following five principles of spiritual perception:

1. I see not just the body but the spirit that it masks.
2. I feel the spirit that animates my being.
3. I sense the love that attracts spirits to each other.
4. I meet the darkness in myself with the light that returns me to my origin.
5. I meet the darkness in others with the light that carries the power of goodness.

It is important to understand that these are not affirmations. Affirmations do not really work. Making affirmations usually means repeating things one does not believe, to convince oneself that one really believes them. Simply repeating things will not truly make one believe them. These are principles of spiritual perception, which need to be acquired through spiritual exercise.

SOME PRACTICAL EXERCISES

Of course, the best way to learn spiritual perception is to practice it. This means, as often as possible, seeing the individuality of self and others. But one must become accustomed to this. A certain kind of meditation will help. It involves contemplation rather than affirmation; it is essentially living with questions. One takes the question into one's heart. One contemplates it with one's whole being, and not just with one's intellect. One does not try to answer it quickly, but instead lets it live inside oneself, gradually revealing its own answers. The questions themselves are inexhaustible, and by surrendering oneself to the question one can keep learning from it indefinitely.

Here are some questions to start with. Others will come to mind as one acquires practice:

1. I see not just the body but the spirit that it masks.

- What is goodness?
- What are the qualities of goodness? Which of these qualities go beyond the five physical senses?
- What does it mean to sense the presence of goodness?
- Can I sense goodness as creative power?
- How do I sense qualities of goodness such as love, beauty, honesty, integrity, truth, justice, and compassion? Of what other such qualities am I aware?
- What does it mean to understand God as Absolute Goodness?
- How does the body express goodness?
- How does the physical express what is not really physical?

- Can I perceive qualities of goodness in the presence of another human being? In myself?

2. I feel the spirit that animates my being.

- Who am I really? How does God, Absolute Goodness, know me?
- What did God create when I was formed?
- What goodness do I sense in my own being?
- Am I aware of any love within myself that does not depend on what I receive in return?
- Am I aware of kind intentions towards others?
- Am I aware of creative activity that fulfills me or others with whom I am in contact?
- Can I find a sense of humor that brings joy to me and others?
- Can I grasp my own unique essence intuitively?
- Can I similarly grasp the unique essence of others?

3. I sense the love that attracts spirits to each other.

- Can I sense the beauty in the nature around me?
- Can I sense the beauty in the smiles and kind acts of others?
- Can I sense goodness in the way my work or the work of others contributes to people's well being?
- Can I sense the wish to be kind, in myself or in others?
- Can I sense the good will that naturally draws people together, even strangers?
- Can I sense the love present in a stranger's kind gesture or offer of help, even in small things?

4. I meet the darkness in myself with the light that returns me to my origin.

- Can I sense in myself that which masks the good?
- Can I sense negative emotions: fear, anger, jealousy, hate, inhibiting or masking the goodness I would otherwise feel naturally inclined to express?
- Am I aware when I go out of control, dominated by these emotions?
- Can I sense these emotional reactions as masking my nature, which would otherwise take form as a spontaneous expression of goodness?
- Can I remember what that nature is?
- How did I experience that nature before darkness began to obscure it?
- Can I begin to recollect it, retrieve it?

5. I meet the darkness in others with light that carries the power of goodness.

- Knowing the dark mask in myself, can I see others' negativity as a mask over their true natures?
- How can I meet that negativity without getting submerged in it?
- Is there any other way besides my darkness screaming at their darkness?
- Knowing goodness as creative power, can I see that power come to bear on a situation of conflict?
- Can this creative power find a way through that conflict other than fear and anger?
- Can the creative power of goodness enable me to meet that conflict with truth, integrity, justice, and compassion?

These questions can be read quickly, but they cannot be practiced quickly. It is best to consider only one at a time. They contain enough material for months or even years of contemplation and, hopefully, transformation. None of these questions is simple, and none has just one answer. They are not mental exercises. They are meant to be lived with, to become a part of one's meditative practice and then a conscious part of one's being. So practiced, they can begin to stop our reflexive emotional reactions and reduce the stress that negative emotions inflict on both our minds and our bodies.

As one works with these principles and ideas, other exercises will suggest themselves, tailored to each individual need. One reader working with these meditations has found the following helpful:

> I just let the idea of goodness hovering around be present with me. I don't have to deny anything, or change anything; I just have to remember that it's there. I find it a gentle, soothing, comforting thing, and a number of times little nuggets have taken shape right in front of me, unexpectedly and most helpfully.

JUDEOCHRISTIANITY "ON ONE FOOT"

This is Judeochristianity in both theory and practice. It tells us that God is Goodness Itself, that we are created in God's image, and that we can find this image through love as a transformation of our perception to detect the true individuality of both ourselves and others.

IV

ETERNAL LIFE

Jesus said to them, "My food is to do the will of him who sent me and to complete his work. Do you not say, 'Four months more, then comes the harvest'? But I tell you, look around you, and see how the fields are ripe for harvesting. The reaper is already receiving wages and is gathering fruit for eternal life, so that sower and reaper may rejoice together."

John 4:34–36

ETERNITY: THAT WHICH ENDURES

IF YOU TALK ABOUT religion with people who are religious, you may hear a lot about "eternal life." In most of these discussions, eternal life is a rather simple thing. It is a state of happiness after we die. And to be assured of entering this bliss, one need only believe the accepted religious doctrine.

While this does sound nice and simple, it is completely false to what the Bible says. Eternal life is not simply a matter of belief. And eternity is not simply a place outside the physical world.

In my music therapy work with hospice patients I often sing a comforting hymn based upon these words from Paul:

> *If we live, we live to the Lord,*
> *and if we die, we die to the Lord;*
> *so then, whether we live or whether we die,*
> *we are the Lord's.* (Romans 14:8)

We are the Lord's. We belong to God, but right now we are here. We have two natures, one spiritual and one animal, one eternal and one temporal. Eternity is the home of our spiritual nature.

It is impossible to grasp what eternity is like. On this human plane our understanding is limited. Also, everyone experiences the eternal differently. But we can still have a sense of it. Jesus said, "Do not store up for yourselves treasures on earth, where moth and rust consume and where thieves break in and steal, but store up for yourselves treasures in heaven, where neither moth nor rust consumes and where thieves do not break in and steal" (Matthew 6:19–20). We can sense what is ephemeral and what has lasting significance. At the end of life, the pleasures of the moment will count for nothing, no matter how intense they may once have seemed. But the love we shared with others will endure, if indeed it was a genuine expression of caring that brought us beyond the narrow limits of self.

While we are here on earth, we are torn between these two possible directions, these two dimensions of life. Through our earthly nature we love pleasure and amusement, but through our spiritual nature we seek something more lasting. A good life on earth consists of a healthy balance of both. Indulging our earthly nature to the neglect of the spiritual leads to emptiness, chasing shadows that never end and lead nowhere. But trying to live only in our spiritual nature may tempt us to cut ourselves off from others, from the daily pleasures and annoyances of family life and other personal interaction. That too is emptiness, since in our earthly life the spiritual is fulfilled through involvement with the world.

THE SPIRITUAL SENSE: OUR SENSE OF GOODNESS

We do have a sense that tells us the difference between that which vanishes with the earth and that which endures—ironically, even if we don't believe there is anything beyond the earth. Often when I get upset about something trivial, I ask myself, "Will this still matter on 'graduation day' (the final day of this life, when we make the transition to whatever lies beyond)?" This immediately puts things into perspective. Some things will matter on that day: the love we have shared, the goodness we experienced, the integrity with which we have lived our lives. All of these are spiritual values.

We all possess this sense, which tells us the difference between what is of preliminary and what is of ultimate significance. We may call it our sense of goodness. We know what is good and what is neutral or evil, whether or not we choose to behave accordingly. Of course there are ambiguous situations, times when it is hard to identify the good or to choose between competing goods. Our sense is not perfect; still, we have it, and usually we know what goodness is. Through this sense I can identify good qualities: love, beauty, honesty, integrity, kindness, compassion, truth, and justice. I believe I know these qualities are good because of this sense of goodness implanted in me as a spiritual being.

This sense of goodness also tells me that God exists. The existence of God cannot be proven. But my ability to sense goodness comes from somewhere. From where?

Some will say my sense of goodness comes from what I have been taught, or from the values of the culture in which I was raised. But through this sense I can identify the good and the bad in what I have been taught, detect flaws in the values of my culture, and perceive the need for change. The sense of goodness is beyond culture and upbringing.

Some will say the sense of goodness simply evolved. But the theory of evolution, applied beyond the limits of biology, becomes pure speculation. I can't think of any reason why the principles of natural selection should predict the evolution of a sense of goodness, but no doubt there is some evolutionist who can. I'm also certain that if we had no sense of goodness, that if everything seemed just as valid—or valueless—as everything else, that some evolutionist could explain that too. Within the realm of biology the theory of evolution makes sense and has explanatory power, but when carried further it tends to start from a conclusion and allow the conclusion to determine the reasons for supporting it. It's far more likely that we are able to sense goodness because there really are things that are intrinsically good. The source of the goodness we perceive is what I choose to call God.

My ability to sense goodness comes from God, who is the source of all goodness, Absolute Goodness, or Goodness Itself. All I can really say with certainty about God is that God is good. "O give thanks to the Lord, for he is good" (Psalm 118:1). The same words may be translated, "for [God] is goodness," or "for goodness is." We can say that a spiritual life consists of recognizing this sense of goodness, listening to it, and trying as much as possible to live by it.

If God is good, then how do we account for the existence of evil in a world that God created? This complex subject requires a separate discussion, which will come later in this book. Briefly, some explain evil by pointing to human free will—God wanted human beings to have free will even at the risk of their misusing it. This explanation is inadequate, since even free will cannot justify the most extreme and sadistic forms of evil. It also cannot explain "natural evil," like the devastation of hurricanes and earthquakes and the misery of degenerative disease. The true reconciliation of God and evil comes from a deeply paradoxical truth: that only through the existence of evil can love become conscious.

Perhaps our deepest consolation is found in realizing that evil does not survive into eternity. Evil is the negation of value. By its very nature it is temporary; it is time-bound. It perishes with the earth. It does not belong to God's Kingdom.

The Kingdom of God is the biblical symbol for eternity, for that which is beyond time. A popular misunderstanding is that eternity is a period of endless time that follows the brief period of time in which we live on earth. This cannot be true, for then eternity would be nothing more than an extension of time. The Bible teaches otherwise: "The kingdom of God is not coming with signs to be observed; nor will they say, 'Lo, here it is!' or 'There!' for behold, the kingdom of God is in the midst of you" (Luke 17:20–21).

Time and eternity are here together, right in this moment. Eternity is another dimension of existence, of which we are usually not aware, but which can enter our awareness as an experience of the sacred or the transcendent. We can experience this in many ways: in loving relationships, listening to inspired music, being of service, or even in profound moments of peace in the midst of a crisis or approaching the moment of death. Once again, an inner sense tells us when we have experienced something beyond ordinary time.

The more we value and practice goodness, the more likely we are to come into contact with the eternal. If we live with these values long enough, we may acquire a sense that the events in our lives are not random but follow a pattern that eventually takes shape as our destiny. One way the eternal dimension makes itself visible in our lives is through the timing of events. At a certain point we can look back in time and notice that many apparent coincidences no longer seem random but part of a direction given to our lives. The emerging consciousness of this directionality is a central aspect of faith.

One of the first patients I met in hospice had this faith. He told me, "God has taken care of me up till now, and will continue taking care of me to the end." From the assurance I felt in him I knew he was telling me the truth. I only saw him that one time. When I returned to the hospice a week later he was no longer there.

Some of us are fortunate to be born into this faith, if our parents have it and succeed in teaching it to us. For others, it can be a lifelong struggle. The way to acquire this faith—slowly and gradually if need be—is to develop our sense of goodness. The suggestions for meditation at the end of the previous chapter may help. We can learn to discern the values of goodness, and so gradually build a sense of the presence of the divine.

The core of goodness is love, and love is the root of faith. "There is no fear in love, but perfect love casts out fear" (1 John 4:18). Perfect love—non-self-interested love—eventually overcomes fear and brings us to faith. It does so by conforming us to God's image, which is Goodness Itself, and God always responds to what conforms to this image. "Just as we have borne the image of the man of dust, we shall also bear the image of the man of heaven" (1 Corinthians 15:49). God "recognizes" God's own image in us and responds to it, and we sense the divine presence in our lives. This cannot be proven in the abstract. It must be practiced for its truth to become real. One practices it by using one's sense of goodness and by devoting oneself, as much as human imperfection permits, to non-self-interested love. This is the kind of faith upon which one can stake one's life.

ETERNITY AND DEATH

The question always arises: What is the relationship between eternity and physical death? What is left after all that is temporal has passed away? No one can say with certainty what lies beyond the moment of death. Even those who have had "near-death" experiences cannot tell us—by the very fact that they survived, they have not really died. Our spiritual senses, however, may be able to give us a tiny clue.

Our sense of goodness tells us that justice is a part of goodness. And justice in this world is incomplete. It must therefore be completed in eternity, if indeed goodness is God's nature. So it seems that some process of correction or learning would continue after death. We cannot know the precise form it will take, but it is highly likely that the more estranged from our sense of goodness we have been, the more difficult our learning process will be—we will have that much more still to learn.

As we've already noted, eternity is not something that happens "after" death. Eternity and temporal existence are intertwined. Yet there is a special connection between death and eternity. One might perhaps say that death removes a mask from the face of the eternal. "For now we see in a mirror dimly, but then face to face" (1 Corinthians 13:12). Often in hospice, as the moment of a patient's death approaches, I can sense a mask slipping away, and feel the peaceful radiance of the soul. I pray that the person finally will see "face to face," and that the seeing will bring healing and joy.

Because I have sensed this so often in my work, I believe that at least for most of us death is a benign process. Death frees the soul to come closer to eternity, after it has begun its learning here on earth. This does not mean, however, that we can shortcut the process by hastening our own death. Justice demands that we be accountable for our lives, and for the effects our actions have had on others. To teach this, the New Testament uses the image of the "steward": we will have to account for how we have managed the resources that were entrusted to us.

What then of the ultimate punishment? What of hell and its fire? It's in the Bible. What does it mean?

A BRIEF HISTORY OF HELL

Nowhere in the Bible does it say that hell is the fate of those who do not believe. (The one verse in English Bibles that does seem to say this is based on a mistranslation.) We will return to this later. First we need to go back a bit in history and see how the whole concept of "hell" developed.

We often think of hell as a place where everlasting fire torments the souls of unrepentant sinners. Many take this literally, but "fire" is an apt metaphor expressing the anguish a soul may experience when one becomes aware of and begins to regret one's transgressions. It is instructive to look at how fire first became associated with hell.

The most common word for "hell" in the New Testament is *gehenna*. This is Greek for the Hebrew *ge hinnom*, "Valley of Hinnom." This valley was a real place on earth; it lay southwest of Jerusalem. As the Israelite monarchy yielded to paganism, children were sacrificed there in flames to Baal. This is the origin of the flames of hell. The Valley of Hinnom became known as a place of slaughter, utterly devoid of God's presence.

Later, when people began to hope for the messiah, the Valley of Hinnom became a symbol. It stood for the place of ultimate torment of the wicked. The apocryphal book of Enoch calls it "a deep pit with columns of heavenly fire" and "a place without the heavenly firmament above it," "a desolate and terrible place" (1 Enoch 18:11–13). Slowly the image of hell current in Jesus's day began to crystallize.

"Hell" became an image for existence away from the presence of God. It is abandonment to guilt, fear, and destruction. It is the moment when our awareness is restored and we confront the results of the way we have lived our lives. "Hell" is an ultimate symbol: Jesus uses it to describe the condition into which one may fall at the end of one's life, if one has not lived it wisely.

Indeed, what will most distinguish our eventual transition from time to eternity may well be a restoration of awareness. This will bring both heaven and hell in a single strike. Becoming aware of how our love and our kindness have affected others in ways we may never have known will bring us heavenly joy. Becoming fully aware of how our selfishness, cruelty, and neglect have affected others will cast us into the flames of remorse and regret, and may truly be an experience of hell. The "afterlife" may simply be a restoration of awareness. That would certainly provide sufficient hell for anyone who deserves it.

In describing hell Jesus never talks about what one believes but about what one does: "I say to you that if you are angry with a brother or sister, you will be liable to judgment; and if you insult a brother or sister, you will be liable to the council; and if you say, 'You fool,' you will be liable to the hell of fire" (Matthew 5:22). Hell is a consequence of having abused others, even of not having treated others kindly. Jesus makes this clear in two parables:

1. THE PARABLE OF THE RICH MAN AND LAZARUS

There was a rich man who was dressed in purple and fine linen and who feasted sumptuously every day. And at his gate lay a poor man named Lazarus, covered with sores, who longed to satisfy his hunger with what fell from the rich man's table; even the dogs would come and lick his sores. The poor man died and was carried away by the angels to be with Abraham. The rich man also died and was buried.

In Hades, where he was being tormented, he looked up and saw Abraham far away with Lazarus by his side. He called out, "Father Abraham, have mercy on me, and send Lazarus to dip the tip of his finger in water and cool my tongue; for I am in agony in these flames." But Abraham said, "Child, remember that during your lifetime you received your good things, and Lazarus in like manner evil things; but now he is comforted here, and you are in agony. Besides all this, between you and us a great chasm has been fixed, so that those who might want to pass from here to you cannot do so, and no one can cross from there to us." He said, "Then, father, I beg you to send him to my father's house—for I have five brothers—that he may warn them, so that they will not also come into this place of torment." Abraham replied, "They have Moses and the prophets; they should listen to them." He said, "No, father Abraham; but if someone goes to them from the dead, they will repent." He said to him, "If they do not listen to Moses and the prophets, neither will they be convinced even if someone rises from the dead." (Luke 16:19–31)

2. THE PARABLE OF THE SHEEP AND THE GOATS

When the Son of Man comes in his glory, and all the angels with him, then he will sit on the throne of his glory. All the nations will be gathered before him, and he will separate people one from another as a shepherd separates the sheep from the goats, and he will put the sheep at his right hand and the goats at the left. Then the king will say to those at his right hand, "Come, you that are blessed by my Father, inherit the kingdom prepared for you from the foundation of the world; for I was hungry and you gave me food, I was thirsty and you gave me something to drink, I was a stranger and you welcomed me, I was naked and you gave me clothing, I was sick and you took care of me, I was in prison and you visited me." Then the righteous will answer him, "Lord, when was it that we saw you hungry and gave you food, or thirsty and gave you something to drink? And when was it that we saw you a stranger and welcomed you, or naked and gave you clothing? And when was it that we saw you sick or in prison and visited you?" And the king will answer them, "Truly I tell you, just as you did it to one of the least of these who are members of my family, you did it to me."

Then he will say to those at his left hand, "You that are accursed, depart from me into the eternal fire prepared for the devil and his angels; for I was hungry and you gave me no food, I was thirsty and you gave me nothing to drink, I was a stranger and you did not welcome me, naked and you did not give me clothing, sick and in prison and you did not visit me." Then they also will answer, "Lord, when was it that we saw you hungry or thirsty or a stranger or naked or sick or in prison, and did not take care of you?" Then he will answer them, "Truly I tell you, just as you did not do it to one of the least of these, you did not do it to me." And these will go away into eternal punishment, but the righteous into eternal life. (Matthew 25:31–46)

In both these parables, which so vividly describe hell's torments, the issue is not what one believes but what one does. Neither has anything to do with believing anything. What both describe are the consequences of the failure to love. This is what casts one into hell, which, as we have observed, is the consciousness of living away from God. Before entering hell, one is not conscious of living away from God. At a certain point one becomes aware, and then one finds oneself in hell.

This discussion would not be complete without addressing biblical passages that seem to suggest eternal condemnation based on belief. The most salient of these comes from the Gospel of John:

> *For God so loved the world that he gave his only Son, so that everyone who believes in him may not perish but may have eternal life. Indeed, God did not send the Son into the world to condemn the world, but in order that the world might be saved through him. Those who believe in him are not condemned; but those who do not believe are condemned already, because they have not believed in the name of the only Son of God.* (John 3:16–18)

This passage sounds "damning," but its use to prove belief as a condition for salvation is based both on selective quotation and misleading translation. The Greek word translated "condemned" ("those who do not believe are condemned [*kekritai*, from *krino*] already") originally meant to "consider" or to "judge." The passage should be translated as follows (with added emphasis to make the meaning clear):

> *God loved the world so much that he gave his only begotten Son, so that all **who have faith** in him may not perish but have eternal life. For God did not send his Son into the world that he might **judge** the world, but that the world might be saved through him. Those **who have faith** in him **are not judged**; but those who do not have faith **are already judged**, because they*

did not have faith in the name of the only begotten Son of God.

We do not have to speculate about what this "judgment" means, or to read into it damnation to an everlasting hell. The Bible itself tells us what it means, and in the very next verse:

> And this is the **judgment**, that the light has come into the world, and people loved darkness rather than light **because their deeds were evil**. For all who **do evil** hate the light and do not come to the light, so that their deeds may not be exposed. But those who do what is true come to the light, so that it may be clearly seen that their deeds have been done in God. (John 3:19–21)

The word "judgment" (*krisis*) in this passage comes from the same Greek root as the word in the previous passage usually translated as "condemned." We are told what this judgment ("condemnation") is, and it has nothing to do with an everlasting fiery hell. It has to do with loving darkness rather than light, trying to hide from the light, and doing evil deeds.

Judgment depends on one's deeds, not on one's beliefs. What then is the role of belief? The Greek word usually translated "believe" (*pisteuo*, from which comes *pistis*, "faith" or "trust") is much richer in meaning than its English equivalent. It does not mean simply assenting to a proposition but rather total commitment resulting from a profound inner transformation. This is how the word must be understood in the New Testament. The meaning of the passage from John is that those who love the light, in other words, goodness, will resonate with Jesus's message, and this will be revealed in their lives and in their deeds. Those who do not love goodness will reject the message, and this too will be evident and will constitute a judgment.

What does Jesus have to say about whether the simple act of professing belief in him confers salvation from the torments of hell?

> *Not everyone who says to me, "Lord, Lord," will enter the kingdom of heaven, but only the one who does the will of my Father in heaven. On that day many will say to me, "Lord, Lord, did we not prophesy in your name, and cast out demons in your name, and do many deeds of power in your name?" Then I will declare to them, "I never knew you; go away from me, you evildoers."* (Matthew 7:21–23)

Jesus could hardly have been clearer. Calling Jesus Lord has nothing in itself to do with salvation. What does? Doing God's will. And what is that? The parables explain it: it is learning to love, in one's heart and in one's actions.

Hell is not a place of literal fire. The body perishes, the spirit endures, and there is no body that can burn forever. Does hell last forever? It lasts as long as one chooses to reject love. However, if one's fate were irrevocably sealed, it would contradict the nature of God, who is "merciful and gracious, slow to anger, and abounding in steadfast love and faithfulness" (Exodus 34:16). "The Lord is merciful and gracious, slow to anger and abounding in steadfast love. He will not always accuse, nor will he keep his anger forever" (Psalm 103:8–9). Hell is not forever. If God could withdraw the possibility of forgiveness forever, with no chance of the lost soul's returning no matter how deep its repentance, then God would be cruel beyond human imagining. Such a God could not be Absolute Goodness.

This seems obvious. Nevertheless many people, including quite a few great religious figures, have not understood it. While professing belief in a God who is good, they seem to have little difficulty imagining a good God meting out eternal damnation even to people who have led exemplary lives. St. Augustine went as far as to teach that infants who die without having first been baptized are eternally damned, because they have not been cleansed of original sin. He also taught a doctrine known as "double predestination": that before time God determined who would be saved and who would be damned, independent of their future actions. The most notable exponent of this doctrine after Augustine was John Calvin, though other Christian theologians also adopted some form of predestination.

These doctrines strongly clash with our sense of right and wrong. How can a merciful God consign people to everlasting flames even if they have led good and moral lives? How can God forever condemn an unbaptized infant who cannot even choose to sin? Does this not take religious symbolism to a bizarre extreme? The answer always given is that these beliefs are based on scripture, and that we cannot apply human standards to the mysterious wisdom of God, whose great mercy passes our understanding.

Such explanations are unacceptable. First, there is no scriptural basis for any of these ideas, as we have seen. The texts traditionally used to justify them must be stretched to the breaking point in order to make them fit.

But there is an even more important and fundamental objection to eternal damnation based on belief. Our sense of goodness is finite and imperfect. There are gray areas, ambiguous situations in which different goods may seem to conflict. However, some situations are so clear that they must violate even a rudimentary sense of goodness. The idea that God endlessly tortures babies, or saves wicked people who believe while damning moral people who do not, certainly qualifies. Since this punishment of the innocent is considered "eternal" and irrevocable, no conceivable good could come from it. No one with an intact sense of goodness can believe such an idea.

God endowed us with a sense of goodness. Why would God want us to ignore it, simply to uphold a received tradition that may be flawed or that we may not even have understood? To justify a bad idea by calling it a "mystery" is bad stewardship, a waste of the mental and spiritual resources God has entrusted to us. A God of forgiveness cannot be eternally unforgiving.

TREASURE IN HEAVEN

"Store up for yourselves treasures in heaven, where neither moth nor rust consumes and where thieves do not break in and steal." "The reaper is already receiving wages and is gathering fruit for eternal life." The goodness in which we participate is the treasure in heaven, and it cannot be destroyed. It is eternal. "Eternal" does not mean "everlasting." Eternal life is not "after." It is now. If we miss it now, we will have difficulty grasping it later.

We often speak of "eternity" and "time" as opposites. Yet time can be an entrance to the eternal. Time is mysterious. We can remember the past, we can anticipate the future, but the present escapes us. As soon as we think about the present, it's in the past. Yet we live in the present moment. And lived rightly, with awareness, the present moment opens us to eternity. The present moment is really outside of time, and removes us from the burden of time. Through the present moment, we can become aware of what is beyond time. In the Gospel of Thomas (5) Jesus says: "Recognize what is right in front of you, and that which is hidden from you will be revealed to you."

Love is remembered in the past, hoped for in the future, but lives in the present. Awareness of the present moment can, by its very nature, bring us the love that belongs to eternity, the love that is not destroyed. This abstract idea becomes concrete only in the world of other people. In this moment, can I be aware of the cashier at the supermarket who checks out my food? Can I be aware of the waitress in the restaurant who serves me? The people I meet at work who often irritate me? The bus driver who takes me home? The beauty of understanding love as awareness is that love can be shared in very tiny as well as in profound ways. This is what it means to know eternal life within our time-bound existence.

At any moment in which we are aware, our vision of the other is transformed, and so also are we. As a hospice music therapist and spiritual caregiver, I learn constantly from my patients. One Dominican family taught me a song that expresses how awareness of the moment shows us eternity. Here is a translation from the original Spanish:

> I have finally met Jesus
> After searching for so long,
> In my brothers and my sisters,
> In their joy and in their cross.
>
> I have met him in the paper boy,
> In the one who's shining shoes,
> In the one down in the garage
> Who cleans the windows of cars:
> It's the image of Jesus.

> I've met him in the worker
> Who toils without rest,
> More than eight hours a day
> For pitiful wages:
> It's the image of Jesus.
>
> I have seen him in hospitals,
> I have seen him in nursing homes,
> In crazy deaf-mutes,
> In the sick and in the blind:
> They speak so much of Jesus.
>
> I've seen him in those people
> So anxious for change,
> Who devote themselves to struggling
> For a more humane world:
> To be the image of Jesus.
>
> I have finally met Jesus
> After searching for so long,
> In my brothers and my sisters,
> In their joy and in their cross.

Our awareness of the ordinary moment transforms it into the vision of Christ. *Just as you did it to one of the least of these who are members of my family, you did it to me.*

AT THE THRESHOLD OF ETERNITY

Eternity is revealed through time, perhaps at no point as strongly as when the moment of death approaches. For then we are pushed up against the boundary of time, and are forced to confront time's limits. In hospice I have shared these moments with many patients, and have often been overtaken by a transcendent peace I sense within them as they prepare inwardly for this transition. This peace may come to believer and nonbeliever alike. What prepares us for it is the way we live our lives. In the heart in which love lives, God lives.

I conclude with the story of one patient, Joanna.

> It was noon. Joanna was lying in bed, her head facing toward the window, her left arm stretched out in front of her. She was comatose, and could not speak. Most of those around her thought this meant she could not respond.
>
> I pulled a chair close to her bed, so that I could see her face. I looked at her and sang songs that would take her to soothing places, a sunny island where she could sing and laugh, or a sailing ship upon whose deck she could rest with the breeze blowing over her. I sang her songs about angels waiting across the bridge to take her home.
>
> Joanna really was young, 30 years old and dying of kidney failure. I could barely notice her soft breathing over the pillow that supported her head as she faced me. I put down my guitar and stroked her arm. I asked her if she enjoyed the music. She gave a slight nod of her head and a barely perceptible movement of her lips. She did this twice, once after each song.
>
> I wondered at the strange, deep peace I was starting to feel. I began to sense Joanna's presence very strongly, and in my need to express it I turned to her mother, who was sitting next to me, and said: "There is a lot of love in this woman." My words startled her, and she asked, "How did you know?" Then she began to tell me things about Joanna.
>
> Joanna seemed born with a loving heart. She gave blood frequently, until she was diagnosed with diabetes and had to stop. She volunteered in nursing homes. She made sandwiches and, in spite of her father's concerns for her safety, distributed them to homeless people near the Port Authority,

not one of New York's best neighborhoods. Her only regret was running out of sandwiches and wishing she had made some more.

I left Joanna to rest and told her mother I would come back. When I returned about 6:00 P.M. I found Joanna moved to a private room, with more space and more quiet. Joanna's boyfriend arrived, and I told him that although she does not seem conscious, she will know he is there, just as she knew that I, a total stranger, had been with her. We entered the room, and I held the railing of Joanna's bed and looked at her. Once again I felt in her a strong presence, something beyond her that both shook me and filled me with peace. I saw something change, and tears came to my eyes. I knew Joanna was not alone. I turned to her mother and said, "Your daughter's angels are working overtime." Within minutes, Joanna died.

I believe that what I "saw" was Joanna's angels coming to take her home. The presence, the deep power and peace that I felt holding Joanna during her last moments, left as suddenly as it came. Joanna died with no anxiety, no agitation, none of the signs of discomfort I see at times with other patients. I let her mother know that I had never witnessed a more peaceful death in all my years in hospice.

The boundary between time and eternity had disappeared.

V

LOVE AND AWARENESS

He entered Jericho and was passing through it. A man was there named Zacchaeus; he was a chief tax collector and was rich. He was trying to see who Jesus was, but on account of the crowd he could not, because he was short in stature. So he ran ahead and climbed a sycamore tree to see him, because he was going to pass that way. When Jesus came to the place, he looked up and said to him, "Zacchaeus, hurry and come down; for I must stay at your house today." So he hurried down and was happy to welcome him. All who saw it began to grumble and said, "He has gone to be the guest of one who is a sinner." Zacchaeus stood there and said to the Lord, "Look, half of my possessions, Lord, I will give to the poor; and if I have defrauded anyone of anything, I will pay back four times as much." Then Jesus said to him, "Today salvation has come to this house, because he too is a son of Abraham. For the Son of Man came to seek out and to save the lost."

Luke 19:1–10

For if you love those who love you, what reward do you have? Do not even the tax collectors do the same?

Matthew 5:46

THE COMMANDMENT TO LOVE

"I GIVE YOU A NEW COMMANDMENT," Jesus told his disciples, "that you love one another. Just as I have loved you, you should also love one another" (John 13:34).

What is so "new" about this commandment? Love has been commanded before, both the love of one's neighbor (Leviticus 19:18: "You shall love your neighbor as yourself") and the love of God (Deuteronomy 6:5: "You shall love the Lord your God with all your heart, with all your soul, and with all your might"). But Jesus both expands the scope of love and makes it more explicit:

> You have heard that it was said, "You shall love your neighbor and hate your enemy." But I say to you, Love your enemies and pray for those who persecute you, so that you may be children of your Father in heaven; for he makes his sun rise on the evil and on the good, and sends rain on the righteous and on the unrighteous. For if you love those who love you, what reward do you have? Do not even the tax collectors do the same? And if you

greet only your brothers and sisters, what more are you doing than others? Do not even the Gentiles do the same? Be perfect, therefore, as your heavenly Father is perfect. (Matthew 5:43–46)

Now, nowhere in the Bible does it say we should hate our enemies. But it is clear that love's reach does not usually extend to everyone. The exhortations in Leviticus to refrain from bearing grudges or taking revenge are expressed in terms of "your own people." What is new about the love Jesus preaches is that its scope is deliberately unrestricted.

The universality of this love may seem astonishing. It just does not seem natural to love everyone. People have enemies, and even though these may be few, most people are strangers to each other. One who loves indiscriminately might appear to be a coward or a fool, someone easily exploited. How else can we understand statements like the following:

But I say to you, Do not resist an evildoer. But if anyone strikes you on the right cheek, turn the other also; and if anyone wants to sue you and take your coat, give your cloak as well; and if anyone forces you to go one mile, go also the second mile. (Matthew 5:39–41)

It sounds like Jesus is telling his disciples to be weak and spineless, to allow others to take advantage of them at will. This would be true if one were to follow Jesus's advice out of any motive except love: for example, out of fear. But Jesus is not talking about fear. His purpose is to shake his audience, to transform our understanding of love completely. What if we felt so secure in God's love for us, that we could make concessions to people who demand the unreasonable without feeling we have lost anything? Then what might appear to others as weakness would really be a profound inner strength.

What kind of love can Jesus be talking about, that appears so weak to the undiscerning while in reality it is the greatest strength one can possess?

To understand this love we need, as Jesus did, to contrast it with the ways we usually love.

"FAMILIAR" LOVE

The love that we normally know, which we may call "familiar love," is limited. "Familiar" love begins within the family. We love our parents because they provide for us and take care of us. Later on, sexual and romantic love may lead us to a family of our own. The bond of marriage is private. Its intimacy sets two people apart from the rest of the world; they share with each other what cannot be shared with outsiders. The family too is very personal territory. "One's home is one's castle," and castles stand apart from other castles, ready to defend themselves against unwanted intrusions.

Beyond the family one may love one's country, one's religious or ethnic group, or any group with which one identifies. Once again these forms of love all distinguish insiders, those who are like oneself, from outsiders, those who are different and who do not belong to the group.

This is what familiar love is like. It is not bad, it is just the way it is. Human love is possessive; it "seeks its own." It has to be that way, to preserve the individual, the family, and the species itself. Freud put it very simply. He said there are two kinds of love: we love those who take care of us, and we love those who are like ourselves. However we love, we are creatures of self-interest. We side with those who are for us, and we distrust and even resent those who are different, outside the circle that our love defines.

Ironically, familiar love seems almost to imply hate. If we love those to whom we feel a special affinity, a sexual, familial, religious, ethnic, or national connection, we become tempted to hate others, to be defensive and suspicious towards them. This is the dark side of familiar love. It lies at the heart of racial prejudice and xenophobia, as well as the hostility towards others we may experience simply in being protective of our spouse or children. It seems only natural to look after ourselves by being afraid of that which is different. Fear, often leading to hate, comes from our desire to protect that which we love.

The ambiguity of familiar love is reflected even in the idiomatic use of language. Consider the following from the King James translation of the Bible:

> *If a man have two wives, one beloved, and another hated, and they have born him children, both the beloved and the hated; and if the firstborn son be hers that was hated: Then it shall be, when he maketh his sons to inherit that which he hath, that he may not make the son of the beloved firstborn before the son of the hated, which is indeed the firstborn: But he shall acknowledge the son of the hated for the firstborn, by giving him a double portion of all that he hath: for he is the beginning of his strength; the right of the firstborn is his.* (Deuteronomy 21:15–17)

The Hebrew word here translated "hated" (*senuah*) does mean this literally, but when used in a context like this one it is an idiom meaning simply "less loved." It does not even mean "disliked," as the NRSV renders it; it is simply a term indicating relative preference. But as the language suggests, that which love does not include is immediately associated in the human mind with hate; it is on the outside, rejected. Familiar love has a tendency to exclude the outsider. This is human reality, which the Bible recognizes by taking special pains to protect the right of the child of the one who is less loved.

NON-SELF-INTERESTED LOVE

Jesus's purpose was to point us towards a love that surpasses the limitations of familiar love. To make clear how this new love differed from the love everyone already knew, he had to make his own life a radical statement of this love. Familiar love is limited, since it involves identification with a specific group of people: a friendship, a couple, a family, an ethnic group, a race, a nation. Thus Jesus's mysterious saying, "Foxes have holes, and birds of the air have nests, but the Son of Man has nowhere to lay his head" (Matthew 8:20): Jesus does not identify with any group; he lacks the security and sense of place that familiar love provides. He can demonstrate only one kind of love: the love he wishes to set over and against familiar love and its underside of hate.

How does Jesus set apart this new, spiritual love from all other forms of love? In two ways: by his teaching, and by his personal example. In his teaching Jesus says that he brings a "new commandment," a commandment of a love that is new and different, love not only toward those with whom one feels a special affinity but toward the stranger and even toward the enemy. But teachings alone are often ineffective. They can invite us to contemplate higher values, but statements about these values are often hard to assimilate. Very often they just bounce off our old habits and prejudices instead of penetrating through them. So Jesus frequently resorted to indirect methods of teaching. He taught in similes and parables, looking for ways to appeal to the hearts of his listeners.

In the concluding chapters of the Gospel of John we find Jesus teaching Peter the meaning of this love in a way that is indirect but striking:

> *When they had finished breakfast, Jesus said to Simon Peter, "Simon son of John, do you love me more than these?" He said to him, "Yes, Lord; you know that I love you." Jesus said to him, "Feed my lambs." A second time he said to him, "Simon son of John, do you love me?" He said to him, "Yes, Lord; you know that I love you." Jesus said to him, "Tend my sheep." He said to him the third time, "Simon son of John, do you love me?" Peter felt hurt because he said to him the third time, "Do you love me?" And he said to him, "Lord, you know everything; you know that I love you." Jesus said to him, "Feed my sheep." (John 21:15–17)*

In this brief encounter, Jesus, to show Peter the meaning of spiritual love, seizes on what Peter holds most dear: Peter's desire that Jesus know the magnitude of his devotion. Jesus surely knows Peter's love for him, but he wants to show Peter just what this love should mean. And so he must frustrate Peter. First he tells him: if you truly love me and all that I represent, you will not love only me but also those who come to seek my message and who may turn to you for help. You must love them whether or not you find them personally appealing, whether or not you find them to be like yourself or take pleasure in their company.

Peter seems not to know what to say, since he makes no response. Jesus wounds Peter by asking him the question three times. Peter, aggrieved, protests his devotion. Jesus's words have touched his heart and so he feels hurt, but this pain opens him to a new way of seeing.

A look at the original Greek text reveals new meanings of this incident. Scholars disagree on how much weight should be put on the original wording, but the author of this Gospel is such a craftsman, and wordplay is so important in it, that it hardly seems likely his choice of words would have been accidental.

In describing this encounter the Gospel uses two different words for love. When Jesus asks Peter "Do you love me?" he says *agapas me*. When Peter answers "I love you" he says *philo se*. *Agape* and *philia* are often taken to refer to two very different kinds of love. *Philia* is the love that exists between members of a family; it is "familiar love." While it is genuine love, it does not easily accept the stranger, the one outside the family circle. *Agape*, on the other hand, is not self-interested; it does not seek the image of oneself in the one who is loved. The basis of *agape*, non-self-interested, spiritual love, cannot be the familiarity or appeal of the loved one. What then *is* its basis?

The story itself provides a clue. The third time Jesus asks Peter the question, he changes his word. He does not use *agape* but instead asks, "Do you love me?"—*phileis me*—and this time appears to accept Peter's answer. This subtle shift in word choice shows Jesus's awareness of Peter. He sees Peter just where he is, he sees the kind of love Peter wishes to express, and he shows Peter that he sees him and that he accepts him. By shifting to the same word that Peter used, Jesus meets Peter on Peter's own ground. He "speaks Peter's language." This awareness of others and responsiveness to their needs is precisely the basis of the spiritual love that Jesus wants to teach.

Non-self-interested, spiritual love—*agape*—is based upon the awareness of another's individuality. This deep awareness lets others know that they are seen, and therefore understood and loved. And in the one who shows this awareness it awakens understanding and compassion. Non-self-interested love cannot exist without this awareness, and where this awareness exists, non-self-interested love will arise.

But, one may say, doesn't increased awareness of another person often lead not to love but to dislike and even hate? Does not "familiarity breed contempt?" Don't we sometimes find in others qualities that make them unlovable, even repulsive?

"Familiarity" belongs to familiar love. Spiritual love is something else. Its awareness goes deeper than merely noticing the flaws and warts. It goes to the core of the soul. Spiritual love can love even what seems to be unlovable. It does not have to accept or approve of another's destructiveness, but it sees what is behind it: usually fear and ignorance. When one can see beneath the surface behavior, no matter how hurtful or hateful, one's feelings change. One can relax into this awareness; while resisting the bad behavior if necessary—love does not mean having to play the victim—one becomes free of any need to destroy the person who behaves badly. One's own reactive, destructive emotions lose their fire. This makes rational response possible.

LOVING OUR ENEMIES

Jesus even said we need to love our enemies. This cannot mean accepting what they do if it is harmful or destructive—this would send a message that such behavior is permissible, which would be contrary to love. For that reason, loving our enemies cannot mean pacifism. Love is an attitude, a state of the soul. Pacifism has to do with behavior. Pacifism holds that the use of force is never justified, even to protect the well-being of others. Since Jesus never addressed this question, there is no basis for insisting that he preached pacifism under all conditions.

Loving our enemies does not mean feeling good about what they do or mistaking them for friends. Not only would this be humanly impossible, it would be foolish. Enemies will not usually stop being enemies even if you love them. But loving one's enemies means *seeing* one's enemies. It means being aware of them on a very deep level, deep enough so that even if the need for self-protection remains, the urge to hate vanishes. One cannot hate a soul one can see is scarred by the desire to be an enemy.

Spiritual love can love even what seems to be unlovable. At the heart of Jesus's message is the insight that the type of perception that sees only someone's unlovable traits does not go far enough; it is perception at a very shallow level. Only a deep level of awareness can serve as the basis of love. And Jesus demonstrated this by the love he showed to a man whom most considered particularly hateful and loathsome.

Zacchaeus was a tax collector. In Jesus's time people despised tax collectors, and for good reason. Tax collectors acted like extortionists. They made their living by taking more money from people than the Roman authorities required and pocketing the difference. More than likely such activity was the source of Zacchaeus's wealth; he was, after all, a chief among tax collectors. It would seem that to know Zacchaeus would be to find a thoroughly despicable human being. How could anyone possibly love him?

What people saw in Zacchaeus was the obvious, surface appearance. He was a man feared and hated, considered by others a sinner. Jesus did not see him that way. Luke gives us only a few clues to tell us just what Jesus saw.

Zacchaeus did not know who Jesus was, since this is precisely what the Gospel tells us he came to find out. But certainly he was aware of the commotion surrounding Jesus, and that Jesus seemed to be some kind of celebrity. Jesus, for his part, knew Zacchaeus's reputation, since he recognizes him and calls him by name. But he sees more than just the reputation. He sees a little man making a big effort to see him by climbing into a sycamore tree. Is this man just curious? Jesus sees something more, in the man's tenacity, his desperation. He calls to Zacchaeus and invites himself over to his house. Far from taking exception to Jesus's forwardness, Zacchaeus receives him joyfully. Jesus touched something deep in Zacchaeus's heart.

When Jesus saw Zacchaeus watching him from the tree, he saw not simply a curious man, but a human being expressing a strong inner need. This must have touched Jesus too. Knowing Zacchaeus's reputation, Jesus surely knew how much this man was hated. In Zacchaeus's determination he saw not only an indication of the man's curiosity but also an expression of the effect all this hatred must have had upon him. He saw both Zacchaeus's pain at being so despised, and his desire to escape it, to find salvation. Underneath the surface, which is all that superficial perception can detect, Jesus saw a deep spiritual need and a desperate yearning to fulfill it. Jesus was aware of Zacchaeus: he saw something beautiful in a man whom everyone else detested.

Jesus's seeing had a dramatic healing effect on Zacchaeus. Zacchaeus pledges half his goods to the poor, and promises to restore everything not rightfully taken. Jesus calls this a sign of Zacchaeus's "salvation." What accounted for this change, and of what exactly does Zacchaeus's salvation consist?

Perhaps for the first time in his life Zacchaeus found himself in the presence of someone who was aware of him totally. Jesus was no Pollyanna. He clearly saw in Zacchaeus the behavior everyone condemned. He knew that Zacchaeus needed healing. He did not condemn him, because he could see more than his behavior. He saw the core of Zacchaeus's being. He saw Zacchaeus's self-hate and his yearning for another kind of life. He saw also Zacchaeus's ability to change, and his capacity for kindness and love. He saw all this in a man who, to all appearances, was a hateful sinner.

LOVE AS TRANSFORMING PRESENCE

In Jesus's loving presence and through Jesus's seeing him, Zacchaeus for the first time could see in himself these same redeeming qualities. He could see that he really was more than his hateful appearance. He could see that not everything about himself was abhorrent, and he could love himself enough to risk making a loving gesture towards others. Love elicits a loving response, which at first may take the form of remorse. Zacchaeus's remorse is a sign that love has touched his heart.

Because he found himself in the presence of love, Zacchaeus became able to love. The love that transformed him was Jesus's awareness of his complete individuality. Such awareness is not self-interested. It seeks no personal benefit, but only the truth of another's being. When possessed by such love, one's own ego seems almost to disappear: and so Jesus has been called a "transparency" through which God's own love is able to shine. Through the purity of his awareness Jesus allowed not his personal desires but divine love itself to become present to Zacchaeus.

This is the basis of salvation. Salvation is the state of knowing oneself in the presence of love. It is transformation through the power of divine acceptance. It does not result merely from belief, but from profound inner change.

Zacchaeus's healing was not physical; it was moral and spiritual. In the presence of Jesus's total awareness, the correction of his hated flaws became possible. His response was unrestrained joy: joy at finding himself accepted, at finding himself known, at finding himself loved. Joy is the response of the spirit to the power of love.

The highest form of love one can express toward another is the nonpossessive, nonjudgmental awareness of the core of his or her being. Awareness at this level always brings forth a compassionate response toward that person. If we do not respond with compassion, if we respond with indifference, fear, or resentment, then our awareness is not deep enough.

Often we do not respond to what the other is, but to our own thoughts that we project onto the other, or to the way the other makes us feel about ourselves. Usually we respond with hurt and anger when another's actions hurt us personally; these are the moments when love is most difficult. This love does not come to us in an instant. It takes time, commitment, and work to get there—and for this we also need to treat ourselves with compassion. But even if we find it hard to be loving, we can still know that a loving awareness is possible that can transform our entire view of the situation, and perhaps even the situation itself. This knowledge can give us hope when love seems beyond our grasp.

Maintaining the awareness that becomes love is simple to understand but difficult to do. It is what distinguishes Jesus's love, *agape*, from Peter's love, *philia*. *Philia* is not a difficult love to maintain. We naturally love those who love us back, or those to whom we feel close ties. Even the love of all humanity, *phil*anthropy, is not really difficult: one can give of one's substance without really giving of oneself. In contrast, *agape*, love of the *individual*, can be hard work. It is often not easy to love an individual with his or her annoying quirks and eccentricities. In fact, it is impossible—unless we can become truly aware of something else beneath the disagreeable surface.

This kind of love is a great inner strength. It enables us to stand firm in trying situations without being swept away by our emotions. It removes us from the control of other people's provocations. It gives us the freedom to respond not in kind but as the situation requires. If we can respond to hate without hating, then we cannot be manipulated by another's hostility. We cannot become victims of other people's efforts to make us feel upset.

But how can we express or even know this love if we have never experienced it? Zacchaeus had Jesus to show it to him. What if we have never known anyone whose awareness of us was deep enough to show us this love?

Love beyond self is really God's love, and human beings are merely its instruments. Even if we have not come to know such love through a person, we can still develop the capacity for it within ourselves. The way to discover just what this love is, if it was never shown to us, is by becoming aware of what its absence feels like.

This means facing the emptiness and the pain that the absence of this love produces. What would it take to fill this void? If we have any idea at all, can we offer it to others? Doing so may turn out to be the best way to find it for ourselves.

To show this particular kind of love to others—not just any love, but a love that respects their individuality and that makes no demands—may in fact be the way toward knowing that we too are loved by God. "God is love, and those who abide in love abide in God, and God abides in them" (1 John 4:16). To find God as a living presence within the soul, we need to know ourselves as active participants in this love.

BLOCKS TO SPIRITUAL LOVE

There is, however, one tremendous block to non-self-interested love, and that is resentment.

It is important to understand the difference between resentment and anger. Resentment literally means feeling something over and over again. It is like a dirty wound that continues to fester. It drains one's vital energy simply to keep itself in operation.

The frustrating persistence of resentment comes from the presence of self-hate. Resentment is an attack on the self; it creates stress on the body, sapping its energy and wearing down its defenses. It is painful to be in the grasp of resentment, and what makes it so painful is the self-hate that always lies at its root.

What we hate in ourselves is the feeling of being unable to cope, of being powerless, of being the victim of something or someone stronger than we are. Resentment is not the same as anger; it fact, it results from the inability to deal with anger. When anger takes no constructive direction it remains trapped inside oneself and acts upon body and soul like a poison. But often it is easier to turn our anger inward, against ourselves, than to endure the futility of not being able to express it openly, or the guilt and fear we may experience if we do express it.

If resentment blocks our ability to love, we need to find a loving presence within ourselves that can overcome it. Love comes through awareness. The kind of awareness that brings us to love is a nonreactive presence that seeks not to judge but to know and to understand. If we are resentful, we need to understand the burden we are carrying.

This burden is anger. Anger need not be toxic, the way resentment is. Anger is a natural human response to the unfairness and the injustice of life. It turns into resentment when our inability to accept it leads to self-hate. One cannot always will oneself to accept what appears to be unacceptable. So when we confront a situation that we can't accept, our anger keeps bouncing off it and right back to us.

If we are to find freedom, we need not to repress but to focus our anger. Far too often in spirituality anger is spoken of as a bad thing, even as something that will invite retribution in a future existence. Anger in itself is not bad; it depends on what we do with it. If we make a global judgment against all forms of anger, then we will only drive it underground where it really can do terrible damage—the history of religion certainly seems to bear this out. To be sure, Jesus cautioned us about anger:

> *You have heard that it was said to those of ancient times, "You shall not murder," and "whoever murders shall be liable to judgment." But I say to you that if you are angry with a brother or sister, you will be liable to judgment; and if you insult a brother or sister, you will be liable to the council; and if you say, "You fool," you will be liable to the hell of fire.* (Matthew 5:21–22)

Clearly Jesus is talking about an anger that becomes personalized and leads to vindictive or even abusive behavior. In other situations (e.g., Matthew 23) even Jesus expresses anger, but it is anger against injustice and the hypocrisy of the religious leaders of his day. This anger is not vindictive; it is a focused anger that can lead to constructive social change.

Too often in spirituality the ideal of "enlightenment" is confused with quietism. Enlightened individuals are described as having no desires, no attachments, no "upsetness." Such people may be good at meditation but are not likely to be found on the front lines trying to relieve human suffering. Those out there doing the hard work are usually the ones who are sufficiently upset by the sight of sickness, poverty, and pain to be motivated to try to do something to alleviate them.

Danger arises not when anger merely exists but when it starts to control us. When that happens, even anger against injustice can be used to perpetrate new injustice. And so Jesus rightly warned us against vindictive anger. Anger is energy, and must become a servant of the good, not a master itself. If that energy is harnessed and properly channeled, it can accomplish great things. But once anger becomes resentment, it can easily be used as a force for evil.

And so we return to the question of finding a loving presence within ourselves that overcomes our resentment. If we can feel only love's absence, we can find love by practicing awareness. We possess a basic capacity for awareness that we may call the "nonreactive observer." When in the grip of strong emotion, we can step back from it and observe it, as if from a distance. This takes practice, and meditation can be a great help. The "nonreactive observer" within us seeks to understand without judging, and so is fundamentally compassionate. From a safe enough distance, we can let go of the anger as if we were suddenly exhaling a huge breath built up far too long. The energy behind the anger will not disappear, but we will be able to see it and to decide what we want to do with it. Awareness brings freedom.

This freedom enables one to be a helpful presence in difficult situations. When carefully focused, saved from becoming hatred of self or others, anger can become a powerful source of creative energy. Awareness can temper anger with love. Even righteous anger, if it becomes hatred, cannot change things for the better. In fact, any situation that we meet with hate we can meet instead with love, if it is a love that settles for nothing less than full awareness of the situation and is willing to use anger's energy to take a firm stand if necessary. The difference between love and hate is that love substitutes awareness for unthinking condemnation.

LOVE AND JUDGMENT

Do not judge, and you will not be judged; do not condemn, and you will not be condemned. Forgive, and you will be forgiven.
(Luke 6:37)

These words have often been mistakenly understood as saying that nothing is inexcusable, that moral values are relative, and that people are not to be held responsible for what they do. It is in this sense that often we associate with Jesus the teaching of "unconditional love."

The word "unconditional" can be misleading. It can appear to excuse the inexcusable, even to imply that we shouldn't punish anyone for anything. We know that Jesus himself had strict moral standards. For example, not only did he condemn the act of adultery but the thought as well. Nevertheless, after saving the life of an adulterous woman whom others were about to stone, he said to her not only "Neither do I condemn you" but also "Do not sin again."

"Unconditional love" is a true spiritual value if it means that we try not to allow any person or any circumstance to prevent us from being loving, and that we not allow vindictiveness to overcome our good will. It becomes a dangerous idea when taken to mean that we should always respond in a kind way to people regardless of what they do. That is why "non-self-interested love" is a better term. It avoids this ambiguity, and also points directly toward love's connection to awareness.

God gave us the capacity to evaluate situations and to make judgments, and Jesus never advocated completely relinquishing this task. Human judgment is always flawed and always involves the risk of being wrong. However, if we made no judgments at all, we would have no justice system, and predators would be free to attack the weak and defenseless at will. This kind of "nonjudgmentalism" is actually contrary to love. Jesus could therefore not have intended it. How then to solve the dilemma, the inherent tension between judging and loving?

We have already seen that Jesus did not denounce anger itself, but personalized, vindictive anger. Judgment becomes destructive when it is motivated by vindictiveness. But judgment can also be motivated by love: love of a compassionate society, love of the citizens whom society is sworn to protect. Therefore judgments can be made and sentences rendered without violating love if the motivation is not revenge but the protection of society. It is important to understand that we can and must make judgments, however flawed those judgments will be because of our human limitations. Life simply does not allow us to escape this responsibility.

And so Jesus said: "Do not judge by appearances, but judge with right judgment" (John 7:24). Some judgments are appropriate, and sometimes life requires us to judge. "Right judgment" sees beyond appearances, taking in the total situation. Right judgment comes through awareness, putting awareness in control over the use of the emotions. Right judgment does not condemn people but addresses behavior, taking measures to limit destructive behavior when necessary. Right judgment is not personal. It is based on values, not on hatred, dislike, or resentment.

Hate and condemnation are always personal, in a double sense: what we hate is usually not sinful behavior or wrong values but another person. And the occasion for our hating is almost always a sense of having been personally attacked. We may disapprove of the wrongs of the world in an abstract sense, but we tend to react with violent, visceral hatred only towards people whom we perceive have harmed us in a personal way. We are likely to become more incensed at the person who cuts in front of us in the supermarket checkout line than at the dictator who has tortured and slaughtered thousands of his people. Most of our judgments are not right judgment.

Thus our hate and our love are usually expressions of our self-interest. Jesus is saying: judge when necessary, but do not judge based upon self-interest. Judge based upon what is right. Have a sound sense of values, and judge accordingly. Do not excuse wrong behavior, but do not condemn individuals. Above all, do not judge others merely according to how their behavior affects your own personal interests. Spiritual love does not condemn individuals, but neither does it release them from responsibility. Spiritual love is therefore best described not as unconditional, but as non-self-interested.

THE SELF AND NON-SELF-INTERESTED LOVE

Jesus made the non-self-interested quality of love most evident when he spoke about the possibility of loving even our enemies. Spiritual love calls upon us to love even when we have no rational reason to love, even when love does not seem to support what we think are our best interests. It is easy, as Jesus said, to love those who love us back, who support us, who take care of us, and who are like us. Even Freud called such love "narcissistic." Such love is really a form of self-love: we love what is advantageous to ourselves, the people whom we feel we need. That does not make it a bad love or a wrong love. All these different kinds of love are how we learn, as human beings, what love truly is. All these forms of love are valuable, but only non-self-interested love can give us God's presence, and can give us faith.

Spiritual, non-self-interested love applies just as much to the family as to the stranger. Just as it asks us to love those who are different, it asks us to love those who are familiar in a new way: not because we derive benefit from them but because we are close enough to them to become intimately aware of them as individuals.

Finally, spiritual, non-self-interested love applies to ourselves as well. Non-self-interested love challenges us to escape the narrow confines of the self, but it does not mean the denial of the self. It is not self-negation, it is self-transcendence. We are not required to sacrifice our own interests for the sake of someone else's. Instead, this love directs us toward something greater than the interests of self and others.

To love outside the circle of our own self-interest makes us aware of a value greater than the self. In this way love brings us God's presence. To devote oneself to spiritual love—a difficult, lifelong task—is to live for something beyond the self, something that becomes an actual presence in the soul, a source of vitality and meaning that no crisis or tragedy can eliminate. When non-self-interested love progresses to the point of becoming a presence within ourselves, then we will know that we, also, are loved.

LOVE'S PRESENCE IN ACTION

The non-self-interested love of others heals us from within: it frees us from the toxic effects of our resentment by revealing to us an individual we cannot hate underneath a situation we may have found hateful. If we can experience such healing, then we know the reality of a love that is greater than mere human desire. The knowledge of this love is perhaps the best "proof" of God's reality we can hope for. If we carry this value within ourselves, we carry God's presence within the soul.

Presence is in fact the very essence of love. To be aware of someone in a loving way means we are present with that person. Through this awareness we let that person know that he or she is understood. Just to know we are understood, that we are not invisible to loving eyes, is healing.

Communicating this presence to another can be as simple as a well-timed gesture. A friend of mine who is blind tells of a moment when she found this love in a teacher's touch:

> I was probably sixteen. There was a choral teacher whom I adored; she was the kind of woman and teacher I thought I'd like to be some day. She knew it, I think. We had a wonderful relationship; she was a mentor in the best sense.
>
> One day after a chorus rehearsal, I had something I wanted to ask her. As usual, she had a crowd around her. I stood there casually waiting my turn, one hand resting on the piano. And then, there was a gentle hand on mine. Just a touch, for a second or two. It said: "I got ya. I know you're here, and I'll be right with you." Forty years later, I still remember it. It was so subtle, so wonderfully nonverbal. For a blind person, such messages are rare, and so very highly valued. She knew exactly what to say, and she said it without uttering a word. It made me feel seen, known, and loved all in a heartbeat.

Underneath every person's appearance is a spiritual need, a yearning towards God (even if the word is never used) that may express itself in an infinity of individual ways but that can be seen with a discerning eye and an open heart. Love is seeing in the other that which connects him or her to God, which even that person may not see. "Blessed are the pure in heart, for they will see God" (Matthew 5:8), even in the souls of other human beings.

Spiritual love, awareness and presence, can become a source of faith in a world in which faith is badly lacking. "Anyone who loves God is known by him" (1 Corinthians 8:3). To love God—to love without self-interest—is to be known by love in return, to receive an indwelling presence greater than oneself, which becomes a source of faith and confidence. Our capacity for this love may develop slowly and not always smoothly, but persisting in the search for it is itself an act of love. As soon as we begin seeking this love we have found it, because the seeking itself is love. Of course, as our search continues, we will discover this love on deeper and greater levels.

The search for this love is a conversation between God and the soul. God speaks to us in every moment in which we discover that awareness and love are inseparable.

VI

COMPASSIONATE SEEING

One of the Pharisees asked Jesus to eat with him, and he went into the Pharisee's house and took his place at the table. And a woman in the city, who was a sinner, having learned that he was eating in the Pharisee's house, brought an alabaster jar of ointment. She stood behind him at his feet, weeping, and began to bathe his feet with her tears and to dry them with her hair. Then she continued kissing his feet and anointing them with the ointment.

Now when the Pharisee who had invited him saw it, he said to himself, "If this man were a prophet, he would have known who and what kind of woman this is who is touching him—that she is a sinner." Jesus spoke up and said to him, "Simon, I have something to say to you." "Teacher," he replied, "speak." "A certain creditor had two debtors; one owed five hundred denarii, and the other fifty. When they could not pay, he canceled the debts for both of them. Now which of them will love him more?" Simon answered, "I suppose the one for whom he canceled the greater debt." And Jesus said to him, "You have judged rightly."

Then turning toward the woman, he said to Simon, "Do you see this woman? I entered your house; you gave me no water for my feet, but she has bathed my feet with her tears and dried them with her hair. You gave me no kiss, but from the time I came in she has not stopped kissing my feet. You did not anoint my head with oil, but she has anointed my feet with ointment. Therefore, I tell you, her sins, which were many, have been forgiven; hence she has shown great love. But the one to whom little is forgiven, loves little."

Then he said to her, "Your sins are forgiven." But those who were at the table with him began to say among themselves, "Who is this who even forgives sins?" And he said to the woman, "Your faith has saved you; go in peace."

Luke 7:36–50

One of the most distinctive and endearing characteristics of Luke's Gospel is the compassion that it shows toward women. In our story one woman, "who was a sinner," approaches Jesus in desperation. Although she does not speak even a single word, she draws our complete attention. The pain and faith she expresses in washing Jesus's feet with her tears and wiping them with her hair moves us deeply. Her lips may be silent, but her tears speak for her; they are at once an expression of her pain and an offering of gratitude.

These tears are a symbol of a universal problem: the problem of self-hate. This woman's image of herself has become so loathsome to her that she is driven to seek forgiveness. What brought her to this extreme state, and what is the forgiveness that she finds?

The Bible tells us little about her life. Some identify her with Mary of Bethany, sister of Martha; others identify her with Mary Magdalene. We cannot be absolutely certain who she was. However, the context makes it clear that she was a prostitute. The Pharisee speaks of her with subtle but deep contempt: "If this man were a prophet, he would have known who and what kind of woman this is who is touching him—that she is a sinner." She is not merely a sinner; she is one whose very touch is abhorrent, whose body has become offensive.

The Pharisee's comments are not particularly exceptional; they merely reflect the thoughts that others in general have about her. To others she is either an object of desire or an object of contempt; often, she is both. This image has, in fact, come to define her human existence; it is the only way she has known herself. No sensitive person can live with such an image of herself without suffering from it deeply. This woman's pain drives her to search for an alternative, even if it means humbling herself completely.

What does Jesus do for her? The only thing he does that we can see is tell her that her sins are forgiven, and this he says after a transforming change has already taken place within her. She has already found her redemption: the ointment, mixed with her tears, is her offering of thanksgiving for having discovered a profound sense of liberation. What could account for this change?

We can find the answer indirectly by looking at the contrast between Simon's and Jesus's thoughts concerning her. Simon the Pharisee had already judged her. He knows nothing of her as an individual; he only identifies her with the image others have of her and that she has of herself: she is a whore, the most distasteful and contemptible thing a woman can become. Jesus does not see a whore. He sees a human being capable of love.

Jesus and Simon saw the woman in radically different ways. It was the way Jesus saw her, rather than any specific action he took, that accounts for her healing. Her experience of forgiveness came from being in the presence of one who did not see her the way all others did. For the first time in her life she found herself in the presence of a man who did not want anything from her, who did not see her as an object of lust or a symbol of degradation. Jesus did not judge her in any way; he did not approve of her behavior as a prostitute, of which he was certainly aware, but neither did he condemn her for it. He saw her as she was in her full individuality, a human being in pain but still spiritually alive, able to love and to change.

This seeing was itself an act of love. The essence of love is to become aware of the individuality of others. It is to recognize others as they are, with their own needs and concerns, instead of projecting onto them one's own desires and prejudices. Spiritual love is the pure awareness of another individual without reference to one's own desires. Such awareness does not leave one unchanged; it calls forth a compassionate, heartfelt response to the other. It may also have a healing effect on the one who is loved. We can experience a sense of peace and well-being when we are recognized for who and what we are, without judgment or condemnation. In the presence of such love we may even discover lost or hidden parts of ourselves.

To be seen as an individual was a completely new experience for this woman. Her image of herself had been built around the thoughts of others; she identified with those thoughts and saw herself as an object to be used by others, and therefore as worthless and contemptible. This was the only self she knew. Through Jesus, she was being seen differently; not by the seeing of the eye but by the seeing of the heart.

In the presence of Jesus's seeing, she was healed. She had always been more than her awful image, but she could not see it until Jesus's seeing showed it to her. This is the power of the special kind of awareness that becomes love. When we are seen for who we are, when we know that we are known without being judged, we feel ourselves in the presence of love. In this benevolent presence we can see ourselves more clearly; we become more able to recognize and to accept ourselves, even those parts of ourselves we were convinced were unacceptable. This love is the way God loves. It is no coincidence that in the conclusion of his hymn to love Paul speaks of knowledge or understanding, an awareness of the individual essence of the one who is loved: "Now I know only in part; then I will know fully, even as I have been fully known" (1 Cor 13:12). Paul's sense of God's presence grows from his sense of loving and being loved, being in the presence of an awareness that knows and accepts him.

Jesus called upon those who would follow him to give the gift of this love to one another: "This is my commandment, that you love one another as I have loved you" (John 15:12). As I have loved you: not as the world loves, not from self-interest or possessiveness, but from pure nonjudgmental awareness. Such love not only liberates the one who is loved, it profoundly changes the one who loves. Awareness of the individuality, the soul, of another human being has a way of touching the heart. It opens one, giving one a deep sense of presence with others, a fuller capacity to respond to others, hence a deeper connectedness to the mainstream of life. We often find this love returned in the warmer ways that others respond to us when we show it, but even if it is not returned, simply to see this love within ourselves and to know that it is based on more than just the gratification of private needs fulfills our deepest spiritual yearning, even the yearning to know God.

Love that is awareness, that is presence, becomes a presence within us, a source of warmth and strength; it is the indwelling presence of God. "God is love, and those who abide in love abide in God, and God abides in them" (1 John 4:16). Love that passes beyond self-interest, compassionate love, witnesses to a higher presence, a power greater than the one who loves and the one who is loved.

Love is seeing; it is compassionate seeing. "Compassion" literally means "suffering with," not in the sense of experiencing the same pain another experiences, but in being with another in spite of it. Often this "being with" must be nonintrusive; at times it must be silent. When not openly expressed, it is still felt as the refusal to abandon others even when they have abandoned themselves. This non-abandonment takes the form of seeing—seeing others as they are, not as symbols of our own desires or hates or as reflections of others' own distorted images of themselves.

Compassionate seeing is beholding God's love for creation. To see compassionately is to participate in God's love for those who do not know that they are loved. This means also participating in God's love for ourselves. The way we discover God's love for us is to become loving ourselves, to find that God's love does indeed dwell within our hearts.

Love is awareness. It is seeing the truth with compassion. This does not mean sympathy; it is not feeling sorry for someone, which only confirms the person's hated self-image. It is, rather, a form of self-transcendence, a way of moving beyond the narrow confines of our own self-interest to see what is there to be seen. If we feel we lack sufficient love in our lives we need not give in to resentment or despair, which would only increase our self-preoccupation. Compassionate seeing takes our attention beyond ourselves. It is active participation in the life of the spirit, to which each one of us belongs.

VII

SELF-ESTEEM

. . . you are of more value than many sparrows.
                                    Matthew 10:31

It was Christmas Eve. I was on my way home from a nursing home visit, where I shared the Christmas spirit with several people who felt especially alone and isolated that night. I was feeling pretty good.

I took the subway home. I got to my station, and headed for the turnstiles. I am legally blind, and did not see two large pizza boxes someone had left perched precariously on the turnstile until it was too late. As I exited the turnstile, the boxes crashed to the floor.

HEY YOU!! PICK UP MY PIZZA!

I turned to find a large, heavy-set man charging towards me. I just stood there for a couple of seconds.

PICK UP THAT PIZZA! I'LL MAKE YOU PICK IT UP! I'LL MAKE YOU PAY FOR IT!

He was standing practically on top of me. His words and manner threatened something quite unpleasant if I did not comply. I picked up the boxes and carefully handed them to him.

NO, OVER THERE, WHERE YOU FOUND THEM!!

I calmly placed the boxes back on the turnstile—he wasn't ready to hear that it was perhaps not the most prudent place to leave them.

Then I walked over to him, looked at him closely and wished him a Merry Christmas. Deeply ashamed, he lowered his voice and wished me one too, and for my loved ones as well.

I admit the incident unnerved me. What an ending to a perfect Christmas Eve!

I walked home slowly, trying to understand what this incident meant, why it occurred when it did.

As it all settled in my mind, I began to see more than just a madman who tried to threaten me. During our brief connection, I actually became very important to him. To have lost control as he did was a sign of a very fragile sense of self. I was the perceived cause of this injury to his self-respect, and only I could repair it.

I also had choices. I could choose how to see myself. I could have become like him, an injured ego fighting for its vindication. How often do we witness people screaming at each other over nothing—"road rage" both on and off the road? I could have felt small and humiliated by his bullying. But I choose not to see myself that way.

We all have this choice, but the choice needs to become clear. If we don't like who we are, we can't simply choose to be somebody else. Our self-image is formed very early, and largely in response to others' perceptions of us. If we don't like the self that results, we can't just simply pick a new one. As a child, I had a disability, which made me an easy target, and I was also too nice. I was frequently bullied and intimidated by other kids. For a long time, these experiences colored my self-image. I couldn't just exchange them for experiences I never had, which would have given me a much more confident image.

We cannot change the way we see ourselves through will power or personal effort. But we can do so with the help of God. God is All-Encompassing, Absolute Goodness. Created in God's image, every one of us has the capacity to embody and to express pieces of this goodness. Even if we are convinced that we fall way short, the desire to express goodness is itself a piece of goodness, and one that deserves our respect.

I had just come from an experience of sharing love with strangers on Christmas Eve. I had seen God's goodness, in the smile of a hundred-year-old man who had lost all his friends and his family and who sadly told me it didn't feel like Christmas. The smile came after we sang a few Christmas carols together. No less endearing was the smile of an old woman who had lost half her teeth. She didn't feel like Christmas either, until she let the music into her heart. Her missing teeth embarrassed her, but I told her the light from her smile would gladden the hearts of the angels. We commented on how the spirit of Christmas can reach even into the darkest places. Goodness was there, in the souls of those two beautiful people trying to make sense of Christmas alone, and I had been given the good fortune of sharing Christmas with them.

I could have chosen to see my experience with the pizza man as another humiliation similar to many I had experienced as a child. But this would have been to deny the goodness I found this Christmas Eve, and that had become a part of me. Knowing that goodness is part of me makes me worthy of respect, because all goodness witnesses to God, who is Goodness Itself. What I realized later that night is that this is the key to true self-esteem. We don't have to become another, more acceptable self. That isn't possible anyway—we are who we are, and we cannot change the past. But we can discover within ourselves that which is not only worthy of our respect, but which demands it.

The key to self-esteem is this: Recognize the core of goodness that is within you, and reverence it, because it comes from God.

If we take seriously the idea that God is Absolute Goodness, and if at the very least we desire goodness ourselves, then it would be slighting God not to regard ourselves with respect and a sense of worth. We can love ourselves, even if we have always felt unlovable, once we know God as goodness and once we consciously value goodness ourselves.

To love God means to love goodness, which includes loving the goodness within ourselves. Do not say there is no goodness in you. If you yearn for goodness, that is good already. And once you know the goodness within you, something about you will change. You will react differently to stressful situations. You may even be surprised at the change in the way others relate to you as well.

This kind of change doesn't happen overnight. There may be temporary setbacks as old images try to reassert themselves. So we speak of a spiritual path or journey, a process unfolding in time. But the change is certain, if we are sincerely committed. "Ask, and it will be given you; search, and you will find; knock, and the door will be opened to you. For everyone who asks receives, and everyone who searches finds, and for everyone who knocks, the door will be opened" (Matthew 7:7–8). These words are God's promise to us, but are often misunderstood because Jesus left out something important that he must have taken for granted. What we ask for must not simply be the object of desire. It must be an expression of goodness. That narrows it down quite a bit, but within that narrow frame the promise is secure.

If God is worthy of reverence, if goodness is of ultimate worth, then we who strive to conform to the image of God are also worthy of love, respect, and honor.

SPIRITUAL EXERCISE: SELF-ESTEEM

Note: The following statements are not affirmations. They are prayers. Do not simply repeat the words to make yourself believe them. Say them with a desire for the awareness of their meaning.

I can see goodness, and I know that this goodness comes from God.

I reverence goodness, as I reverence God.

I can see in myself the yearning for goodness and the realization of goodness.

I know this goodness as God's presence in me.

I value this presence. I respect this presence. I reverence this presence.

The presence of God in me is sacred. As the embodiment of God's image, I am worthy of respect.

The presence of God in others is sacred. As the embodiment of God's image, others are worthy of my respect.

When I feel attacked, let me recall this presence of God. The divine presence needs no justification, it needs no defense, it needs no explanation.

I let this divine presence speak for me.

VIII

PRAYER

Likewise the Spirit helps us in our weakness; for we do not know how to pray as we ought, but that very Spirit intercedes with sighs too deep for words.

Romans 8:26

PETITIONARY PRAYER

In my hospice it is not unusual to see people praying. Prayers are as individual as people. But often the prayer will go something like this:

> O Lord, we know you can do anything, and we pray that you heal and give her a speedy recovery. Dispel this sickness and grant her perfect health so that she may leave this bed and leave this hospital and return to her family. We know You have the power to do this, and we ask it in Your name. We need only believe, and You will answer and make her well again. Thank you Lord for this miracle.

I have heard very many such prayers. Not once was one ever answered in the way that people expected.

Prayer is a mystery. Paul captured the experience of many when he said that we do not know how to pray as we ought. We may feel a need to pray, but wonder what kind of prayer can be heard or can even bring an answer.

The way we pray says much about the God in whom we believe. Perhaps the most common type of prayer is asking God for things. This is called "petitionary prayer." We can ask God for trivial things, like a parking space, or important things, like the health of a loved one. But let us reflect a moment on what this form of praying says about God.

Most people who offer petitionary prayers also believe that God is all-knowing. But if God knows all, then why do we need to tell God what we need? Wouldn't God already know? Why would God so trifle with us, to make us beg for what God already knows we need, and then often still not give it to us?

Some justify petitionary prayer by saying its purpose is not to remind God of what God already knows, but to remind us of our dependence on God. But if that is the purpose of prayer, then we are talking to ourselves and not to God.

Petitionary prayer separates us from God. It presents God as a totally separate entity, whom we must approach in just the right way to obtain just the right things. And since we don't always know what the right way is, we play a guessing game and often guess wrong.

It is hard to measure the success of petitionary prayer. If we get what we ask for, we say the prayer was answered. If we don't get it, we say that God said no. But perhaps that is not how we are intended to pray.

THE LORD'S PRAYER

Many people are frustrated by petitionary prayer, wondering why God doesn't seem to hear them. We may need to examine our assumptions about prayer and its purpose.

Jesus knew that people often have difficulty with prayer, and so he offered this guidance:

> *When you are praying, do not heap up empty phrases as the Gentiles do; for they think that they will be heard because of their many words. Do not be like them, for your Father knows what you need before you ask him.*
> *Pray then in this way:*
> *Our Father in heaven,*
>   *hallowed be your name.*
> *Your kingdom come.*
> *Your will be done,*
>   *on earth as it is in heaven.*
> *Give us this day our daily bread.*
> *And forgive us our debts,*
>   *as we also have forgiven our debtors.*
> *And do not bring us into temptation,*
>   *but rescue us from evil.*
>
> (Matthew 6:7–13)

The first thing one might notice about this prayer is its simplicity. It does not go on at length with a list of things for God to do. In fact, it begins: "Your kingdom come, Your will be done."

The "kingdom of God" is the biblical symbol for what we have elsewhere called "eternity." It is the intangible but real dimension of existence that is the source of life's meaning. It is all that endures even after the material world has passed away. We can grasp the eternal through our sense of goodness. Acts and expressions of goodness reverberate; they move far beyond their point of origin and even signal to us a different world, where all that has true value is not lost but endures.

We cannot prove this, but I think we can sense it. In our hospice, after a loved one has died and a certain amount of time has passed, the family can, if they choose, come back and participate in a special ceremony. On one wall of the hospice we have an artistic representation of a tree, with long, flowing wooden branches. The family members come for a brief service of song and prayer, during which they place upon a branch a gold leaf with their loved one's name inscribed upon it. I ring a special bell. The sound of that bell reverberates for many minutes, and if one's ear is close enough, it seems almost as if the ringing never ends.

The bell's reverberations symbolize the spirit's enduring nature. They continue to sound, symbolically, throughout eternity, even after we can no longer detect them. So it is with the spirit. We may no longer be able to detect its presence—at least not with the physical senses—but we may still sense that it endures. No one can prove this scientifically. Yet somewhere inside us we may know, if we have known a true and genuine love, that the goodness that love expressed cannot be destroyed. "Love is strong as death" (Song of Songs 8:6). Love belongs to a life that is eternal.

At its deepest level, as Jesus's prayer shows us with disarming simplicity, this is what prayer is meant to be:

Prayer is the endeavor to bring ourselves into the awareness of eternal life.

The most effective prayer changes our perspective. It transforms our state of being. It brings us, if only briefly, from time to the edge of eternity.

In this way prayer brings us to faith. Faith is the awareness of eternity's power. Faith enables us to meet life's accidents and tragedies with a conviction that we will not be destroyed by them, that there is something beyond them that continues and that reaches out to us and helps us in our weakness—and even more, that we are a part of something greater than the time-bound experience in which our being seems continually threatened.

How can prayer do this? If we understand God as Absolute Goodness, then what brings us closer to goodness brings us closer to God. If we don't immediately know how prayer can bring God closer to us, or us closer to God, then at least let prayer bring us closer to goodness.

How do we enter the awareness of goodness? What is good in our lives? We can start by what we have to be grateful for.

The rest of Jesus's prayer sounds petitionary. But it is much more than that. It asks for our daily bread, and for forgiveness. The request for our "daily" bread is a simple one. It reminds us that each day, each moment, we are dependent on something beyond ourselves. We are not self-created, and we are not self-sustaining. We also ask for no more than our simplest need: to be sustained throughout each day. And we ask for nothing beyond this day. If we are in faith, in the awareness of eternal life, we have no urge to look beyond this day. The children of Israel were told to gather up manna for this day only, and not for the next day. We are grateful for the manna of today.

We ask also for forgiveness, but something is asked of us as well: that we be prepared to forgive in return. Forgiveness is a mystery, and much misunderstood. On the deepest level, we are directly accountable to God for how we have lived our lives. No one can relieve us of that responsibility. But we can view others with charity, trying not to hold their shortcomings against them. As we try to understand their frailty, we better understand our own. Forgiveness does not mean excusing everything people do, or not acting to correct a mistake—but it does mean letting go of personal claims, choosing to uphold sound values rather than self-interest.

If we are in the awareness of eternal life, our personal claims become inconsequential—it is God, not others, who sustains us. What remains are the values, the goodness we try to preserve.

The rest of this prayer represents a hope: we wish not to be tested, but when such moments come, may we be kept from evil and preserved in goodness. We have reason to hope for this if we are in faith, in the awareness of eternal life.

The prayer ends as it began: with a recognition of God's kingdom. Some sources add: "For the kingdom and the power and the glory are yours forever." Eternal life is the true reality. We are included in it, even while still in our physical existence.

A DEEPER LOOK

This very simple prayer Jesus taught us contains the essence of true prayer: the recognition of God's goodness as the ultimate reality, and of the need to remind ourselves of this and to bring ourselves into the awareness of this goodness. It gives us even more: It provides an opening to an awareness of reality that is deep and even healing. It deserves a closer look.

The prayer begins and ends by mentioning the "kingdom," the biblical symbol for eternity. It calls upon us to be mindful of eternal life. Therefore it asks us to expand our understanding of reality.

For most of us, reality is what we see, hear, and live every day. It is the people we meet, the things that happen to us, our joys, our fears, and our tragedies. It is experience unfolding in time.

This is only part of reality. There is something else, above, beyond, and around us. It is called eternal life. How do we know it's there?

Not all moments in time are alike. Many seem quite unremarkable. Others bring pleasure or pain. Still others have a power to transform us, and afterwards we know we are not the same. We experience this in both large and small ways. In larger ways, we may find a deep connection with another human being, an experience of love or of mutual understanding that seems to have a life of its own. In smaller ways, even a simple kind word exchanged with a stranger can make a moment stand out. We can sense such moments belonging to a dimension of existence beyond the tedium of daily life.

Sometimes transformation is found in moments not of height but of depth. In larger ways, we may experience the loss of a loved one, or a serious setback in our health. In smaller ways, a misunderstanding or clash with someone who offends us can upset us and ruin our day. These moments also transform us, even positively, if we are willing to allow ourselves to be opened and changed. They too can become entrances to this other dimension, if we pay proper attention to them and use them rightly.

That is the paradox of eternal life. It makes its presence known both positively and negatively. Sometimes the only way we can become aware of this larger dimension of reality is to be profoundly shaken by a negative experience.

Actually, eternal life is present in every moment of existence. Usually we are not aware of it. The purpose of prayer is to bring us to this awareness.

An expanded view of reality clarifies the purpose of prayer. Reality understood as experience in time is one-dimensional: a sequence of events arriving from the future and stretching back into the past. This is temporal life. Eternal life takes the temporal into itself, but is also above and beyond it. In the right moment, we can sense its presence and also that we are a part of it.

In eternal life we are still individuals, not an undifferentiated mystical "oneness," but we are not separated or isolated from each other, as we experience ourselves to be in temporality. Eternity joins us together, not in identity but in participation. That which is good within each of us is connected in the Absolute Goodness that is God. There is only one God, so there is only one goodness. By appreciating the goodness in others, we participate in it and are united with it.

This is how the forgiveness in the Lord's Prayer becomes possible. It is possible only if we have enough awareness of eternal life to see the connection between ourselves and the other that is made through the goodness that we share. In the consciousness of eternal life the other is no longer completely separate, completely alien, foreign, strange. If we condemn the other we condemn part of ourselves, because we also condemn the goodness in the other that is united with the goodness in ourselves. Prayer, as exemplified by the Lord's Prayer, gives us an eternal perspective in which the impossible gesture of forgiveness comes to seem inevitable.

The emphasis on "daily bread" is also symbolic of eternity. "Give us this day our daily bread" is another way of saying "In this moment we are sustained." We look to this moment, and not to the next one. When we worry, we live in a moment other than this one, in a fear about the future or regret about the past. When we fail to live in this moment, we miss its intersection with eternal life. Jesus's prayer calls us to this moment. It looks for eternal life within a moment of time. Time and eternity are not separate domains. They interpenetrate. Time belongs to eternity.

And since time belongs to eternity, so do we. The consciousness of eternal life assures us we are not alone. We can access this consciousness through the appreciation of goodness. That which is not good—all forms of selfishness—is separating. But all expressions of goodness are connected, through God. When we feel alone, cut off, afraid, we need to return to the awareness of goodness. We can even become aware of goodness to the extent of experiencing our connection with every expression of goodness, and knowing that connection exists in eternal life. Then we know we are not lost. This is how to know God. This is what prayer really means.

ONE WOMAN'S PRAYER

No one is excluded from God's love. I would like to tell the story of Ileana, a patient of mine, who expressed her prayer in music.

Ileana was only 56, and dying of AIDS. Her husband, who was promiscuous, had given her the disease. She didn't complain. She told me she used to sing in her church, and even write songs for the people there to sing. I asked her to teach me one song. I brought a tape recorder to her bedside, so I could catch every word. She was so weak she could hardly utter the words. I kept asking her if she wanted to stop, if this was too much for her. Perhaps we could do it tomorrow, I offered, although in her condition there was no guarantee she would have the strength tomorrow. She wouldn't hear of it. She insisted on doing it now. She had barely the strength to get through the final verses of the song and sing me the melody, but she did. I took the tape home and learned the song that night.

The song is in Spanish, with a sad, haunting melody. In English it begins like this (the complete words are included at the end of this chapter):

> When I gaze up at heaven
> I feel that I can see You.
> I know that one day
> You will make it a reality...
>
> Then from this heaven
> Will come your Savior,
> Whom for so much time
> You have been waiting here.
>
> When I gaze up at heaven,
> When I gaze up at heaven,
> When I gaze up at heaven....

When I came back to see Ileana, she was in terrible pain, and very weak, too weak to sing her song. She asked me to sing it for her. I did, and she fell into deep sobs that shook her whole body for several minutes. I just held her and after a while reassured her that God must love her very much to have given her such a beautiful song. She gave me a silent nod.

The next time I found Ileana shivering under a thick quilt—the air conditioning was just too cold for her. I got her an extra blanket, then sat with her as she cried and told me she was worried about her mother, who lives in Florida and was very ill. There wasn't much I could say, so I just listened with my hand on her shoulder. Ileana was also upset because she couldn't eat the dinner the hospital provided. She kept some special food in her room, but someone threw it out by mistake. What she really wanted was a slice of cheese pizza! I went out and got her one. She sat up in bed and ate it heartily—little things like that make a big difference when you don't have much left.

Ileana mentioned her song, and said she hoped it would help

others. I told her I had already shared it with other people, and it lifted their spirits. That moved her deeply. Then she sang it herself while I accompanied her on my guitar. I left her underneath her blankets, and asked if there was anything else she wanted. There was—just a kiss goodnight.

A few days later I entered Ileana's room and found her in an awkward, twisted position, propping herself up by an elbow and looking like she wanted to go somewhere. I asked her if she was in pain and she just started to cry. I put my arms around her and just let her cry for a while. She was still worried about her mother. She talks to her mother every day—I expressed the hope that it would be of some comfort. I sang to her, in Spanish, to help her sleep, a song on the words of St. Teresa of Avila:

> Let nothing disturb you,
> Let nothing frighten you.
> Those who have God
> Want for nothing.
>
> Let nothing disturb you,
> Let nothing frighten you.
> Only God fulfills you.

Ileana went home, and I wasn't sure I would ever see her again. But she came back to the hospital a few weeks later. Much weaker, she had hardly the strength to talk, and slept most of the time.

When I went to see her I found her just barely awake. Her head was turned towards me. I wasn't sure whether I should disturb her or just let her sleep. I stayed. She could not utter a word, but I saw the recognition in her eyes. I went to get my guitar.

I sat by her and sang her song, "When I gaze up at heaven.

..." I stroked her hair, then softly told her in Spanish that I loved her and that God loves her too, and that I would be back. She still didn't say a word, but there were tears in her eyes.

In spite of all the pain Ileana went through, she had a deep quiet faith that she affirmed sincerely, a sense of God's love that helped her and saw her though to the end. But like all of us, she needed a way to reconnect with her faith, to find it again when she felt alone and afraid. That song was Ileana's prayer. It brought her back to her faith and to the awareness of eternal life. In spite of all she had suffered, just before she died she said she was ready, and her death was peaceful.

HOW WE MIGHT PRAY

There is no one right way to pray. Even a prayer that takes a petitionary form can become a true prayer if it opens us to the awareness of God's goodness. We can also pray by recalling moments in our lives in which we experienced goodness touching us—the Bible calls this "grace." We can be thankful for these moments—that makes them more real to us. We can also pray by opening our hearts to the experience of goodness in the present, by cherishing it and aspiring to it. We can sense how moments of goodness in our own lives are connected to all moments of goodness and even to God. Then we can know we belong to God.

Mindful of this, if we do not know how else to pray, we can always pray this basic prayer:

Remember that God is All and Absolute Goodness.

Ask to be conformed to God's image of goodness.

Ask to see God's goodness manifest in your own life and in the lives of others.

Ask to know that you are included in God's goodness and in eternal life.

If we pray like this regularly, we might be able to build an awareness of this greater dimension of reality called eternal life. At this level prayer brings us to faith: the awareness of eternity's power. It takes regular practice, because without the awareness of eternity, our experiences in time may seem to testify there is no God. Then we are thrown into fear, and may have a hard time finding our way out. The way out consists of little steps: following the traces of goodness we can detect in our own experience, the signs that something beyond and greater than ourselves may have touched our lives. Considering these moments of goodness precious, trying to practice more of them: this is how we lay up those treasures that cannot be destroyed, of which Jesus spoke.

Before concluding we must say a word about the greatest enemy of prayer, which is fear. Fear is a sign that we are rooted in the temporal. We cannot see beyond it. We feel cut off from others and cut off from God—if there is a God. We are Adam and Eve thrown out of the garden. This is when we most need prayer to bring us to the awareness of eternal life. But prayers at this time can easily increase our sense of separation. Imploring God to save us or to change a threatening circumstance can increase our feeling that we are cut off from a God who is foreign to us and who either does not hear or does not care.

Suffering is an inevitable characteristic of temporal life. However, it is not suffering but fear that removes us from God's presence. Fear is the false witness to God's disappearance. Paradoxically, sometimes through experiences that cause us the greatest fear we can find the deepest experience of God, and our sense of belonging will be restored. Paul reminds us of this: "Not height, nor depth, nor anything else in all creation, will be able to separate us from the love of God" (Romans 8:39).

Fear may still try to separate us from God's love. We may know many moments when the eternal breaks into our lives, but through fear we may try to push them away, doubting them, not feeling worthy to receive them. We need to stop struggling and open our hearts to the possibility that God has touched us. Moments of knowing goodness may be unrecognized messages from God.

Jacob was afraid when he fled his angry brother Esau. On the road, at the end of the day, he lay down, placed a rock under his head for a pillow, and dreamed. He saw a ladder, upon which angels were ascending and descending between earth and heaven. Then he knew that time and eternity are not separate. As they are joined, so we are joined to God. Jacob exclaimed: "Surely the Lord is in this place—and I did not know it!" (Genesis 28:16). God may be with us in ways we barely suspect, until we reflect on our experience and sense the presence of a good beyond human capacity and effort.

Eternal life may come to us either through height or through depth. If it comes through depth and we are afraid, demanding the removal of the source of our depth will further entrench us and increase our fear. Instead, prayer consists of opening our hearts to the possibility of goodness. The Bible has a term for goodness that comes to us even in the experience of depth. It is *resurrection*.

Whatever may happen to life, or to the body, the experience of resurrection is the knowledge that we belong to God, and that we ultimately return to God. We are all connected. There are none who do not have goodness, or the potential for goodness, within themselves. Some may be more estranged from it than others, and their pathway back may be longer. But none are irredeemably cut off. God wants all of us to return from this painful journey that seems to afford the only way we can truly learn the meaning of compassion.

So let your prayers bring you to God through the awareness of goodness. Let them give you a sense of connection to a greater whole that embraces you and will always be present for you. Know that goodness by its very nature must be eternal. Sense it in your prayers. Know that all forms of goodness point to its highest expression, which is non-self-interested love, of which eternally you are a part. At that point your prayers will have opened your heart and brought you to faith.

ILEANA'S SONG

Cuando miro al cielo,	*When I gaze up at heaven*
Siento que te veo.	*I feel that I can see You.*
Se que algún día	*I know that one day*
Tu lo harás realidad,	*You will make it a reality,*
Cuando tu la iglesia	*When You look for the church*
Busque aquí en la tierra,	*Right here on earth*
Y nos lleve al cielo,	*And bring us up to heaven*
Al trono de Dios.	*To the great throne of God.*
Cuando miro al cielo,	*When I gaze up at heaven,*
Cuando miro al cielo,	*When I gaze up at heaven,*
Cuando miro al cielo ...	*When I gaze up at heaven ...*

Mira hermano mío, *Ponte tu a mirar* *A ese cielo lindo,* *Inmenso para ti.*	*Look, my brother,* *Pay attention and look* *At this beautiful heaven,* *So immense for you.*
Pues de ese cielo *Vendrá tu Salvador,* *Que por tanto tiempo* *Tú has esperado aquí.*	*Then from this heaven* *Will come your Savior,* *Whom for so much time* *You have been waiting here.*
Cuando miro al cielo, *Cuando miro al cielo,* *Cuando miro al cielo . . .*	*When I gaze up at heaven,* *When I gaze up at heaven,* *When I gaze up at heaven . . .*
Afírmate mi hermano *Y busca más de Dios,* *Pues sólo hay un camino* *Al gran trono de Dios.*	*Have faith, my brother,* *And keep searching for God,* *For there is only one way* *To the great throne of God.*
Y ese Jesucristo, *Mi Rey, mi Redentor,* *Que pronto da su viaje* *Por ti que te llamó.*	*And this Jesus Christ,* *My king, my redeemer,* *Will soon make a path* *For you whom he has called.*
Cuando miro al cielo, *Cuando miro al cielo,* *Cuando miro al cielo. . . .*	*When I gaze up at heaven,* *When I gaze up at heaven,* *When I gaze up at heaven. . . .*

IX

THOUGHTS ABOUT AN AFTERLIFE

Surely goodness and mercy shall follow me all the days of my life; and I shall dwell in the house of the Lord for ever.

Psalm 23:6 (RSV)

Perfect love casts out fear.

1 John 4:18

TWO PATHS

No one wanted to be in his room when his wife was present. The two of them would argue constantly, undermining each other in ways only available to those who have been married for decades. He would criticize everything she did, fight with her, berate her. And while she took care of him faithfully, she cut off any attempt by him to express his feelings, good or bad, as if responding to him as a person would take too much of her energy. At moments he would relax, give in to his fear and start to cry, saying he was afraid and sorry he had hurt her. She would just tell him to stop acting like a baby.

She wanted to control him, and he wanted to control himself. But his fear defied control. His obsessions ruled. He needed to know where every little thing was, at every moment. Write down his wife's cell phone number. Is it correct? Must try it out, even in the middle of the night. Can't dial the phone. Need help dialing the phone. Too many wrong numbers. Too tired, can't quit.

Can't rest until it works.

He was 62 years old, and dying of bladder cancer. He had to be fed intravenously, and every day he'd go into a panic an hour before the IV was due to run out. Would the nurse remember to replace it? She had always been on time, but this is today, one never knows, she might forget. Go remind the nurse. So many reminders, for nurses already busy doing their jobs. I had to use my judgment: when did the nurse really need to know, and when did he just need to be reassured?

But no amount of reassurance seemed to register. He would ask the same things over and over again, even after receiving an answer. One night he had me spend an hour looking for his store of ostomy pouches, even though he didn't need a new one and they were always in supply. He had to know where these particular ones were, and right now. Telling him one could always be found when needed did not satisfy him. Finally I found them, to his great relief, though he still wouldn't stop griping about the nurses who couldn't find them when he wanted (though not when he needed) them.

He could be manipulative. When his wife was absent, I became his wife. When I got ready to leave one night, he loudly complained, "You're a liar! You said you would stay!" I had already spent much extra time with him. His fear didn't care.

He had no spiritual preparation for facing a crisis; his background was Ethical Culture, and it wasn't helping him. He refused the care of a minister, saying "It's too late for me now to go back and start from square one." He had no belief in eternity, or in anything following this life. The most I could do to comfort him was to help him see he was less afraid of death than of isolation. At times he drew solace from the thought of death being like an endless sleep.

Now he is entering his terminal coma, and the end is approaching. Drugs and physical weakness finally neutralize his defenses. It takes a lot of energy to fight. If one cannot win the struggle and find peace through one's spiritual resources, eventually the exhausted body simply gives up.

Two doors down there is a woman twenty years younger, from Honduras, and dying of cervical cancer. She shows no signs of stress—at most a few tears when she hears a sentimental song. She smiles at every visitor, and loves to joke. She sings with me even if she doesn't know the song I am singing, and she makes beautiful harmonies singing songs of faith with her sister.

Thinking of my patient down the hall who lives in constant panic, and knowing that usually the younger patients have the most trouble accepting their disease, I ask her, how does she maintain her spirit? *"La fe es número uno"* she replies—"Faith is number one."

Her faith is genuine. Some consider faith a placebo—a comforting deception. But I was not just witnessing a defense mechanism. This woman's spirit was very much alive.

FEAR

The concept of death as the cessation of existence is impossible for the mind to grasp. We all know intellectually the fact of death, but some protective layer of denial seems to insulate us from total awareness. This protective ignorance makes normal life possible: it would indeed be difficult to function if we were always conscious of the actuality of death and the suffering that usually precedes it. But eventually the moment comes when the prospect of death seems real, and the protection falls apart. And when that moment comes, we may not be prepared.

> *Then he told them a parable: "The land of a rich man produced abundantly. And he thought to himself 'What should I do, for I have no place to store my crops?' Then he said, 'I will do this: I will pull down my barns and build larger ones, and there I will store all my grain and my goods. And I will say to my soul, "Soul, you have ample goods laid up for many years; relax, eat, drink, be merry."' But God said to him, 'You fool! This very night your life is being demanded of you. And the things you have prepared, whose will they be?' So it is with those who store up treasures for themselves but are not rich toward God." (Luke 12:16–21)*

Our possessions often take on a symbolic significance. They become a magical protection against death. Possessions are durable, they can outlast death, so by having them we immunize ourselves from death. Having things enables us to deny life's impermanence. For a while, anyway.

Of all species, only humans seem to be aware that one day they will die. Because of this, we suffer anxieties that animals are spared. We can usually keep our awareness of death at a distance, but no defense is strong enough to shut it out indefinitely. Like the man in Jesus's parable, we become exposed when our defenses are breached, forced to confront how we have prepared, or failed to prepare, to see the truth of our existence.

Anxiety over the prospect of nonbeing seems a singularly human preoccupation. What good does it serve? The obvious answer is self-preservation, but if that's the answer, then our anxiety, which at times can overwhelm and immobilize us, is definitely overkill. Such anxiety is not helpful; it only makes it harder to do what we must to protect ourselves. Could it be this anxiety signals a genuine need, a need to know that life in a body here on earth is not all there is, and that we are really part of something greater than we can imagine? Perhaps faith is a placebo to this symptom of anxiety no more than food is a placebo to the "symptom" of hunger.

But what could be the content of this faith? There are many specific ideas about the afterlife, and many of them contradict each other. The specific belief cannot be what really matters. It must be something behind the belief.

The beliefs themselves are not knowledge. Almost always, they project this current life onto the next one, because this life is all we know and all we can imagine. Thus heaven becomes an everlasting experience of the greatest consolation or pleasure we can picture here on earth. Many visions of heaven draw upon imagery from earthly nature scenes: "He makes me lie down in green pastures. He leads me beside still waters": such images describe the way many think about heaven. We may also think of heaven as the best we know of earth without the imperfections: being reunited forever with our loved ones, living together in a harmony we never knew here.

This is a Western view of the afterlife. In the East the prevalent view is reincarnation. This belief also has many variations, including the time between incarnations, whether and how they come to an end, and the relation of one's present experience to one's past lives. But this belief also is not knowledge, and it too is a projection of current life onto the next, in a nearly endless repetitive cycle. Like the ideas of heaven already mentioned, it seems too simple, too much like our human imagination. Reincarnation has great appeal. It gratifies our desire to transcend our limitations, to experience everything and to be everything. If we are poor in one life, we may be rich in the next; male in one life, female in the next; ordinary in one life, gifted and famous in the next. Something in reincarnation seems to want to deny our human finiteness, our being tiny parts of a greater whole rather than the whole itself.

Belief itself is but a pale imitation of faith, but belief can symbolize the content of a faith that our human minds cannot grasp. The belief, then, is not important for itself, but for the underlying faith that it represents.

FAITH

Once again we are thrown back on the question, What is the content of this faith? Beliefs are the clothes that faith may wear. Underneath the garment, pure faith is awareness of eternity itself—the intangible dimension of existence, which is characterized by enduring qualities of goodness. Perhaps the anxiety we experience when this awareness is absent is a mark of the way we were designed. Our spiritual nature needs this awareness as much as the body needs food.

Faith is the awareness of the power of eternity. Beliefs have power when they become symbols of this awareness. Separate from this awareness, beliefs become empty. Or they may become defense mechanisms. One may flee to belief to escape a reality that is too frightening to face. This kind of belief is betrayed in one of two ways: either it is so shaky that it is easily undermined, or so rigid that it stifles growth and leads to intolerance.

Understanding the difference between faith and belief leads to some important conclusions. A belief that is grounded in true faith is a sign of that faith; it is not faith itself. Anxiety about our nonbeing is not resolved by adopting a belief—we cannot make ourselves believe what we don't really believe, except at the expense of cutting off our awareness of that which makes us afraid. This will last only until we can no longer avoid facing it. Anxiety about our nonbeing is not resolved by asking the question, What happens after death? Faith is not merely about "after death." Faith, as the awareness of eternity, is about every moment of life.

> *The kingdom of God is not coming with things that can be observed; nor will they say, "Look, here it is!" or "There it is!" For, in fact, the kingdom of God is among you.* (Luke 17:20–21)

The Gospel of Thomas is even more explicit:

> *It is not coming in an easily observable manner. Rather, the Kingdom of the Father is already spread out on the earth, and people aren't aware of it.* (Thomas 113)

Eternity is not some event in time that arrives at a certain moment, after we die. It is a whole other dimension of existence, which is always available to us and to which we always belong. To know this dimension is to know what we need to know to resolve the anxiety of death.

But how can we know it? We never know it with certainty. We cannot know it through our powers of observation. We cannot know it through our powers of reasoning. We know it through our sense of goodness.

To know goodness in any form gives us awareness of a source of meaning and value in which we participate. We can sense this most strongly in the greatest good of all, non-self-interested love. Familiar love does not give us this awareness; it is limited, to our family, our circle of friends, or group of identification. But love that pulls us beyond self-interest gives us a glimpse of limitless good. To know this love is to come into contact with a dimension of existence that exceeds human limitation. It is eternal reality. And conscious contact with this reality produces faith.

This is not certainty. It is not proof. Eternity does not tap us on the shoulder and say, "Look, here I am!" or "There I am!" Rather, it makes impressions on the soul. It gives us a hint, a glance, not hard evidence. There is a reason. We must come to love goodness for its own sake, because it is good, and not because it saves us. Religion that promises "Do this or think that and you will be saved" misses the mark. Many who are "saved" in this way still do not know how to love. We do not love in order to be saved. We love, because love itself is the greatest good.

HOPE

Loving beyond self-interest is the best way to know of a reality beyond the impermanence and decay of the physical world. We can follow the soul's awareness of this love to the awareness of eternity itself. We can practice this. We can become conscious of this love, we can let it place its mark upon the soul, and eternity will be revealed. Then we will know eternity as a very present aspect of our lives, grasping and guiding us in this life and in whatever is "after"—for to eternity it is all the same, it is all of one piece, it is all one life.

Nobody knows what the afterlife is really like. Every description of it is a symbol. "Heaven" is a symbol of the goodness we perceive undiluted by the impurities of human intention. "Hell" is a symbol of the justice and balance needed to complete the goodness that is only partially realized on earth. "Reincarnation" is a symbol of the need for learning to continue after the conclusion of earthly life. All of these should be taken seriously; none should be taken literally. Nobody knows precisely what happens after death. Accepting this requires courage, and more than that, faith. Facing death without faith, we need some specific idea of what to expect or we may collapse into panic. But with faith, all we need to know is that eternity is good because God is goodness, and we place our trust in that.

What, then, of reunion with our loved ones? Do we have any hope of that? We do not know in what form we or our loved ones may survive this life on earth, and those who claim otherwise speak without knowledge. However, our sense of goodness tells us that genuine love shared is eternal, it is limitless, it does not get lost. It will survive, in ways we cannot imagine. "Love is strong as death" (Song of Songs 8:6). Similarly, there is no hell as an actual place of burning or torture for the unrepentant - such tortures have no meaning when the physical body no longer exists. But justice, which is a part of goodness, demands an accounting, and it will be easier for us to judge ourselves and return to goodness through our own free choice than to wait for the judgment that goodness one day will require.

We were not meant to speculate on the specifics of what comes "after." There is much work to be done here on earth. Still, we do need a sense of eternal reality—we need faith—if we are to do this work efficiently. Our fears cannot be eased through certainty, for certainty is unattainable, but we do not require certainty for our fears to be healed; we require hope.

LOVE

In my hospice experience I have accompanied many people through the last days of their lives. It is no coincidence that those whose faith was deepest, who most easily found peace, were also the most loving. I could see it in the way they treated their families, or the members of the staff, or in the way they greeted me. I have been with others who professed faith, who believed all the right things, who were sure about heaven, but their faith did not protect them from the torments of anxiety. Their love never took them outside their own world, so they could not perceive—or receive—the comfort of an eternal good, which only genuine love can reveal.

Genuine love shared is eternal, and survives the limitations of earthly existence. That is the basis of our faith and of our hope.

If a specific example is needed, here is one:

> Lillian had been a nurse when she was healthy. Now a patient in hospice, she was suffering from a very rare form of cancer with a name so long I had no chance of remembering it. As she told me herself, she never did anything the usual way.
>
> I met Lillian when she was admitted to the hospice unit. She could still walk then, and would visit the other patients, asking how they were and what she could do for them. Only her bathrobe marked her as a patient rather than a volunteer.
>
> One patient whom Lillian visited was a very tiny, frail woman, 104 years old. Thick blankets covered the woman. Her feet bothered her the most; they were always cold. Lillian entered her room, and in her thick European accent asked her, "How are your feet today? Is there anything I can do for your feet?" Then she found an extra little blanket to cover the woman's feet.

In a few days Lillian went home, but several weeks later I saw her again. Now it was her turn to be the one always in bed, accepting the ministries of others.

Lillian knew she was dying. She raised her hands toward the air in a gesture of embrace. She kept saying how happy she was, how grateful for her life. This was not a time to grieve; it was a moment of awesome joy. Lillian had touched life's other dimension. She seemed to look right through her surroundings, and she kept repeating that she saw the face of an angel.

Lillian's love, which had no limit, which reached out even to strangers, returned to accompany her like a friend waiting nearby, holding her hand and keeping her safe.

The deepest faith is rooted in love. "Those who abide in love abide in God, and God abides in them" (1 John 4:16). The path to faith for those who have no faith is devotion to non-self-interested love. This is the "narrow gate," which leads to a life both in this world and as part of something greater—a life beyond life.

PART 2

Obstacles on the Path

X

SELF-HATRED

Now Joshua was dressed with filthy clothes as he stood before the angel. The angel said to those who were standing before him, "Take off his filthy clothes." And to him he said, "See, I have taken your guilt away from you, and I will clothe you with festal apparel."

Zechariah 3:3–4

Is this you?

Your alarm goes off on time, but you're too tired to get up right away. Half an hour later you rise, look at the clock, and feel an adrenaline rush. You gulp down a quick breakfast, then it's out of the house and into the morning traffic. An accident on the freeway slows you to a crawl as two lanes are blocked. You feel your heart pounding, and you start to sweat. You can hear the clock ticking in your head, and imagine it showing forty-five minutes late as you enter the office. You want to scream at the slowpoke driver in front of you, even though your head tells you he's as frustrated as you are. Screaming at him solves nothing; you know you are mad at yourself. You curse yourself for missing the alarm, for staying up too late the night before watching that late movie, for not having the discipline to get up when you knew you should. You imagine your boss's disapproving look. What will he say? That very important meeting was supposed to start on time. Now everyone is already there, wondering where you are, and whether you'll even show up. Maybe they'll figure they can do their job just as well without you. Maybe they'll finally discover you really don't contribute anything essential. What will happen to your status in the company? Will they start looking for ways to ease you out? To bring in someone younger and more creative? What a dumb idiot you are! Loser! Blowing your job because you were too lazy to get out of bed!

If this is not your situation, do you do something similar to yourself on some other occasion? How exaggerated is this scenario, considering how you feel once your internal watchdog starts howling?

Welcome to the torments of the superego. The Big S can pop up anytime, sometimes when we least expect it, and ruin our day. The effect can be trivial, or it can be severe. It might be just a mild discomfort at the far edge of consciousness. Or it might be a depression so deep it can even lead to suicide.

There are many names for this mental self-attack. Psychologists call it the superego, but it is also known as the internal critic, the judge, or the "inner mother-in-law" (just kidding). Its attacks vary in severity. Some people don't seem disturbed by it at all. In fact, they are only too happy to cast responsibility for everything onto others. They may be so afraid of the internal critic that somehow they manage to block it out of existence. But the critic dies hard, and its presence often becomes evident if you succeed in challenging these people's innocent self-image, after which they become ready to shoot you dead.

SUPEREGO VS. CONSCIENCE

Internal critics can be a nuisance, but they are poorly understood. They are often confused with conscience. But the inner critic has very little to do with conscience. Your true conscience won't drive you against yourself for trivial infractions or even for a social faux pas. It may even seem like your superego would kill you in order to save you—that's not how conscience behaves.

The superego is a false conscience, which can obscure and compete with our real one. To see this more clearly, let's look at how the superego works.

While many of Freud's theories today seem outdated, they actually throw much light on the workings of the superego. Psychoanalytic theory sees the superego as essentially a protective device. The child, afraid of the disapproving parent, internalizes the parental voice, to make sure of never committing a transgression that would incur the parent's wrath and rejection. Of course, this defense is not foolproof. Sometimes one makes mistakes, and to the superego every mistake is potentially fatal. Therefore the superego cannot forgive mistakes. So never mind if you really were exhausted and needed a little extra sleep. In the deep recesses of the primitive mind, arriving late to work is equated with losing status, getting fired, thrown out into the street, and totally abandoned. That is a child's worst fear. To prevent this fear from becoming reality the superego clamps down mercilessly, attempting everything it can to undo the mistake, which may include pretending it never happened, trying to undo it in fantasy, or simply screaming it out of existence.

What the superego is best at is beating you up. It will flog you without pity, to make sure you never make a mistake that might put your life at risk. And if you do make a mistake, even a small one, the superego tries to make you feel so stupid and miserable that you'll never do it again.

It's hardly any use trying to fight back. The superego is bigger than you are. It's the internalized voice of every figure in your life who was more powerful than you: your parents, teachers, peers, anyone capable of criticizing you and cutting you down to size. Developing a superego is the way a child copes with the threats such people present: do it to yourself before they do it to you. Unfortunately this process happens so early and so unconsciously that usually we mistake the voice of the superego for our own: "I'm so mad at myself!" is how we often react when we fail to meet an impossible internal standard. Freud so understood this self-inflicted pain that he claimed an adult's greatest fear is fear of the superego's disapproval.

One reason this pain is so hard to escape is that we don't always realize it is self-inflicted. Sometimes we beat ourselves up, and don't know how to stop. But other times, we think it's the other person who causes us pain by judging, insulting, or demeaning us. What others say to us can't hurt unless we identify with it. The pain comes not from another's judgment, but only when we side with that judgment and make it our own. Someone calls us stupid, we feel pain only if we believe it. As Eleanor Roosevelt said, "No one can make you feel inferior without your consent." We do to ourselves as others have done to us.

This pain lies underneath all kinds of ridiculous behavior, from bar fights to road rage to attacking others when one feels "dissed." We feel judged by others. We see our own judge in them. So we try to silence our judge by silencing them. We "take it personally": what this really means is that we identify with the judgment. If we stand firmly within ourselves, know that we are clean, and that the other person's judgment has nothing to do with us, then we don't need to react. When the other's judgment scrapes against our own self-doubt, then self-defensive rage may carry us away.

EFFECTS OF SELF-HATE

Perhaps the worst examples of self-hate I have seen were people living in nursing homes and similar institutions. I once worked in a hospital for people with neurological disabilities. One wing of the hospital was for rehab: relatively short stays for people who expected to get better. In the other wing lived people with serious permanent disabilities who were there for the long term.

In the rehab wing, whenever someone got well enough to be able to go home, we would celebrate. But not everybody got better. Sometimes it became clear that someone's condition wasn't going to improve, and in fact would only get worse. Such people would also leave rehab, but they didn't go home. Instead, they went to the long-term wing.

Of course we didn't celebrate such a person's departure. It would go almost unnoticed—the person was there one day, then gone the next. The empty bed was soon filled. But while the other patients on the rehab floor never saw them again, I could visit the transferees in their new surroundings. Almost always, what I found was a sharp deterioration not only in the patients' physical condition but in their emotional state as well. There was much less activity in the long-term wing. Some recreation was available, but the patients' functioning was much lower and they could not do nearly as much as the healthier ones in rehab. The building was older and the lights were much dimmer, very unlike the bright new lighting on the rehab floors, and the staff seemed less attentive. For those patients who came from rehab, the contrast was devastating. On rehab they had hope of getting better, seeing home again; in long-term there was no such hope. They were treated like human discards, and so they came to see themselves.

Eleanor was a member of my music therapy group on one of the rehab floors. She was overweight and diabetic, and had lost a leg because of poor circulation. She felt completely useless and became severely depressed. She said that if she ever lost her other leg, her life would be worth nothing. She didn't yet know that soon she would need regular dialysis, because her kidneys were starting to fail.

In time Eleanor became too sick to come to the group, so I would go to her room and sing for her there. One day I noticed she was gone. I looked for her name on the door and it was missing. Carmela, her roommate, told me she had just been transferred to the long-term wing.

I found Eleanor at the other side of the hospital, in the long-term building. She knew she had no more hope of rehabilitation. Although her mind was clear, they placed her in a dementia ward (there was really little choice; very few long-term patients were clear-minded), and she had no one to talk to. Her depression became overwhelming.

Eleanor identified with the confused and isolated patients she now lived with. She showed them a compassion often missing from the staff. One patient, Miriam, suffered severe dementia and would often yell things no one could understand. With a fond smile Eleanor would reach out her hand to Miriam, who would quietly take it into her own. Miriam could not speak her gratitude, but clearly Eleanor's touch was comforting.

Staff neglect and the drastic change in environment added to the toll of Eleanor's illness. Her mental condition badly deteriorated. She became paranoid, convinced that staff members were speaking about her with hostile intentions when they might just be casually conversing in the halls. Eleanor would yell and curse at staff members, accusing them of lying and abusing her. This lost her even more sympathy and increased her isolation. Only during music did her mood ever improve.

I was walking towards the old building one day when I heard screaming. It was Eleanor, sitting in the lobby, waiting for her dialysis. The pickup was late and she was upset. She shouted at the security guard, calling him a liar and a son of a bitch. The guard lost his patience and shouted back: "Now you've done it. You've lost your privileges and you'll have to wait upstairs in your room." He roughly grabbed her chair and started wheeling her into the elevator when I told him I knew where she lived and offered to take her up myself. He was only too happy to get rid of her.

Sitting next to her in her room, I could practically feel the tension in her body. She kept talking about how much she hated herself. Her body was failing her, her mind also, and she didn't know how to react anymore. I pulled out my guitar and started singing, songs about friendship, about trust, about how we can lean on each other when we're at our worst. I just sang until I felt her whole body sighing and saw the muscles in her face finally relax.

When she heard words that she knew, Eleanor sang with me. It made her feel good, she said. For the first time in a very long while she smiled. I made her promise to remember how our singing made her feel.

Eleanor died the next day. She developed an infection, apparently from the stress and invasiveness of the dialysis. She died from complications of diabetes, but her strong self-hatred was also undoubtedly a factor. In spite of it, she could break through to some good moments. When others rejected Miriam and made fun of her, Eleanor showed her love. I also found comfort in knowing that Eleanor could still feel a little love for herself through music. But those were isolated, tiny undulations in the atmosphere of rejection, by self and by others, in which she lived.

It is very difficult to resist our tendency to adopt and internalize the disapproving or rejecting voices we hear. We can't fight this tendency directly. There are lots of books and professional advice that seem to think we can—just tell the judge to get lost (putting it mildly). It isn't that simple. Fighting the judge only gives it reality. Even trying to disengage from it is still a form of engagement, unless we really have somewhere else to go.

A BIBLICAL PERSPECTIVE

The Bible actually has something to say about this problem. It is woven in symbolism, which is the Bible's way. Let's begin with the book of Job, a rich text that can be understood on many levels. One way of looking at it speaks directly to our issue.

We have been calling the severe superego an "inner judge." But judges are supposed to be fair and impartial. This judge never cuts you any slack, hears only the evidence against you, and stacks the deck. It's hardly even a judge; it's more like a prosecutor. The Bible, written many centuries before Freud, does not speak about a superego. It does speak about a prosecutor. The prosecutor's name is Satan.

"Satan" originally meant the "adversary," the "one who opposes." In the Bible he appears as a symbolic figure, one's opponent on the path. His greatest appearance takes place in the opening dialogue of the book of Job. The entire book is a dialogue, between

God and Satan, Job and his friends, God and Job. Let's listen to these dialogues, and for our purposes let's imagine them all taking place within Job's soul:

Job, we are told, was "blameless and upright, one who feared God and turned away from evil" (Job 1:1). That made no difference to his prosecutor. Satan tells God it doesn't matter what good Job has done or how good he seems. Just keep probing, and you'll see how worthless Job really is. So God probes. He deprives Job of his possessions. Job doesn't change. He deprives Job of his health. Job remains faithful, but he does complain. How can such things happen to an innocent man? Job wants to know.

Job's friends come to comfort him—but they side with the prosecutor! Job is suffering—therefore he can't be innocent. He must have bad karma. God doesn't punish the innocent. The discussion begins in a civil manner, but the friends become impatient with Job's stubbornness. How dare he resist the prosecutor! Job himself must be evil! "Is not your wickedness great? There is no end to your iniquities" his friends tell him (Job 22:5), ignoring everything good Job ever did in his life—just like the superego, who doesn't care even if you are a saint.

Job continues arguing with God. He never does get a clear answer about why those bad things happened to him. But one thing is plain: God repudiates the prosecutor. "My wrath is kindled against you and against your two friends; for you have not spoken of me what is right, as my servant Job has," God tells Job's companions who condemned him. God loves and values Job. Wherever that voice inside Job's head comes from that keeps picking at him and accusing him, it does not come from God.

Then where does it come from? We have seen, ironically, that the inner prosecutor actually is meant to protect us. Its purpose is to restrain us before we do anything that would incur the disapproval of others, and thus their rejection. The problem is, it does its job too well. Even after we have long outgrown the need to keep the approval of significant others, the inner prosecutor has become so automatic it may still not leave us alone. Its demands also become so global and so contradictory that we have no hope of ever fulfilling them. Trying to resist this accuser, screaming at it, telling it to get lost, may only seem to feed it more energy.

Once again the Bible gives us a striking insight. Without the language of psychoanalysis, and perhaps not even realizing the deeper implications of his words, Paul addresses the issue. He is in Galatia talking about the relationship between faith and action. We cannot get faith through action, or as Paul puts it, through "doing the works of the law." The law alone, specifically the laws of religion, will not bring us directly to God. Then is the law without purpose? By no means! Paul would say. Here are some of the most important lines Paul ever wrote:

> *Now before faith came, we were imprisoned and guarded under the law until faith would be revealed. Therefore the law was our disciplinarian until Christ came, so that we might be justified by faith. But now that faith has come, we are no longer subject to a disciplinarian, for in Christ Jesus you are all children of God through faith.* (Galatians 3:23–26)

To those who may be troubled by the Christian language, let us remember that for Paul, Christ is the teacher of faith and the means by which he reaches this realization. Now let us focus on the realization itself. Paraphrasing, for "law" let us read "should," specifically, external standards telling us how we should act. The "law" in this interpretation encompasses the "shoulds" that both guard and imprison us. They guard us by keeping us in line so that we behave properly and so that others won't reject us. They imprison us in that their harshness and inconsistency make it impossible for us to succeed, to break out into the freedom of accepting ourselves as we are.

As Paul says in Romans, the law is a good thing. The law wants us to act right and be good. "So the law is holy, and the commandment is holy and just and good" (Romans 7:12). But from a spiritual perspective, the law was not intended to represent our final stage of development. It is a stepping stone to something better. As long as human beings are imperfect, we will need guidelines for behavior to insure the functioning of society (so we cannot behave in ignorance of the law, as if we could take grace for granted). But through spiritual development we can reach a stage where we no longer need the law to tell us what to do, because from our own motivation and without struggle we will act right and fulfill the law's purpose. This is not something we achieve through behavior. It results from an inner transformation.

If we no longer view the superego as a "prosecutor" but as a "disciplinarian," then our perspective changes. A disciplinarian can be harsh, as we may remember from actual childhood, but we need a disciplinarian while spiritually we are still children. When we reach adulthood and understand more, we can replace this disciplinarian with something else. Once we know what that is and how to make the replacement, we are on the way to freedom.

The disciplinarian is harsh because our motive for complying with it is fear. What if we didn't need fear to drive us into acting in ways that are good for us? What if we could find another motive?

The Bible tells us about such change, in another allegory. It is a vision from the prophet Zechariah:

> *Then he showed me the high priest Joshua standing before the angel of the Lord, and Satan standing at his right hand to accuse him. And the Lord said to Satan, "The Lord rebuke you, O Satan! The Lord who has chosen Jerusalem rebuke you! Is not this man a brand plucked from the fire?" Now Joshua was dressed with filthy clothes as he stood before the angel. The angel said to those who were standing before him, "Take off his filthy clothes." And to him he said, "See, I have taken your guilt away from you, and I will clothe you with festal apparel." And I said, "Let them put a clean turban on his head." So they put a clean turban on his head and clothed him with the apparel; and the angel of the Lord was standing by. Then the angel of the Lord assured Joshua, saying "Thus says the Lord of hosts: If you will walk in my ways and keep my requirements, then you shall rule my house and have charge of my courts, and I will give you the right of access among those who are standing here." (Zechariah 3:1–7)*

Once again we meet Satan the Prosecutor. Satan accuses Joshua, who stands for the entire people here. That is Satan's nature, to accuse. But God does not side with him. God says to Satan, step aside. My angel will take your place. My angel will show Joshua a new way of looking at himself and learning how to act. Now under the angel's direction, Joshua takes off his "filthy clothes"—the old image of himself he has learned to hate—and puts on "festal apparel." Now the angel, not Satan, directs him how to act: walk in God's ways and do God's will.

Under the Disciplinarian we tried to be good out of fear. With the Angel's guidance, we follow the good out of love.

This is really all there is to it; nevertheless, actually accomplishing this change is not a simple matter. It requires a profound

Self-Hatred

inner transformation. But we will be helped, if we search for it rightly.

Let's look closely at what Zechariah's vision tells us. The prosecutor accuses us mercilessly. We feel unworthy, we feel filthy. God's angel comes and says, Begone Satan, this is a "brand plucked from the fire," who has suffered enough. Your services are no longer required. So Satan leaves, and the angel says: "Thus says the Lord of hosts: If you will walk in my ways." We don't need the nagging disciplinarian, but to keep the disciplinarian away we must learn to walk in God's ways. What does that mean?

THE PRACTICE OF SELF-COMPASSION

The perspective we have developed about seeing God as Absolute Goodness is of tremendous help in finding the practical application of this passage. It shows us how we can replace self-hatred with self-compassion. Specifically, it tells us what to look for to replace the disciplinarian in our minds. If our sense of goodness is well developed, we will have a standard of behavior that can replace the disciplinarian. It will be gentle and compassionate, yet guiding and firm. The basic exercise is: Identify the disciplinarian/judge/prosecutor/superego, then do a shift in consciousness to your sense of goodness, the awareness of what goodness, not the superego, requires. This is your true conscience.

The exercise is easily stated, but both parts take a lot of work. Identifying the superego is not always a simple matter. The superego has many disguises. One of them is conscience, which we have seen is really something very different. But the superego may be present whenever we experience a sensation of discomfort with ourselves. Sometimes the superego works in secret, and all we know is that we feel anxious or depressed, or simply a restlessness within the soul. We need to allow these feelings to speak, and tell us their self-critical message if one is present. Often we hear the superego speak through the words of others. When others' words sting, usually it is because we identify with them. We take others' critical words and use them as weapons against ourselves.

It is important to be self-observant, to get to know the superego and the many voices with which it speaks, by identifying one example at a time until the complete picture comes into view. Likewise, we need to practice our awareness of goodness, so we will have something solid and reliable to replace our internal critic. We practice the perception of goodness until it becomes meaningful to consider how Goodness Itself would solve the problem that our superego has attempted to address. This practice acquaints us with the qualities of goodness culminating in non-self-interested love, the one form of goodness that has true saving power.

As in Zechariah's vision we can think of the Angel of God—the Angel of Goodness—replacing the superego. Any time the superego gets us down, depresses us, or attacks us in anyway, we can become aware of it and say, Disciplinarian, thank you for your help, but I don't need you anymore. Please leave. I turn instead to the Angel of Goodness. And the Angel of Goodness will respond that any correction, if needed, must come with compassion, because compassion, not self-attack, belongs to goodness. If we have gotten ourselves into trouble, it may be that in some way we have failed to express goodness, we have not lived up to our nature as God's image. If so, the correction is to see it and turn to goodness to find out how to change it. This is a very different and much kinder way than attempting to flog ourselves back into shape.

Like any spiritual practice this must become a daily exercise, and life itself will give us many opportunities to use it. The basic shift we need to make is to place ourselves in the awareness of goodness as a substantial reality. This is the purpose of the exercises. From within this awareness, replacing self-condemnation with goodness makes sense. Every time the Angel of Goodness replaces the Disciplinarian, we come closer to God and we strengthen our faith. We also get a taste of the freedom of accepting ourselves as we are. Even in the worst cases, if we think we are totally worthless, our appreciation of goodness can save us, because if we are striving for goodness, that itself is good and that itself makes us worthy. This will work only if our meditations on the meaning of goodness have given us a deep sense of what it means. A well-practiced sense of goodness gives the idea the feeling of reality and makes it more than just an empty word.

The result of this inner work is a transformation of our motivation from fear to faith. We progress from the superego, whose motto is: "Do the safe thing because it will protect you," to our true conscience, whose motto is: "Do the right thing because it is good."

When our motive for action is not fear but the love of goodness we are entering the realm of faith, because the love of Goodness Itself is the love of God.

SPIRITUAL EXERCISE: SELF-ACCEPTANCE

Note: The following statements are not affirmations. They are prayers. Do not simply repeat the words to make yourself believe them. Say them with a desire for the awareness of their meaning.

(Remembering that God is All Goodness:)

Creator God:

- You have created me as I am.
  You know my name.
  By your will I am what I am.

- Help me to be what you created.
  Help me to see what you created.
  Help me to love what you created.

- Though I am finite, a point in the universe,
  No other can take my place.

- My destiny has brought me here.
  My destiny needs me here.

- Could I become other, what I think I desire,
  I would leave my own place empty.

- God works through me here, not elsewhere.
  God shows through me here, not elsewhere.
  God walks with me here, not elsewhere.

- As I see God's face
  In the place where I was born,
  I will love this very same place.

XI

OVERCOMING ANGER

When you are angry, do not sin.

Psalm 4:4

Scoffers set a city aflame, but the wise turn away wrath.

Proverbs 29:8

The following story turned up in a Dear Abby column from 1990:

A young man from a rich neighborhood had just graduated from high school. He was expecting to receive as a graduation gift the car of his dreams. He had spent months picking it out, and told his father which model he wanted.

But at the graduation his father presented him with a small package, beautifully wrapped. Beneath the wrappings was a Bible!

This so enraged the son that he tossed the Bible on the floor and left, slamming the door behind him. He never spoke to his father again.

He came back home only after hearing that his father had died. Going through his father's possessions, he found the Bible. He wiped the dust off, opened it, and found inside a cashier's check made out for the exact price of the car that he wanted.

Anger hurts those who are angry far more than their intended targets. And so Jesus cautions us against anger.

Jesus's words do not fall easily on the modern ear. They go against all we have learned from psychology. We believe that feelings are OK as long as you don't act them out; that denying our feelings is unhealthy. How can we make sense of Jesus's words, and how can they help us in modern times?

THE ONE WHOM ANGER HURTS

Anger is self-destructive because it robs us of awareness. Once anger grabs us we can think of nothing but hitting our target, and we screen out any information that might help us see the situation differently. When we act out of passion, we often say or do things we regret. And we stand to lose a lot more than a new car.

But what is the alternative? Repressing our feelings is no solution. Repressed feelings often find indirect ways to express themselves. They can also be self-destructive, both mentally and physically.

We therefore need to take a closer look at what Jesus is saying. The Sermon on the Mount is one of the most difficult passages in the entire Bible. It seems to hold up a standard of conduct impossible for mere human beings to fulfill. We need to understand the spirit of the words, beyond their literal meanings.

Here is the full context of our passage:

> *You have heard that it was said to those of ancient times, "You shall not murder"; and "whoever murders shall be liable to judgment." But I say to you that if you are angry with a brother or sister, you will be liable to judgment; and if you insult a brother*

or sister, you will be liable to the council; and if you say, "You fool," you will be liable to the hell of fire. So when you are offering your gift at the altar, if you remember that your brother or sister has something against you, leave your gift there before the altar and go; first be reconciled to your brother or sister, and then come and offer your gift. Come to terms quickly with your accuser while you are on the way to court with him, or your accuser may hand you over to the judge, and the judge to the guard, and you will be thrown into prison. Truly I tell you, you will never get out until you have paid the last penny. (Matthew 5:21–26)

Now let's contrast this with the following:

Woe to you, scribes and Pharisees, hypocrites! For you clean the outside of the cup and of the plate, but inside they are full of greed and self-indulgence. You blind Pharisee! First clean the inside of the cup, so that the outside also may become clean. Woe to you, scribes and Pharisees, hypocrites! For you are like whitewashed tombs, which on the outside look beautiful, but inside they are full of the bones of the dead and of all kinds of filth. So you also on the outside look righteous to others, but inside you are full of hypocrisy and lawlessness. . . . You snakes, you brood of vipers! How can you escape being sentenced to hell? (Matthew 23:25–28, 33)

What is the difference between the caution against anger in the first passage and the expression of anger in the second? Was Jesus a hypocrite?

Jesus is instructing us on the meaning of anger and its proper use. The second passage presents a number of difficulties for Bible scholars. First, it is doubtful that Jesus is describing typical Pharisee behavior. Second, there is reason to suspect that these words might not actually go back to Jesus. These questions are important; however, they need not concern us here. The lesson on anger still stands.

The crucial difference between these two passages is this: the first talks about anger that is personal, and the second about standing up for a principle. In the first, Jesus talks about being angry with a brother or a sister, insulting or abusing that person. He advises people to settle all personal grievances. The repercussions of personal anger are certainly like a "hell of fire." Personal anger can destroy friendships and families. It can greatly damage the one who is angry.

In contrast, Jesus had no personal relationship with the Pharisees whom he criticized. They had not done him any harm. His complaint against them was that they were poor leaders, bad shepherds. Instead of offering the people spiritual nourishment, they were leading them astray. Jesus was not standing up for himself, but for the people and for a principle. He was driving home a hard truth: the leaders failed in their leadership role. But he was not acting from resentment, which is the anger felt when one's ego has been wounded. His act was clean, free of egotism. If Jesus had been raging against the Pharisees from a wounded ego, because they insulted him personally, then he would have fallen under the same condemnation he gave in the Sermon on the Mount.

This difference is beautifully illustrated by a story from the Buddhist tradition.

> A Samurai warrior made a vow to find and kill the man who had murdered his master. It was considered a great honor that he do so. After spending years hunting for the man, finally he found him. He raised his sword, but just as he was about to strike, the man spat in the Samurai's face. The Samurai low-

ered his sword and walked away.

The man ran after him, incredulous. "Why did you not kill me when you had the chance?" he asked the Samurai. "Were you not waiting years for the opportunity?"

The Samurai responded: "Until you spat in my face, I could have fulfilled my duty. But after that, I was angry."

The Samurai knew the difference between upholding a principle and acting out a personal grudge. That is the same distinction Jesus wished to teach us. Once anger becomes personal, it becomes a passion that controls us, preventing clear thought and dragging us down to the level of our antagonist, if not even lower.

Never take any action in raw personal anger.

THE ANATOMY OF ANGER

Then what to do with our anger? The first thing is to be aware of it.

We begin by being aware of what anger does to us. It literally takes us out of our right mind. Anger magnifies out of all proportion any perceived insult or injury, and impairs our judgment. So the person who takes our parking space becomes the devil incarnate, deserving of torture and even death, instead of what is much more probable, a basically good person who committed a selfish and thoughtless act. Road rage is a form of temporary insanity. Anger kills the rational mind and reduces us to reacting automatons.

It is therefore important to catch the signs of anger as soon as they begin to appear. We can do this by training our capacity for observation. A practice of observation meditation can be very helpful. As soon as we feel the signs of anger arising, we can shift our focus before we lose control.

Anger has two components: a physical sensation and a verbal interpretation. In meditation, or in the simple act of observation, we can become aware of both. Usually what we first experience is physical: the body reacts even before we're fully conscious of what we perceive. The stomach may tighten, the breath may get shorter, the heart may beat faster, we may feel our adrenalin rushing. We can become so attuned to our body that we notice the signs of anger beginning to arise at the very earliest tremor. That is when we go into action.

The simple act of observing places a distance between ourselves and the impulses of energy we see arising within us. From this distance we can watch these impulses and choose not to channel them into anger. Instead, we "call them back home." The distance created by observation gives us the ability to withdraw our energy from its originally intended target. This defuses its intensity, and it no longer controls us. We can send it in another direction.

If someone offends me and I feel my body tensing, I know that anger is arising and will have me in its grip if I do not intervene. I shift my awareness, from the target to the impulses arising within me. From the distance of awareness I can watch these impulses calmly. I remember that I do not wish to lose my rational mind. I reflect on the distorted image of my target that anger gives me. I reflect on how anger robs me of my humanity by usurping my free will.

If we practice this regularly, starting with the minor irritations that occur every day, we can develop a habit of maintaining self-control and not reacting automatically when provoked. We can find more effective ways to deal with provocative situations.

Simply telling the truth is one. That has much more power and brings more respect than an angry outburst.

What also gives anger its power is the story we add to those physical signals. We are always telling ourselves something: the other person did this or that, should have behaved differently, is horrible, even evil, and so on. Often we construct imaginary dialogues in our minds that only stimulate more anger. It is important to be aware of the story as it unfolds, and simply observe it. That will already neutralize much of anger's power.

There is no shortcut. To be willing to do this is already a big first step. We need to stay with it until we find our thoughts becoming clearer, and the impulse to thoughtless action becoming weaker. Before this can happen we may need to sit for a while until, through the process of observation, the story separates from the physical energy and we cease identifying with either.

As we continue to observe, the energy behind the anger will remain. It doesn't disappear, but it no longer controls us. As it recedes from the object of our anger, it loses its mindless drive. We can then decide what to do with it. We can direct it towards other things. We can, as Jesus taught us, assert a principle rather than a limited self-interest. It is very easy, however, to deceive ourselves that we are standing up for a noble value when we are really just trying to impose our own will on someone else. Our bodies reveal the truth: if we still experience tension and a compulsion to react, we are still under anger's control. A good practice of observation can help us tell the difference.

Through this practice we can transform and reverse the way we usually react to anger signals. Once we sense the first hints of arousal, instead of letting them take command and dictate our behavior, they can become cues for us to stop and observe. We develop a heightened sensitivity to what is happening in our bodies and minds, and this helps us respond appropriately and creatively to stressful situations.

What is the best thing to do with our energy, once we recall it from the target? It is to contemplate goodness. Withdrawing angry impulses from their objects does not mean we stop caring about anything and just give up. Instead we regain our composure, and are free to shift to a higher perspective, considering the role of goodness in our lives and in the present situation. Simply attaining a state of equanimity is goodness. The return of anger from its object, defanged and harmless, brings joy. That is goodness. The retention of self-control is goodness.

The highest goodness is non-self-interested love. We can even direct our energy into the contemplation of love, what it means in general and in this particular situation. Instead of seeing the targets of our anger as symbols of all that has gone wrong in our lives, we can behold them in love, aware of their individuality. At this level our heart is opened, which is the true sign of spiritual progress. Anger closes the heart. The practice of non-self-interested love—the awareness of the other's individuality—opens it.

EASTERN AND WESTERN PERSPECTIVES

This is a key difference between Judeochristianity and Buddhism. We in the West have much to learn from Buddhism, specifically its insight that attachment causes pain and enmity, and must be overcome. However, unlike the Buddhist ideal of relinquishing all attachments, Judeochristianity recognizes that attachments are expressions of human needs that persist as long as we are human.

Attachments are signs that we are looking for permanence—for the eternal—in that which is temporal. A new possession, or even a relationship, may afford the illusion of permanence. We imagine that the object of our attachment will last forever, and that therefore so will we. This inevitably leads to suffering, because it is based on self-deception. At this point Buddhism and Judeochristianity are still together. But after this point they diverge.

Attachments are signs we are looking for the eternal within the temporal. The answer is not to stop looking, but rather to look in the right place. We cannot simply relinquish our attachments to temporal objects. If we have nothing to take their place, we will fall into fear or into depression, and the need for attachment will return. We can't go without food without being hungry. We need nutritious food. If we can't find it, then junk food will do, even if it does not promote our well-being. But simply renouncing the junk food will not solve our problem.

We can be liberated from attachments only through being anchored in something else, in eternity. We know eternity through our sense of goodness. When we recall our energy from its attachment to things that don't last, we can also recall the presence of goodness. This fills the need left by our attachments, brings us to the eternal, and so gives us faith.

At the center of goodness is love. Love cannot exist without the presence of individuals who are separate and independent but capable of seeing and cherishing each other. In contrast, a basic doctrine of Buddhism is *anatta*, or "no-self." There is no independently existing, abiding or eternal self. What we experience as self is basically a collection of thought formations, or a "karmic appearance." The Buddhist ideal of love is detached compassion—and even then it is not clear just exactly whom or what we love.

Judeochristianity does not have a doctrine of no-self. As we have seen, we do need to rise above the demands of the ego, the aspect of self that Buddhism identifies as self, that is attached to things and that grasps itself in a desperate effort to achieve persistence and gratification. But beyond this self there is not nothing. There is the *individuality*, the unique essence of each one of us, which belongs to eternity, which we can perceive through spiritual sense, and whose awareness naturally stimulates the response of love. The highest level of spirituality in Judeochristianity is therefore not the extinction of the self but the awareness of the individuality, especially of others, to the point where the heart is completely open.

As the Psalm (4:4) says: Be angry, just don't sin. Perhaps saints never get angry, but we are not obligated to become saints. We are here only to use the energy we were given to help build God's Kingdom.

XII

A SPIRITUAL RESPONSE TO FEAR

Even though I walk through the darkest valley, I fear no evil; for you are with me.

Psalm 23:4

FEAR IS THE GREAT obstacle we face on the road to faith. It provokes doubt and breaks our confidence. At times it seems to tell us that God is nothing more than an image we invent to help us cope with the difficulties of life—and we may well believe this when we are afraid. At other times, its message is that even if God does exist, God cannot really affect our lives, cannot or will not help us in any meaningful way. Fear, especially when chronic, can undermine our faith and rob us of the vitality we need to live productively. Yet, paradoxically, fear can also become the door to a deep, abiding faith—if we know how to respond to it in a way that preserves our own presence of mind, and with it our sense of God's presence.

SEARCHING FOR CERTAINTY

Fear is the sign of an uncertain situation. It is hard to live with insecurity, and so we struggle for certainty in ways that usually only increase our fear. We may turn for reassurance to people who understand our situation little better than we do, even if they appear to be experts. We may turn for company and support to friends who cannot be with us all the time, who have problems of their own, and who cannot provide the solutions we seek. Even the closest members of our family never understand completely what it is that we experience, and though they may genuinely wish to help us, they may simply lack the power or the resources to provide an answer that will reassure us in our anxiety.

If we find no relief from fear by turning to other people, we may seek it by turning inward to our own thoughts. We may try to find certainty in uncertain situations by imagining the worst possible outcomes we might face; we hope that by preparing ourselves for these outcomes we will protect ourselves from fear. Instead, we end up frightening ourselves even more. By letting our imaginations run wild we easily fall into obsessive worrying. What we imagine scares us, but we cannot let it go because our need for certainty requires a specific image on which to focus. Worry is the struggle to control frightening situations with our thoughts. It is actually an attempt to escape from fear, but only draws us deeper into it. Instead of the control we seek through worrying, we find only a self-perpetuating cycle of worry and fear: what we imagine when we worry only frightens us, and becomes a cause of further worry.

THE NEED FOR INNER SILENCE

Where then shall we turn? If we look for another human voice to reassure us, we may find one, but no human words can stop our fear for very long. Unless we are totally self-deceived, we soon discover that another person's understanding and insight, like our own, is limited. If we turn for assurance to our own inner voice, we find a buzz of thoughts churning in our minds, groping for knowledge where we have no knowledge, in a wishful grasp at certainty that merely increases our anxiety. The only alternative left, then, is to listen for God's voice.

But what is this voice of God, and where can we discover it? It is that "still, small voice" (1 Kings 19:12, RSV), discernible only in moments of inner solitude and quiet. Such silence requires that our own inner voice be completely still, that the inner monologue that calculates, imagines and worries be quieted. We cannot, however, simply tell ourselves not to worry, and worrying about worrying will certainly do no good. We need a deeper understanding of ourselves.

LEARNING TO BE PRESENT

Many today speak of the importance of "being present to our own experience." To become silent and receptive to the divine voice we need to maintain a presence with ourselves, and within ourselves. This means staying with our present situation, in this case staying with the fear. When we worry, we try to escape fear by fleeing into a false sense of certainty, which is actually an abandonment of ourselves at the critical moment. Maintaining a presence with ourselves means remaining aware of the raw experience, the fear, and not allowing our minds to race in a frantic search for escape. In this regard, practicing an attitude of watchful, meditative observation is helpful. Observing ourselves as if from a distance, seeing without reacting, can help us remain present with ourselves even when we are conscious of our fear.

Remaining still within ourselves, we may discover the quiet moment that lies within the heart of fear. The great paradox of fear is that it often contains such moments. To find them, however, we must do a most difficult thing, which is to drop the demand for certainty. This is one of the hardest challenges we face, but it is possible, provided we are honest enough to see that a sure knowledge of the outcome is beyond our grasp. Living without certainty means being open to the unexpected—even the unexpected good. Fearful situations change us, and they can change us for the better if we meet them on the ground of truth, maintaining our presence even when the situation seems hopeless.

We may have to live in darkness for a while. Our lack of knowledge about the future, about the way our problems will resolve, makes the way obscure and difficult. But we can learn to live through the "dark night" if we cease our frantic efforts to escape. We will then find ourselves alone, with no external source of support to which we can confidently turn. All we have is the silence—but this silence is God's dwelling place.

ONLY BE STILL

If, by maintaining our presence and stilling our useless mental activity through watchful contemplation, we can find a quiet place within ourselves, then we can establish a communion with God even during our anxious moments. The stillness and calmness we can find in a fearful time, when we would really expect ourselves to be agitated, are not signs of mere emptiness. They are active; they speak to us. The contrast between this stillness and our previously agitated mental state speaks to us of a higher presence that can even grow into a source of assurance. If we listen, we may begin to sense something: "Fear not, for I am with you" (Isaiah 41:10); "The battle is not yours but God's" (2 Chronicles 20:15); "The Lord will fight for you; you need only be still" (Exodus 14:14). We may not hear actual words, but we may find an insight, a new way of looking at the situation that had not previously occurred to us. Or we may find nothing more specific than the sense of a presence of love, of acceptance even during a time of great difficulty.

Such moments are moments of grace. There is no method by which we can be certain of capturing them. No one can tell us precisely how to bring them about; here, too, certainty fails. Nevertheless, we can prepare ourselves for these moments. We do so by meeting our difficulties with truth and love. We meet problems just as they present themselves to us. We keep watch over the mental activity through which we usually try to escape. We maintain our presence in the situation by remaining aware and resolving not to deceive ourselves. We find a calm observing presence within ourselves that "sees us through it." By maintaining this sense of presence we show love to ourselves and towards others who may also be affected by the difficulty of the situation. If we have this love, then we have the strength to carry the cross.

The inner stillness that meets fear with love is more than just our presence with and to ourselves; it is God's presence with us. In this presence we can converse with God, the inner monologue of our frantic thoughts giving way to a healing dialogue with a transcendent source of wisdom and peace. We can speak to God, express our deepest concerns, and then spend most of our time listening.

We cannot listen, however, if we still try to control the situation or calculate the outcome. We can listen only in a state of perfect, childlike trust in the center of calm beneath the storm, as Elijah listened to the "still, small voice." We may then find the assurance of a deeper presence, a friend who remains with us when it seems we have left all of our other friends behind.

GOD DWELLS IN DARKNESS

Perhaps we need moments of fear and doubt in order to find this inner presence. Without such moments we would never question ourselves, we would never pause to reflect, we would never really become aware. It is therefore no accident that the first verse of Psalm 91 can be translated in two starkly contrasting ways, each of them faithful to the original Hebrew: "He who dwells in the secret place of the Most High, shall abide under the shadow of the Almighty" (NKJV), or "The Most High dwells far off; the Mighty One abides in darkness" (*Gates of Prayer* [New York: CCAR Press], 1975). The paradox of fear is that these two radically different translations of the same verse fit together perfectly. The "secret place of the Most High," God's dwelling place, is the dark, quiet place in our own consciousness where we drop our concern for certainty and confront ourselves in perfect solitude. In this dark, quiet place we accept our lack of knowledge about the course our lives will take, and trust the stillness that comes to us in spite of it. As dark as this place may seem, once we know that God abides here with us, we will be in no hurry to leave.

CONFRONTING OUR GUILT

God will not abandon us, if we do not abandon ourselves. Even in the dark and fearful experience of guilt, when we seem to turn actively against ourselves, God remains with us. Guilt cannot simply be psychologized away as the product of neurosis. Sometimes our sense of guilt may be exaggerated, but sometimes there is a genuine recognition that we have violated authentic standards of integrity. In these cases, too, we need to maintain our presence in the situation. By not running away, we may be able to learn something that will help us to set the situation right, or to do what we can to alleviate the harmful consequences of our actions. If it is too late to repair the situation, we can learn from the wound in our heart and resolve to respond differently to similar conditions in the future—that will be our penance. No sin is unforgivable, as long as we are sincerely searching for the truth. We can easily take ourselves out of God's presence if we demand of ourselves a perfection that no human being can ever hope to have. But if we can return to the stillness with compassion for our own limitations, we find that God is still there and has always been there.

A SECURE INSECURITY

If we can maintain our solitary friendship with God we may become blessed to find even the most difficult situations resolving in unexpected ways. No one can give us this as a guarantee, and we cannot make it the object of a willful quest. It is ultimately a matter of grace. Nevertheless, we can know that whatever the outcome of the situation we can emerge from it stronger, more loving and more whole, as long as we maintain a loving presence with ourselves and with God. In this way "all things work together for good for those who love God" (Romans 8:28): this, not the promise of a forever peaceful existence, is the basis of our trust and our hope. It is our lifeline of strength in time of fear.

XIII

THE TRANSCENDENCE OF GRIEF

A voice is heard on high,
lamentation and bitter weeping:
Rachel is weeping for her children;
she refuses to be comforted for her children,
because they are no more.
Thus says the Lord:
Keep your voice from weeping,
and your eyes from tears.

Jeremiah 31:14–15

SUFFERING IS OUR GREATEST stimulus to the search for a redemptive meaning in life. It is also the greatest threat to the realization of such a meaning. Perhaps no form of suffering challenges our faith more, or is anticipated with greater dread, than grief over the loss of someone we love. Especially if this grief results from a tragic situation, a violent or untimely death, or one accompanied by much pain, it may seem that all notions of God's goodness vanish like wishful fantasies or futile attempts to deny the true harsh nature of existence.

How can a good God—or any God—coexist with the reality of grief? We can talk about the theology later. When grief afflicts us we need more than a theological discussion: we need to know whether there is a response to grief that can preserve our faith and heal our souls.

People who lose loved ones may find their faith falling apart. They may fall into despair, every attempt to approach God seeming futile. They may try to impose a meaning on the tragic event, or may just give up and conclude that what happened is meaningless. At that point they may find themselves falling into darkness.

FACING DESPAIR

Despair literally means "without hope." Hope is a vision of good that has not yet materialized. It is looking towards the realization of what now seems only possible. It is a way into the future. Despair is a response to catastrophe that says, "There is no future." Those who are in despair have given up the struggle. Their plans have been shattered. They see no action that can transform their hopeless situation. They have lost their future.

Despair can be redeemed if it becomes an attitude of patient waiting. But there is a danger within despair, which always threatens to emerge. Despair risks giving way to a related condition, with which it is often confused. This related condition is depression. On the surface, despair and depression have much in common. In both, the sufferer experiences a sense of powerlessness.

However, there is an important difference. Despair is a response to a situation that seems hopeless. Even though they may see no options, people in despair can face their experience. But once depression sets in, people lack the energy to respond. Depression, literally, means "pressing down." Depressed people are "pressed down"; they may want to strike out but cannot, and so they turn their energy against themselves. People in despair may continue to search. But those who are squeezed by depression are immobilized, anaesthetized, paralyzed.

Is there a way to prevent despair from becoming depression? Can we hope for even more: to find a path from despair back to faith? Before attempting a response, we need to consider possible reactions to grief.

STRUGGLING WITH GRIEF

Reactions to grief can become complicated, particularly if there are already other unresolved losses or traumas in the person's life. The present loss can reawaken the experience of these traumas, giving grief a self-perpetuating energy. Attempts to resolve it bring only more pain. One may turn increasingly inward, alienating oneself from life, perhaps even using grief as a refuge.

It is also not uncommon, if the loss has been severe, to feel we have been thrown out of the divine scheme, no longer to have an active share in the life around us. It may seem that if there truly is a God, then our suffering at least proves God's indifference, and perhaps even God's rejection of us. One way to preserve this God in the presence of our pain is to demonstrate our guilt. We search our imaginations to discover what we must have done to deserve this pain—we are convinced we must have done something, simply to justify what we cannot otherwise comprehend. We focus increasing attention on ourselves, assuming power and blame for what was really beyond our control.

Another way of preserving our image of God is to direct our anger against it. This can actually be healthy. Anger is a natural consequence of grief, and it needs a place to go. God will not be harmed by it—although we might be, if our anger turns into festering resentment. Our anger needs a way to resolve. It becomes complicated when we refuse to let go of it, when it becomes a continuing unwillingness to accept our experience, a flight into futility. We fight with God the way Quixote fought his windmill or Sisyphus his rock. We condemn God for not living up to our expectations. We become bitter in spirit.

This reaction may reveal certain assumptions we make about God: that God is an omnipotent person to whose support we are entitled, who must conform to our standards of justice, but whose actions are arbitrary and capricious just like any human being's. Nevertheless God must be on our side, must feel our pain, perhaps even cry with us. This God may die in the experience of grief. It is just as well, for this God has no reality, but is a servant of human desires.

Finally we may react to grief by trying to escape it completely. We may try to deny it, find ways to divert our attention from it, or insist to others and to ourselves that we are strong when in fact we may be on the verge of collapse. If this approach to grief does not lead to an actual breakdown, it may place us back on the road to depression.

Grief can be a heavy weight totally crushing the spirit, or a fire consuming the last particles of dross that separate the soul from an awareness of itself and its God. What determines which it will be? Is there a healthy response to grief that can preserve the consciousness of God?

A CRITICAL CHOICE

When there seems to be no alternative to despair but depression, when every attempt to make sense out of life, to pray, to approach God, breaks down, then there is no longer any action one can take to save one's spiritual life—except one. One can choose to endure one's pain.

At first this sounds absurd: the very nature of one's plight seems to imply that one has no choice but to face it. However, as we have already noted, people have many ways of trying to escape their pain. But if one chooses to face one's pain fully, one may come again to know the capacity to appreciate life.

A word of caution. Facing the pain does not mean fixating on it and immersing oneself in self-pity. This is not really facing one's pain but trying to remove its sting by turning preoccupation with it into a pain-killing drug. To face one's experience means feeling the grief just as it is, neither diminishing it by denial nor embellishing it with self-indulgent fantasies. By enduring one's pain exactly as it comes, one prepares the way for three profoundly paradoxical consequences.

GRIEF AND FAITH

The first consequence is that, in the light of a receptive attitude, *grief reveals the character of faith*.

What is faith? "Faith" is a word that has nearly died on the bloody battleground of religious dogmatism. Most commonly "faith" is confused with belief. However, belief alone does not determine the quality of spiritual life. The mind's assent to a given proposition does not guarantee the inner transformation that comes with true faith. Being a fearful or unloving believer is just as easy as being a fearful or unloving nonbeliever. Many people who believe demonstrate little spirituality or love. Historically, religious belief has often been used as a weapon to dominate others. Belief can even be used—and often is used—to escape the true awareness that comes from faith. By itself, belief has no saving power.

Faith is the awareness of the power of eternity. Eternity is timeless, spaceless spiritual reality. It is what Jesus called the "Kingdom of Heaven." It is not accessible to the senses, but is described by the prophets in their visions, and all religious experience points toward it. Eternity is not "endlessness," since that is a concept defined in terms of human time. Eternity is God's original creation, from which our material universe derives. Eternity penetrates time; it dissolves time; it is the reality that lies beyond the veil of experience. Eternity comes in the realization that "Many waters cannot quench love" (Song of Songs 8:12). When we are able to perceive the effect of eternity on human life, we experience it as healing.

Those who are crushed by grief often have no perception of eternity. They do not begin their journey hearing voices of angels. They begin it on a path of darkness. Can the dark road lead us to faith's illumination? Instant enlightenment is an illusion: the dark road is the only road from experience to faith.

We have a natural human tendency to place conditions on our experience. None of us wants to suffer. When we do, we may become angry, resentful, and bitter. Our tragedy seems monstrous to us, perhaps uniquely so, and should never have happened. We may condemn others whom we hold responsible for our suffering, or who somehow escaped the pain. We may direct our anger towards God: either condemning God outright or defining God in a way that keeps us believing comfortably. All these conditions that we place on our experience are limited human judgments, and all are attempts to avoid the dark road.

The dark road that leads to faith is the choice to experience one's pain without imposition of judgment or placement of conditions. Psychologists have described the first few steps along this road as "stages of grief": first may come shock, then denial, then anger, then withdrawal, then working through—but not necessarily peace and healing. The psychological journey must be accompanied by a spiritual one. Grief begins in the psychological world, the world of emotional pain and broken relationships. The journey ends in the world of awareness of eternal reality.

From here to there the gap may seem unbridgeable. But if our response is authentic, if we have truly allowed our former beliefs, judgments, and desires to be shattered by grief's assault, then we have already entered the circle of faith, even though we may not know it. We have let go of the temptation to define reality the way we want it to be—and this renunciation is not easy. Sometimes the self-serving use of grief seems the only comfort available to us. But there is something that gives us the power to do without it.

Here is the paradox of despair: Despair is a response to the non-fulfillment of our desires. If we accept our grief just as it comes to us, maintaining our silence before the temptation to judge our circumstances, then our desires no longer enslave us. We then become free of despair, for we suffer more from these judgments than from grief itself. The dark road seems dark because traveling it means giving up our vision of the world as we would have it be. Until now we may have looked towards this vision for solace. But giving up the dreams of the past is a step away from despair—it enables us, once the wind and the earthquake and the fire have passed, to become open to the sound of the "still, small voice."

Accepting our grief without judgment brings us within faith's reach. What empowers us to make this impossible gesture of acceptance?

GRIEF AND LOVE

There are two possible reactions to a tragedy, which are often confused. One is acceptance; the other is resignation. Outwardly both appear to face the situation, but there is a critical difference.

If we are resigned to our loss, our energy does not flow freely; there is a sense of paralysis. The love we felt for the one we have lost could still be an active force in our lives but is blocked by rage or by immobility, which are both expressions of powerlessness. The resigned person does not really give up the wish to judge or to deny the experience, although it may appear so. The wish survives but is concealed by feelings of helplessness.

In contrast, those who can accept the tragic situation—who can face it without judging self, others, or God—can keep their love alive within themselves, and can draw upon its energy to embrace a world whose apparent cruelty they may not understand.

What enables us to pass from resignation to acceptance? The answer is given in the second paradoxical consequence of the decision to experience one's grief just as it is: *grief reveals the character of love*.

The very source of the intolerable sharpness of grief's pain is our essential resource in the struggle towards acceptance. *This is the love one still feels for the one who has died.*

Love is a source of strength, a wellspring of tremendous energy. It does not disappear after the one we loved is no longer with us. In fact, we are likely to experience our love towards that person with stinging intensity. No matter how we may try to prepare, nothing brings to our attention the sweetness of something beautiful as sharply as the pain of no longer having it. Nevertheless, if the love was genuine, a true appreciation of the other's individuality, then it can still be redeemed. It will supply the strength to save those who grieve from the paralysis of resignation.

Simply facing the emotional experience is the beginning of the redemption of love. In the normal course of mourning it is helpful to allow oneself to relive one's memories in minute detail—a gradual and painful process. This is the beginning, but more is needed, since one still must deal with the fact that we can no longer express our love in the ways we did when our loved one was still alive.

When a loved one dies, love does not disappear. Quite the opposite: what usually happens is that love intensifies. We reexperience our love with a new sharpness that can seem overwhelming. The contrast between these intensified feelings of love and the absence of the loved one is what makes grief nearly unbearable. We can respond by trying to suppress these feelings, thus killing off a part of our soul. We can also respond by allowing this love to channel itself back into life.

The fate of the love that seems to be lost forms the ground upon which the transcendence of grief will stand or fall. To the extent the love was real—a true unconditional expression of goodness—it can continue to transform the life of the survivor. Love is more than emotion; it does not perish after we lose the source of good feeling in our lives. "Love is strong as death" (Song of Songs 8:6); even from beyond the grave those we have loved can inspire us to fulfill our lives. This preservation of love has nothing to do with the very common use of grief to justify living in the past. Some react to their tragic loss with "My life is over now"; "Nothing will ever be as good." This does not honor the dead. It taints their memory by using it to constrict one's life. In contrast, the love that now seems to be lost can become an inspiration to continue moving forward. It need not lead to fixation on the past but can become a way into the future.

How can one find the love that seems to be lost after the separation of death? Does one find it by seeking a new relationship? The love that has the power to survive death cannot be confined to any one relationship. Love wants to express goodness, and the goodness in a relationship interrupted by death still needs to express itself. Love does not perish, but we can obscure it by insisting on a painless existence. Love does not ask to be spared the experience of pain (1 Corinthians 13:7). A mother embraces her new-born infant in spite of the pain that its birth has caused her. She wants only to be the first source of goodness her child discovers in a strange and lonely world. In the same way, the love that survives the grave does not expect the absence of pain but desires to contribute creatively to life, even in the uncertain world of grief's aftermath. What begins as love between two human beings finds fulfillment as a movement outward and towards the world. It is the same energy, transformed and grown. It provides strength to the weak survivor, "a spring of water, whose waters never fail" (Isaiah 58:11).

The experience of love's loss brings pain. The realization that love is not lost, that it continues to flourish and inspire growth even when no longer expressed in the same way, makes the pain bearable and gives us the power to accept life after tragedy. In biblical terms, the love that survives a personal attachment may reappear as God's presence. Rachel's love was originally a mother's love for her children, but it lived after her and became a heavenly voice inspiring Jeremiah to compose a beautiful hymn of consolation for a people who thought they had lost God's love.

Love's transformation and reemergence prepares us for the final, most surprising consequence of grief faced with an open heart: *grief reveals the character of joy.*

GRIEF AND JOY

Grief is not merely a painful experience; it is a journey. The journey begins with the experience of separation. In this sense the journey of grief is the journey of life itself. The book of Genesis, with its story of the separation from paradise, encapsulates the separations we experience as human beings. The first of these is the separation at birth, the physical separation from mother. Afterwards, through the process psychologists call "separation-individuation," we learn to perceive ourselves as individuals separate from one another. Thus the thought of separation becomes a basis for our understanding of the world—so basic that we are not normally conscious of it. The perception of separation is also present in all forms of suffering. If we are separate as persons, then our interests are also separate—making fear and suspicion inevitable. The most acute experience of separation is grief: the apparent separation from sources of love.

If separation were the ultimate state of reality, there could be no consolation. Yet we do try to console those who are grieving, and we hope to be consoled when it is our turn to grieve. Perhaps the anticipation of consolation reveals something about grief, and finally about reality itself.

"With weeping they shall come, and with consolations I will lead them back; I will let them walk by brooks of water, in a straight path in which they shall not stumble" (Jeremiah 31:8). This is the journey of grief. What are these rivers of water, and from where do they come? They are the "living waters" that come when the response to grief makes no effort to escape the darkness but follows it to the end. That response to grief is love itself, a love that is willing to bear the consequences of death and so survives death's finality.

A response to grief that tries to escape the darkness of separation will not find true relief. It cannot, because it does not become transformed in love. Instead it increases the sense of separation. It is only natural to ask "Why me?" but if we persist with that question, empowering it with our resentment, it will create further division in our minds, perhaps even suggesting that somebody else's loss would not have been as tragic. Such reactions are a self-defeating grasp for comfort, keeping the energy of our attention focused on the self at a time when it needs to learn to redirect itself towards the world.

There is a response to grief that creates not separation but healing. We can respond to grief with faith if we allow it to shatter our judgments of what should be. We can respond to grief with love if we allow our love for the person we have lost to continue to inspire our lives. These two responses lead to a third, revealed through love's patience over the course of time but as inevitable as it is incomprehensible: *we can respond to grief with joy.*

THE TRANSFORMING POWER OF LOVE

Any loving relationship both serves the self's needs and draws the self beyond itself. To the extent that love participates in the spiritual—the love that is greater than the self—it transforms the one who loves even after the one who is loved has been lost. The intensity of grief is the measure of the gift that was shared. The response that does most justice to the gift—difficult to reach in the beginning, but gradually revealed by the transforming power of love—is *gratitude*. Gratitude can arise as we overcome our attachment to the specific form of love we have received, when we become fully aware of its value, and realize it never was our personal possession. Like grief, gratitude is more than an experience. It is the recognition that through the love that one shared, one has been touched by a reality deeper than separation. Gratitude is an understanding of the world that dissolves the appearance of separation, an understanding that love is not consumed by death. It is the sign that grief has finally been healed.

Gratitude is the pathway from grief to joy. The joy attendant upon grief's resolution preserves the love of the past without living in the past. Love actually knows neither past nor future; it is eternal. The joy of grief's resolution realizes the eternal in the love that once was associated with the past.

For most mourners gratitude does not—cannot—come right away. It can take a long time before it comes. It requires the willingness to give up our "false friends": the anger, resentment, possibly even hatred, that may first seem to be grief's only solace. But at the path's end we find that it was dark only because of our inability to see. Eventually the day arrives when we discover that consolation is inevitable. Grief alone testifies to a false reality, false because it gives up on love.

The love we felt has a life that never dies. We may be surprised at the ways it continues to express itself. It can be very comforting and healing to break off tiny pieces of that love and give them to everyone we meet. Love is inexhaustible; we need not ever fear losing it or using it all up. The love that once caused us so much pain can redeem us, if we can let go of the notion that the way we once experienced that love must be the only way it will ever be experienced. Our loved one would not want that. A love that was born in a strong loving bond between two people can continue to motivate us and change our lives, even years after our loved one has vanished from sight, even to the end of our own lives.

"Blessed are those who mourn, for they will be comforted" (Matthew 5:4). Who is the comforter? The comforter is the self-transcending love that remains after personal love has disappeared into the obscurity of death. Love cannot be confined within a single personal relationship. Its nature is to expand and to give. The love we experience within any given relationship reflects only a single facet of the principle of Love—which we call God—that governs the universe. If we become more interested in this greater

Love than in the specific personal attachment through which we experienced love, we will find that attachment slowly evolving into a general attitude of love and compassion. This loving attitude does not depend on the existence of any particular personal relationship, and so is not threatened by its absence. It is the way into the future that was missing in the hopelessness of despair.

The healing of grief consists in this: that we can still use the love we experienced in our relationship with the loved one who has died. *This love is still a living energy that can direct itself towards the world and can make us an expression of goodness to others.* As we allow it to do so, it will bring us to new and unexpected places of healing we could not have anticipated.

Faith is awareness of the eternal, an awareness that spans the chasm of separation. At the end grief's journey our sense of separation is overcome by love—a love that grows from the very same love we feared we had lost. Allowing this new and greater love to flourish brings us to faith, because it brings us to the eternal through making contact with God's own nature.

Love outlasts every consequence of loss, because it is eternal. When grief is finally healed, our faith informs us that separation has no power, because it has no share in eternity. Our human needs and fears may forever tempt us to resist it or deny it, but the amazing paradox of grief and joy has belonged to our experience even since earliest history. Only the heart's secret knowledge of an eternal truth could preserve the song of consolation from the dust and ashes of the accumulation of time.

> *They who sow in tears*
> *shall reap in joy.*
> *Though weeping they go forth,*
> *carrying seed to sow,*

with song of joy they will return,
bringing home their sheaves.
      (Psalm 126:5–6, original translation)

XIV

THE PROBLEM OF SUFFERING

And not only that, but we also boast in our sufferings, knowing that suffering produces endurance, and endurance produces character, and character produces hope, and hope does not disappoint us, because God's love has been poured into our hearts through the Holy Spirit that has been given to us.
Romans 5:3–5

No, in all these things we are more than conquerors through him who loved us. For I am convinced that neither death, nor life, nor angels, nor rulers, nor things present, nor things to come, nor powers, nor height, nor depth, nor anything else in all creation, will be able to separate us from the love of God.
Romans 8:37–39

THE NATURE OF THE PROBLEM

THERE IS NO GREATER resource than faith in time of stress. But an overpowering obstacle awaits anyone who sincerely desires to have faith: there is so much in our experience that seems to teach us that faith is groundless.

Spiritually sensitive souls have always tried to reconcile their belief in God with the existence of suffering. The Psalmist cries: "Why, O Lord, do you stand far off? Why do you hide yourself in times of trouble? In arrogance the wicked persecute the poor... all their thoughts are, 'There is no God'" (Psalm 10:1–2, 4). The prophet Habakkuk questions: "Your eyes are too pure to behold evil, and you cannot look on wrongdoing; why do you look on the treacherous, and are silent when the wicked swallow those more righteous than they?" (Habakkuk 1:13). Job, himself the symbol of this problem, laments: "It is all one; therefore I say, he destroys both the blameless and the wicked.... If it is not he, who then is it?" (Job 9:22, 24).

Such questions are no mere intellectual exercise. They express our need to organize our experience and make sense out of it. How we deal with these questions can affect our faith, our temperament, and our attitude towards life. Those who are totally without faith live in despair, "without hope." They lack the energy, which faith provides, to effect any meaningful change in their lives. Faith is energy: to feel that life is futile or has no meaning, that nothing makes sense, can sap our strength and make even trivial chores seem overwhelming. Perhaps the most concrete sign of faith's absence is simply an inability to get out of bed in the morning and face the day.

This is why the question of God and suffering is so important. When we look at the need from which the question arises, we can see that it affects even the energy we need for living. To lack faith is to lack a connection to life.

To be precise, we really should speak of the problem of the suffering of the innocent. This generalizes what is sometimes called the problem of evil. Innocent people may suffer from evil acts committed by others, or from events in nature such as diseases, storms, and earthquakes. Sometimes these natural occurrences are also called "evil," and so the term "problem of evil" is often used. Philosophers also speak of the problem of *theodicy*, a term coined by Leibniz meaning "divine justice": how can a just God coexist with evil in the world?

Here is the classic way of presenting the problem: to preserve our belief in God while remaining true to our experience, we would like to say three things:

1. God is good.
2. God is all-powerful.
3. There is evil in the world.

Any two of these three statements fit together. Once we add the third, a tough contradiction appears to arise: How can a God who is both good and powerful allow suffering and evil to exist?

Most attempts to solve this problem do so by denying one of the three propositions. Let's see what happens with each one.

WHAT IF GOD IS NOT GOOD?

Throughout history the first proposition, that God is good, has been denied in a number of ways. Zoroastrianism and Manichaeism are examples of dualism, in which the world is seen as the arena of conflict between cosmic forces of good and evil. It is hard to see how this type of theology can lead to faith. It would seem to foster insecurity, since the forces of evil pose a constant threat to the survival of goodness.

The modern version of denying that God is good is to consider God, if you can still even call it God, as some kind of morally indifferent natural life force. Nature doesn't care about good and evil, or about you or me. If nature cares about anything at all, it can only be self-perpetuation. Moral values do not apply to the animal world, nor to ours, which is a part of it.

This way of viewing God is not implausible given our scientific world view and what we observe in our experience. It also is not a very good foundation for faith. Just like dualism, it holds little hope of God's being involved in our lives in any meaningful way. It is hard to know how to approach such a God in prayer. Nature is inexorable. In its determined motion it continues to discard the weak at the side of the road, just as it always has.

Of course, just because a certain view of God may not give us the results we want doesn't make it false. Far too much theology works on the basis of wishful thinking: we want to believe something; therefore we assume it to be true. Theology must be more than just saying things about God because they make us feel better. Perhaps we really can't expect any more of God than this morally neutral life force. If that is the truth, then we must confront it. But Judeo-Christian tradition has always considered such a view of God limited and false. God must be in some way actively involved in our lives; otherwise faith is meaningless. We will have to consider whether, on the basis of our actual experience and not just our theological wish list, it is possible to go beyond an amoral God. But for the time being we can observe that this view of God is bound to lead to insecurity in one who takes it with the seriousness it deserves.

There are of course other ways of denying or at least modifying God's goodness that are common in religion. Sometimes we say that God's ways are inscrutable: everything that happens is good and is also the will of God; it just does not conform to human standards of goodness. But God has not given us a sense of goodness for nothing. It makes no sense to say, on the one hand, that morality is divine and Godlike, and on the other, that God can behave immorally as a matter of whim. If God's permitting the most radical, brutal evil is somehow "good," then concepts of good and evil lose all meaning. God becomes the devil, sending tragedy and destruction to people solely according to fancy. Such a God should not be worshiped but abhorred.

The classical way of getting around this problem has been to say that since God is just, God punishes only sinners. But this is the answer of the friends of Job, which the Bible discredits. It is the least compassionate response of all, blaming those who suffer for their own suffering; yet it is extremely common. It is comforting to think that people who suffer must somehow deserve it—it makes sense out of chaos, and gives us the illusion of control. The price we pay is the encouragement of a harsh judgmentalism, which is contrary to love.

Reincarnation, another attempt to reconcile justice and the existence of evil, similarly denies the suffering of the innocent. It maintains that all suffering is earned, even though its earning may have occurred in a previous life. It therefore also leads to blaming suffering on the one who suffers.

These attempts to resolve the dissonance between justice and the existence of evil are a little too neat. From an existentialist perspective, these approaches are wrong because they deny the tragic aspect of life: often people do suffer unjustly, tragedies that they have not earned and do not deserve. The Bible recognizes this: "For he makes his sun rise on the evil and on the good, and sends rain on the righteous and on the unrighteous" (Matthew 5:45). For reasons hard to understand, the innocent do suffer. It is only by accepting this that we can develop compassion to the fullest extent. Love is a higher value than security. Only the ability to see that people do suffer innocently truly opens our hearts.

WHAT IF GOD IS NOT ALL-POWERFUL?

In our time own time it has become fashionable to put limits on God's power; this has been the theme of some popular books on the problem of suffering. God would love to help us but simply can't, either because God chooses not to out of respect for our free will, or because God is limited like we are and is only able to do so much. But at least God's feelings are in the right place: God sympathizes with us, weeps with us, "feels our pain." This picture of God appeals to sentimentality; still, it is completely unbiblical.

The Bible tells us that God is "a very present help in trouble" (Psalm 46:1) and is involved in our lives in very decisive ways.

If God really cannot overcome evil, then evil, not God, is the real God. This would be unthinkable, and so many who limit God's power claim that it is God's own choice.

Why would God impose such self-restraint in the face of evil and the terrible suffering it causes? The universal answer to this question is: human free will. Such is God's great love for us that under no circumstances will there be any intervention, out of respect for our free will. God is often compared to good parents, who do not overprotect their children but respect their independence and allow them to make their own mistakes.

There are several problems with this response. The argument from free will fails to explain why God allows innocent people to suffer so intensely from disease or natural catastrophes, which have nothing to do with human will. But there is an even deeper problem. Let us grant that we have free will, however limited it may be by psychological or environmental influences. We are responsible for our decisions. That is not the issue. The issue is whether preserving this freedom at any cost can serve as a justification for divine inactivity in the face of radical evil.

If God's allowing our free will to reign absolutely is an act of love towards us, what about love for the victims? Are they not God's children, too? God may be understood as a good parent, but would any sane parents allow their children to maim, rape, torture, and kill each other just for the sake of respecting their free will? The "free will" solution sets up a false dichotomy: that either we allow human free will or we don't. The obvious answer is to allow free will to operate but within limits. Is that not why we have laws?

The solutions we have so far seen to the problem of God and evil portray God as immoral, irrelevant, or stupid. What else is left?

WHAT IF THERE REALLY IS NO EVIL?

A final possibility, which would preserve both God's goodness and power, is to deny the reality of evil. This option is taken by metaphysical approaches to spirituality. They maintain that the world we experience with our senses is an illusion. It is a product or projection of thought, and as such has no more reality than a dream. It has nothing to do with God, who did not create it and is not involved with it.

Therefore to overcome suffering we need to change our thinking, to see the perfect world that "really" exists in place of the painful one we experience. Often this means turning our attention away from, or tuning out, the "erroneous" thoughts that manifest as unpleasant experiences. If through God's perfect mind we can see God's perfect world, we will experience it in all its glory. Our suffering will come to an end.

This theory has some obvious contradictions. If God is the only Mind, as metaphysics likes to claim, then how could erroneous thoughts even exist? "But they don't exist," is the usual answer, "they aren't real"—a disingenuous response, to say the least. Someone or something is conscious of these erroneous thoughts, or else we could not even talk about them. God certainly couldn't entertain them: God is Perfect Mind, and also the only creator. So there seems to be no possible way the illusions that create so much strife could even have arisen.

But the real problem with this approach is more psychological than philosophical. It encourages a life based on denial. People do have experiences and emotional reactions. One cannot make them go away simply by declaring them illusions. If we try to abolish the world without honestly confronting it, we risk creating a false reality in which we are unaware of our true concerns and those of other people. We become distant both from our own suffering and the suffering of others. We may neglect physical and emotional problems instead of attending to them and treating them as "real." The problems do not disappear; they just go into hiding, to crash down on us later when we can no longer avoid them.

If the world that "carnal" or "mortal" mind creates is not real, then God has no connection to it. Once again we cannot expect God's involvement in our lives, unless we manage to believe that we see a perfection way beyond the reach of human existence. If we can't see it, then we are lost. God cannot help us in a dream God did not create. Ironically, in searching for a perfect spiritual world, followers of metaphysical theologies only create a deeper separation between themselves and the world of ordinary human beings.

THE REAL QUESTION

It seems that none of these options will allow for belief in a God who is not only good but who remains actively involved in our lives. The problem of suffering, in its customary form, cannot be solved. One might as well try to divide by zero. The problem of suffering, when taken seriously, destroys traditional forms of faith.

However: What we really need to consider is not whether the original question can be answered, but whether something might be wrong with the question itself. Questions are not neutral; they carry assumptions. What are the assumptions behind the question: "How can a good and all-powerful God permit the existence of evil?"

One cannot ask this question without thinking of God as a self-conscious being, with a separate autonomous will and set of reactions. In other words the question itself implies that God is a person just like ourselves, differing from us only in not having a body but having unlimited power. In spite of these differences God is a creature, albeit one who may have total control over our lives. It is hardly possible not to resent, at least in secret, another creature in such a position of power over us.

The problem of suffering is not really a theological problem. It is an existential one. We may try to reduce it to abstract speculation about God, but this only trivializes it and leaves the real question behind. The theological question is relevant only in its impact on the existential question, which has to do with our lives as we actually live them. Those who ask the question of suffering with true sincerity and from a broken heart are driven to ask it not by theological curiosity but by both compassion and fear. They feel compassion for those who suffer, and experience the fear of living in an uncertain world where a tragic accident can knock one down at any moment.

And so the real question becomes: How can we make sense out of a dangerous world? How can we live our lives with confidence when terrible things happen with little predictability? And if we phrase our beliefs in terms of God, the question becomes: What can be the source of our faith? How can we maintain trust in God in spite of fear?

THE NEED FOR FAITH

The problem of suffering is really about faith. No matter how devastating, suffering destroys us only if it destroys our faith. So to understand how to deal with this problem, we need to understand faith.

The faith that overcomes tragedy must be more than belief in some religious doctrine. Belief alone does not provide the strength of character necessary to overcome catastrophe. Without the foundation that true faith provides, beliefs may crumble under suffering's weight. Belief alone tends toward rigid rather than creative responses.

Faith is more than belief. It is an internalized conviction that ultimately things make sense. Faith is a sense of order in spite of the appearance of disorder. The confidence of faith is the confidence to move forward in life because, in spite of the risks involved, we count on something that supports our movement.

FAITH AND TRUST

The most rudimentary form of faith is trust, the trust children have that enables them to explore their environment and try to master it. They learn to trust the order they encounter in the world, which enables them to live in it with some degree of safety and predictability. They trust the presence of their parents, who will catch them if they fall. Almost everyone has faith to some degree, since if we completely lacked faith, fear would overwhelm us to the point of immobilization.

There are many levels of faith. The first level is the child's basic trust, a type of faith hardly anyone develops to perfection.

Perfect basic trust is impossible, since one's own parents are not perfect, and accidents will happen as part of the very process of living. Even if one has the best of parents, one does not have them forever. If one does not lose them through death, one loses them simply through growing up and becoming aware of their frailty. The child's faith must therefore change if one is to continue to live with confidence. As we grow older we acquire other sources of faith: faith in parental substitutes, such as teachers or other role models, and faith in our own abilities. Later on in life we seek faith in lasting relationships, marriage and the family, which provide a safe structure that continues to nurture our growth.

All these sources of faith are, however, finite, fragile, and fallible. They do not provide perfect security, and on some level of consciousness we know it. The time may come when we lose them, once more finding ourselves thrown back into the need for a faith that can give us a sense of order and meaning sufficient to keep us standing even in times of crisis. Such faith is our only protection against fear of the danger and chaos inherent in human existence.

THE THREAT TO FAITH

Those who ask the question of suffering do not need a tidy theological explanation of divine justice, but rather a sustaining faith in God, an awareness of Ultimate Order, that can withstand the threats life makes against any finite source of faith.

Often the faith we do have cannot stand against these threats. We don't always respond to our suffering with courage and perseverance. We may not know how to respond at all. If we are hit hard enough we may even lose the will to live. What determines whether our response to suffering will be positive or negative, perhaps so negative as to lead to the loss of all hope and enthusiasm for life?

Intellectual speculation about the role suffering plays in the cosmic scheme of things does not help. We cannot drain the mystery out of suffering—nor can we ever find a complete solution to the problem. There will always be things we do not understand, things we question, things that threaten our faith. Lacking certain knowledge of what occurs after death we can make no sure pronouncement, either positive or negative, concerning the resolution of human suffering. But we do not need certain knowledge. We only need enough clues pointing towards an eternal, redemptive reality to keep our faith intact, and to keep us going.

If we can find these clues, we will find a God who survives the doubt that suffering always brings. This God may turn out to be very different from the one we questioned when we first began struggling with this problem. We may find ourselves quite surprised.

THE CHARACTERISTICS OF FAITH

To see how faith can be preserved, let us look at it closely. Faith's characteristics can be described symbolically in terms of three spiritual qualities: light, truth, and love. In practice these correspond to awareness, self-honesty, and compassion.

AWARENESS

There is no spiritual life without awareness. Awareness is the ability to see one's own thoughts. It is the ability to know oneself as separate from others, which means seeing others' concerns as well as one's own. It is the knowledge of where one's own self ends and others begin. It is the capacity to sift reality from illusion, to recognize deception and self-deception, to tell the true from the false. It is consciousness of the world that exists beyond the boundaries of one's own self, one's own needs, sensations, interests, and desires. Without awareness we could not realize the higher spiritual qualities, such as faith and love. If we were always in a state of sleep, or enveloped by dreams and fantasies, we could not see the separate existence of others. We could not love them or have compassion for them. We could also have no knowledge of the deeper strength, presence, and love within ourselves and beyond ourselves, which are a witness of God's presence.

Without awareness there could be no faith—and without suffering, there could be no awareness. Without suffering we would never come to know any reality outside ourselves. We would know nothing outside our own pleasant sensations. We begin life tied to another person, mother, whom at first we do not recognize as a separate being. If she could always perfectly fulfill every one of our needs, we would never come to know her as anything more than an extension of ourselves. Our "ego" in the strict psychological sense, which is our sense of ourselves in relation to others, develops precisely because mother cannot always satisfy our needs. The mother who is "good enough" (Winnicott) does fail to meet her child's needs, but gradually over a period of time, failing just enough to enable the child to grow but not so much as to destroy the child's faith (trust) in an orderly world. Eventually the child recognizes its mother as a separate person, with needs of her own. As the child grows older it learns to love her not just as someone who provides care but as an individual in her own right. Our very early experiences teach us to see others as separate from ourselves, showing us that their wills do not always coincide with our own. Without this elementary awareness we could not perceive the individuality of others, and for this very reason we would be unable to love them.

This awareness is born in suffering: the suffering of experiencing needs that are not met, of breaking the symbiotic tie with mother, of exploring the wider world and confronting the fear this separation produces, of experiencing a similar separation from others. Seeing others as separate individuals, with different wills and different needs, is both a cause of suffering and essential to love.

Any experience of suffering, even beyond these childhood separations, has the power to increase our awareness. Suffering drives us out of our hiding places; it pries us loose from our most cherished illusions. It makes us question; it makes us search for a higher meaning that makes life worthwhile in spite of our pain. If we respond well to suffering, it makes us more aware of ourselves; it makes us examine and question ourselves, thus deepening our self-knowledge. It tests our limits, often revealing in us strengths we might otherwise never have known. All this is not to make excuses for suffering or even to call it good, but to point out the role it plays in our development.

Suffering shows us our own strengths. If we are willing to face our pain and the fears that surround it, without asking for immediate solace but seeking only to increase our awareness of ourselves and the meaning of our situation, then we have the possibility of self-discovery, growth, and even faith. To approach suffering without demands but only with a search for awareness is in fact a prayer. In this prayer we surrender our own will and become open to what the experience has to reveal to us.

Suffering produces endurance. Suffering makes us not only discover but practice our strengths, even if the only strength we possess at the moment is to endure what we are facing without trying to make it disappear. "Enduring" does not mean passively feeling pain without hope. It is a positive response to suffering that allows it to be, lives with it, tries neither to escape nor deny it, but does seek to become aware of all the hidden issues that extreme pain inevitably raises. This already is faith. It is being open to revelation, even if there is no confidence that this revelation will come or that when it does come it will bring a redeeming message. This is *dark faith*, the most difficult but deepest kind of faith.

Dark faith does not try to strike bargains with God or seek the false solace of martyrdom. It just wants to see what is there to be seen, and then it waits.

Endurance produces character. By not expecting immediate comfort, but through the willingness to live with our struggles, we find our spiritual strengths.

While awareness of ourselves and others is a prerequisite for love, it is never perfect. We all carry illusions and ignorance from our earliest years. If we are receptive, suffering makes us aware of them. It brings to the surface lost pieces of ourselves, memories, unresolved conflicts, grievances, and archaic fears that need reclamation and healing. The awareness that results from suffering can make us more resilient, more resourceful, and more compassionate.

Character produces hope. The very fact that this process of awareness, self-discovery, and strengthening of our character takes place is evidence that our world is not total chaos, that a certain wisdom and guidance are available to us, and that perhaps there really is an Ultimate Order.

There are gradations of awareness: awareness of self, awareness of one's environment, awareness of the existence of others, awareness of the individuality of others (which is love), and through love, the awareness of the eternal. At this point awareness truly becomes faith.

SELF-HONESTY

Awareness directed towards the self becomes self-honesty. Self-honesty is the practical application of the quality of truth. Truth is the correct perception of reality, including our own thoughts and experiences, and also the deeper spiritual qualities (awareness, inner strength and guidance, compassion and love) that give life its meaning.

Self-honesty is the cultivation of truth within oneself. It is the resolve to become aware of one's own self-deception. It is the willingness to question oneself when confronted by the possibility that one might be wrong. It is the willingness to examine oneself, to admit to oneself exactly what one may be thinking or feeling. It is a refusal to be comforted by platitudes or placated by clichés. It is an allegiance to the truth in all its forms.

Truth is not some abstract notion that God exists or that the universe would appear to us as perfect if only we understood it. If our ideas about God do not penetrate to the core of our experience, then they have no meaning. Truth is radical honesty with ourselves. Truth is the willingness to admit to ourselves that we are lacking in faith, if we find our faith wanting when we need it most. Truth is the willingness to question any false idea of God we may have cherished but that has failed to save us. Truth is the refusal to rely on sources of authority we cannot verify for ourselves in our own daily experience and struggle for spiritual growth. Truth therefore implies courage, since it is a lack of courage that makes us run from truth and that drives us toward false sources of consolation, ideas and objects that would comfort us by masking our awareness of the truth. As a spiritual quality, courage is the resolve to live with the truth, to face what must be faced, to accept our responsibilities, even if doing so means that for a while we must live with pain and fear rather than the easy consolation that comes from believing in our wishes.

Self-honesty makes prayer sincere, which in turn makes it effective. We find an instructive example in the life of the prophet Jeremiah, at a time when he was struggling with his own crisis of faith. It was Jeremiah's burden to deliver a message of warning to a corrupt people about whom he cared deeply. This was an act of love, but the people responded with a deep, personal hatred. Rejection by his own people tore at his heart and threw him into despair. And so Jeremiah prays, a prayer that is rather astonishing:

> *Woe is me, my mother, that you ever bore me,*
> *a man of strife and contention to the whole land!*
> *I have not lent, nor have I borrowed,*
> *yet all of them curse me....*
>
> *O Lord, you know; remember me and visit me,*
> *and bring down retribution for me on my persecutors.*
> *In your forbearance do not take me away;*
> *know that on your account I suffer insult.*
>
> *Your words were found, and I ate them,*
> *and your words became to me a joy*
> *and the delight of my heart;*
> *for I am called by your name, O Lord, God of hosts.*
>
> *I did not sit in the company of merrymakers,*
> *nor did I rejoice;*

under the weight of your hand I sat alone,
for you had filled me with indignation.

Why is my pain unceasing,
my wound incurable, refusing to be healed?
Truly, you are to me like a deceitful brook,
like waters that fail.

Therefore thus says the Lord:
If you turn back, I will take you back,
and you shall stand before me.
If you utter what is precious, and not what is worthless,
you shall serve as my mouth.
It is they who will turn to you, not you who will turn to them.
And I will make you to this people a fortified wall of bronze;
they will fight against you, but they shall not prevail over you,
for I am with you
to save you and deliver you, says the Lord.
(Jeremiah 15:10, 15–20)

This prayer is worth a close look, because it is not the kind of prayer one would expect from an enlightened or holy man, and yet it receives an answer.

Jeremiah complains. He is angry. He indulges in self-pity. He expresses hopelessness. He accuses God of betrayal. And God answers him!

Whatever else this prayer may express, it has one overriding quality: self-honesty. Jeremiah does not say what he thinks God wants to hear, what would make him sound pious, or what would conform to most expectations of a religious man. Nor does he present God with a list of favors, as is common in worship today. He says only what is in his heart. If he cannot praise God, he doesn't.

If he is angry, so be it. He does not rush to be consoled. He asks, "Why is my pain unceasing?" He does not say, "Please take my pain away, and the sooner the better." Jeremiah chooses honesty over the appearance of spirituality—and the result is a surprisingly spiritual prayer!

What does it mean to say God answers? The answer is presented as if it were a heavenly voice actually speaking to Jeremiah. This is a symbolic representation. Most likely it was an inner sense of assurance that could be translated into words, and that Jeremiah knew came from beyond himself. That is how prayers are often answered. And if prayers have two qualities—honesty and love—they will be answered. Jeremiah was completely honest about what he thought and felt, and was torn by love for his people, who he saw were destroying themselves.

How can we understand this response to prayer, particularly when so many prayers that are phrased just right, with good, respectful, religious language, seem to go unanswered? A prayer that expresses divine qualities will draw a divine response. When God's nature is in any way reflected in us, it draws God's presence like a magnet. This is a spiritual principle: the Kingdom of God is neither "in heaven" nor simply "within you": it is both. When divine qualities become visible in our hearts and in our souls, God does also. And we know it.

The divine qualities Jeremiah expressed in his prayer are truth and love. When we are truthful with ourselves we come closer to God—even though we may hardly suspect it. By facing his despair honestly and by being willing to live with it, Jeremiah found within himself an endurance and courage that enabled him to become a source of strength to those few who were looking for someone like him to give them guidance in a troublesome time. Meanwhile Jeremiah knew that his own guidance came from a source far greater than his limited perception.

There is another great figure of the Bible who was saved by his allegiance to the truth. His name was Job, and he became a symbol for the problem of suffering. At the beginning of his story the devil's witnesses are very much in evidence, and they are powerful: Job, who was rich and prominent in his community, first loses his possessions, then his children, then finally his health. His body covered with painful sores, all he can do is sit among the ashes scraping himself to find relief. His wife represents the temptation to lose faith completely and give in to despair: she tells him to "Curse God, and die" (Job 2:9). And Job almost gives in. He curses the day of his birth, lamenting that it would have been better for him had he never left his mother's womb. He questions and doubts the God in whom he once fervently believed. He protests his innocence, but without hope of getting any response. He condemns God as cruel and immoral:

> *Though I am innocent, I cannot answer him;*
> *I must appeal for mercy to my accuser.*
> *If I summoned him and he answered me,*
> *I do not believe that he would listen to my voice.*
>
> *For he crushes me with a tempest,*
> *and multiplies my wounds without cause;*
> *he will not let me get my breath,*
> *but fills me with bitterness.*
>
> *If it is a contest of strength, he is the strong one!*
> *If it is a matter of justice, who can summon him?*
> *Though I am innocent, my own mouth would condemn me;*
> *though I am blameless, he would prove me perverse.*

> *I am blameless; I do not know myself;*
> *I loathe my life.*
>
> *It is all one; therefore I say,*
> *he destroys both the blameless and the wicked.*
>
> *When disaster brings sudden death,*
> *he mocks at the calamity of the innocent.*
>
> *The earth is given into the hand of the wicked;*
> *he covers the eyes of its judges—*
> *if it is not he, who then is it?*
>
> (Job 9:15–24)

Job's faith seems to disappear. God is no longer present for him:

> *Even when I cry out, 'Violence!' I am not answered;*
> *I call aloud, but there is no justice.*
>
> *He has walled up my way so that I cannot pass,*
> *and he has set darkness upon my paths.*
>
> (Job 19:7–8)

There is an irony here, which makes Job's prayer unexpectedly effective. Job only seems to have lost his faith. *Even in the moment of his deepest despair he continues to talk to God.* Like Jeremiah, he tells God exactly what is in his heart. He is completely honest, and his prayer expresses truth. Job is in fact more honest than the friends who came to comfort him. They simply spout platitudes about God that they have never tested, but Job expresses the true concerns of his heart, even if they contradict the faith he once had.

This in itself is an act of faith; it is an awareness of truth far deeper than any false religion or spirituality that one has not made nor can ever truly make one's own.

To accuse God of faithlessness, as Job does, is still to search for God. This anger towards God is therefore the most paradoxical expression of faith. Job's faith is still very deep, in spite of his confession that he has lost all faith. *Even in the moment of his deepest despair he continues to talk to God.* Job's suffering reveals how deep his faith has always been.

Job's circumstances force him to abandon the false comforts of simple religion, but he does not abandon his allegiance to the truth—in this case, the truth about the falseness of his former faith. And so his dialogue with God remains unbroken. Indeed, Job's prayer expresses the second quality next to honesty that makes prayer effective, and that is love.

What Job still loves is goodness: he cries out for justice, and condemns God for not being good. But the God Job condemns is the God of religion. There is another God, the real God, beyond the God of religion, and that is Goodness Itself. And so to love goodness is to love God, even if it leads one to reject the God of religion. This explains how God—the *real* God—could eventually answer Job. Job never stopped loving God. The dialogue was never really broken.

But what kind of an answer does he get? Job never receives a response to his original question. God never does explain why the innocent suffer. Instead, God takes Job on a tour of the mysteries of the universe, showing him wonders beyond anything he has ever imagined. The one thing Job does learn is the limit of his own understanding.

God's answer to Job will not satisfy all of us. Some may even feel that God is being cruel and dismissive, as if to say, "Job, don't you dare question me, for you know nothing." But we need to look deeply at the meaning of God's response to Job. Job himself is satisfied, for he says: "I had heard of you by the hearing of the ear, but now my eye sees you" (Job 42:5). And we know that the very persistent Job is not satisfied easily. What does Job see that we do not?

While Job never receives an answer to his question, he does find something much more valuable: God's presence. In spite of his pain he can still devote himself to something greater than himself. His suffering has not taken that from him. Continuing to talk to God even in the darkness, when the answer doesn't come, is love, and love always draws a response from God. Job discovers God alive in the midst of dark faith.

Ironically, God vindicates Job: "After the Lord had spoken these words to Job, the Lord said to Eliphaz the Temanite: 'My wrath is kindled against you and against your two friends; for you have not spoken of me what is right, as my servant Job has'" (Job 42:7). These friends of Job defended God. Job blasphemed, he condemned God—and God stands up for Job! Job's religious God had to die so that Job could find the real God who is Absolute Goodness even in the midst of suffering. The God whom Job now knows is not the God of his spiritual infancy, but a God who dwells in truth and desires the expressions of the heart.

Many have objected to the book's ending, in which Job's fortunes are restored. Job does not find the same family he had before—that will forever remain an empty place in his life—but a new family and a new fulfilled life. While this might seem like a fairy-tale ending, it should not be taken that way. It is a symbolic statement that in some way God always does respond to those divine qualities present in the human heart: to awareness, truth, and love. The response may not come in the form of what we expect or what we want, or even as with Job, in the restoration of what one has lost. But it will come in the form of a sense of God's presence that, to the faithful heart, will be unmistakable.

COMPASSION

Awareness and self-honesty ("light" and "truth") prepare us to approach the mystery of suffering. At the heart of this mystery we find the connection between suffering and love.

Suffering and love are joined in the word compassion. "Compassion" literally means "suffering with." It is the ability to be with another when that person is suffering; that is, to be present without flinching or hiding from that person's pain.

Our ability to understand and to feel for others' pain begins with our own knowledge of what it means to suffer. If we did not suffer ourselves, then the pain others feel would make no impression on us. Just by itself, suffering does not make us loving: we also need awareness. Without the awareness of others' separate individuality we could not know compassion but only identification with others' painful experiences. This would not be love; what we think we love would only be the image of ourselves that we see in others, not others as they really are. Their pain would become our pain, and their fear our fear. As a result we may become afraid to approach and comfort others who are suffering, or we may make false assumptions about them based only on our own experiences. We cannot truly love others until we can see clearly where we end and they begin.

Making a clear difference between what others suffer and what we experience does not mean that compassion for others is not painful for us as well. Becoming aware of others to the point of seeing their pain and feeling for it can be heartbreaking; at times it can hurt us even more than the pain of our own suffering. This may be one reason why we can be so reluctant to respond to others who suffer. To be aware of the soul of a suffering individual can be overwhelmingly painful, but we need not be afraid of it. This is because responding to others through their pain hut as separate individuals is a form of love. When we are conscious of sharing love with others, their pain may hurt us but will never harm us. (This is something professional caregivers need to understand, so that they can be truly present with their patients without suffering burnout.)

Compassionate love, while painful, strengthens us as long as we maintain our loving presence in spite of the awareness of otherness. The pain we feel at seeing the suffering of someone we love can rip the heart, but if it contains no fear, hate, or guilt it is a clean wound and will heal cleanly. Often the pain we feel for ourselves is not clean; full of self-pity and resentment, it festers and burns. A wound free of such impurities always heals cleanly, leaving one spiritually stronger.

"Compassion" is not to be confused with another word that sounds just like it: "sympathy." It is ironic that both words literally mean "with suffering"; one derives from Latin, the other from Greek. Sympathy, however, means "suffering with" in the sense of feeling sorry for people who are hurting, a condescending attitude that may even take secret pleasure in another's misfortune. Sympathy is not healing; it only confirms the low self-esteem and sense of inferiority of the person who is its object. Unlike compassion, sympathy is not based on the awareness of who and where the other person really is. Instead, it takes at face value the other's sense of victimization and gratifies those who offer it with a feeling of superiority at their ability to help one who is needy. When we are trying to be helpful it is important to be able to look at ourselves and know whether what we feel is compassion or sympathy.

Compassion is a form of love, and love is a form of awareness. If we are not aware of others as separate individuals with their own histories, interests, concerns, perceptions, needs, and fears—if we see them only in relation to ourselves—then we cannot love them. If we think that we love, most likely what we really love is a reflection or extension of our own self.

If, however, we have the clarity and awareness that allow us to see others in all these dimensions of their individuality, then that awareness has a way of touching the heart. We discover an appreciation of others' separateness and uniqueness, a respect for their struggles, a desire for their well-being, a sense of warmth when we see them blessed, a sense of happiness when they are happy. Our capacity to respond to others in this way, from the heart, depends directly on our ability to become aware of them as full and separate individuals, without referring or comparing them to ourselves. Love is therefore the awareness of others' individuality. This love cannot be willed, but is a natural response to others when our awareness reaches beyond the limits of our own self-interest.

Without suffering we would never develop the capacity for love. We have already observed that through suffering we become aware of others as separate from ourselves. More than that, if we did not experience suffering ourselves, we would not know what it might mean for someone else. We would be unable to understand or even see whole aspects of others' lives. Of course this does not mean that we should or even can understand others' experience by comparing them to our own, but only that our own struggle through life opens us, broadens our perception, and sharpens our awareness of the struggles of others even though they may be very different from our own.

This kind of awareness, a special form of love, is what compassion truly is. Compassion is the awareness and acceptance of the tragic aspects of human existence. It is seeing that weakness and suffering are part of the human experience, and that no one escapes them no matter how pure a life one tries to lead. Compassion is seeing the imperfections of the human will and the human heart, and consequently knowing we cannot perfect ourselves no matter how hard we try—and that we may not even know how to try. Compassion is seeing others' weaknesses without judging or resenting them, and even with a loving response toward them, a heartfelt response that sees others limited by their desires and fears, struggling as best they know how under conditions they may barely understand. Compassion means maintaining a respectful, nonintrusive presence with others. It is a refusal to abandon others even when they are at their worst.

Real love begins with compassion, and compassion begins with suffering: this is our greatest clue to unraveling suffering's mystery. Without suffering we would have no reason to seek outside ourselves, or even to become conscious of anything besides our own pleasure. Suffering forces us out of our shelters and makes us question. We question God, we question life, we question others, we question ourselves. And if we are fortunate, we find a connection between our own pain and the pain of others. We could not even see others if we didn't suffer. Suffering, used wisely, sheds its disguise to reveal itself not as the face of death but as the teacher of love.

COMPASSION AND FORGIVENESS

WHAT FORGIVENESS IS—AND IS NOT

Perhaps the highest, and certainly the most difficult, form of compassion is compassion toward someone who has hurt us personally. We call this *forgiveness: the ability to see with compassion those who have trespassed against us.*

There is a lot of misunderstanding about forgiveness, and a lot has been written about forgiveness that simply makes no sense. This is because of the way forgiveness is usually presented: without an understanding of non-self-interested love, forgiveness can become self-centered, something we do for ourselves to reduce our own discomfort. True forgiveness of the other becomes a nearly impossible undertaking, and the meaning of forgiveness is lost.

Forgiveness is often presented as an obligation: we are commanded to forgive and so we must, no matter how serious the offense. We may feel guilty if we can't forgive; then forgiveness becomes an impossible burden and a judgment on ourselves. To "forgive" usually means to pardon, to release, to absolve. To "forgive a debt" means to cancel it. So forgiveness is taken to mean telling the offender he or she has no need to account for anything; the offense no longer matters. Very often we cannot sincerely deliver this message but believe that we should. So people say things like "I forgive, but I can't forget." This is a less than honest way of saying "I can't forgive." If you still harbor resentment, then you have not forgiven. And a command to forgive that cannot be obeyed is bound to increase resentment.

To forgive by releasing others from the claims their offenses make upon them is considered a virtue. It is anything but. There are two huge problems with this kind of forgiveness: First, we cannot do it. Second, it would be arrogant to try.

The little transgressions of daily life—a careless word, a thoughtless gesture—are not usually real challenges to forgiveness. The big ones—deep betrayals, serious crimes—test our notion of what it means to forgive. Forgiveness can actually be harmful if it means releasing people—figuratively or literally—who have committed serious offenses and are likely to do so again. We also clearly have no right to forgive anyone whose actions have affected people other than ourselves.

The consequences of any serious violation of goodness are between the individual and God. If we attempt to forgive someone for extreme cruelty and that person has not reformed, the cruelty still remains a stain on the soul. We cannot change that and we cannot relieve anyone of the need to atone for it. Atonement is not just a moral requirement; it is something the offender's soul needs, with which we have no right to interfere. Releasing others from responsibility for their actions is not humanly possible, is not loving toward the victims, and is not even loving toward the one who committed the offense.

If the person does truly reform, then divine forgiveness may already be won even if we cannot see it and even if we don't wish to accept it. "To err is human, to forgive divine"—this is truer than we may realize. Forgiveness in the sense of releasing someone from a karmic debt belongs not to us but to God. No human being can tell others exactly for which sins they may or may not need to account. Only God can cancel a person's debt, because only God sees truly into the heart.

No one can say to someone who has murdered, maimed, raped, or robbed: What you did no longer matters; your offense has been pardoned. And what a relief not to have this burden! We are not God, and are not required to make such pronouncements in order to lead a spiritual life. However, we still need to practice forgiveness in a spiritually healthy way, and for this we need a different understanding of forgiveness.

FORGIVENESS REDEFINED

Some may protest this limitation on forgiveness. Often we hear the advice: "Even if the other person does not repent you should still forgive, because you are not doing it for that person's sake, you are doing it for yourself." Forgiveness thus seen is not a loving act towards someone else; it is a psychological self-help technique. It is also a misnomer. It should not be called "forgiveness," but "letting go." There is much to be said for the healthy effects of letting go of resentments, but that does not constitute forgiveness.

Forgiveness cannot be primarily a quest for relief. Forgiveness is above all an act of love; otherwise it has no meaning. Fortunately our definition of love leads to an understanding of forgiveness that is not only humanly possible but desirable as well. Love is the awareness of the individuality of others. We can find a new understanding of forgiveness if we read Jesus's words in this light:

> *You have heard that it was said, "You shall love your neighbor and hate your enemy." But I say to you, Love your enemies and pray for those who persecute you, so that you may be children of your Father in heaven; for he makes his sun rise on the evil and on the good, and sends rain on the righteous and on the unrighteous. (Matthew 5:43–45)*

Loving someone who has wronged us, even loving an enemy,

does not mean having to feel good about that person. It means becoming aware of that person. Seeing the other as an individual is all that is required. We do not need to pass judgment on a person's innocence or guilt, or to release that person from responsibility. We could not even if we wanted to.

We can learn much about the meaning of forgiveness by revisiting someone we met in chapter 5: Zacchaeus the tax collector. Zacchaeus must have trampled on a lot of people, because the impression we get is that he was generally hated. The people have not forgiven Zacchaeus; they "grumble" when Jesus welcomes him (Luke 19:7). Jesus does not forgive Zacchaeus; he sees that Zacchaeus has already been forgiven. Forgiveness is between the individual and God. It does not depend on our desire to forgive, and it does not depend on our desire not to forgive.

How do we know Zacchaeus has been forgiven? He has clearly experienced a transformation. He feels genuine remorse, and he offers to make restitution "four times as much" (Luke 19:8). His heart has opened, and he can feel what he did to those whom he hurt.

What then does it mean that we are asked to forgive? Jesus said:

Be on your guard! If another disciple sins, you must rebuke the offender, and if there is repentance, you must forgive. And if the same person sins against you seven times a day, and turns back to you seven times and says, "I repent," you must forgive. (Luke 17:3–4)

One cannot ask for forgiveness without first having repented, and from the Zacchaeus story we learn that one must make restitution when possible. If one is repentant, we must forgive. But forgiveness cannot mean the same thing when applied to God and to human beings. The New Testament word "forgive," *aphiemi*, originally meant to "send away," and later on acquired the meaning of pardoning sins. The first meaning, in the sense of taking leave or letting go, is the one best applied to human forgiveness.

The forgiveness Zacchaeus received had no human source. He had already put himself right with God, and to his fellows he made his offer of restitution. Yet Jesus still modeled the forgiveness that was expected from the members of Zacchaeus's community. That forgiveness was not the remission of Zacchaeus's sins. It was the call to behold Zacchaeus in love.

To forgive humanly means to love the offender in spite of the offense, which means *to be aware of that person's individuality*.

When we become aware of another's individuality, we cannot hate. Even those whom we may hate have an individuality, a soul. As long as we hate them we cannot see it; their destructive behavior has gotten in the way. They may in fact have many unloving qualities; however, it is not their possession of such qualities that prevents us from loving them but rather our own sense of having been personally violated. We can love—or at the very least not hate—if we can see beyond the limits of our own self-concern. This does not mean we must condone another's destructive behavior, or do nothing to prevent it or defend ourselves against it. Often we cannot remain passive in situations that call for a corrective response, but we can make such responses out of awareness and not out of hatred.

Even while we keep a necessary distance between ourselves and an enemy, our awareness can grow into compassion. In becoming aware of others, we see what their actions have meant to them. Those actions may remain unacceptable, but by seeing what they mean to the other we can let go of our own personal sense of hurt.

And if we are even granted the grace to see into the heart of an enemy, that person may cease to be an enemy. Forgiveness does not mean having to accept the unacceptable or pardon the unpardonable. Love, even toward one's enemies, is the awareness of the other's individuality. Forgiveness is simply the expression of love toward someone who has wronged us. It is the ability to see the other as an individual, and therefore with compassion.

ACQUIRING COMPASSION

Compassion, inconceivable without suffering, is the one quality that can redeem suffering and restore our faith in spite of it. Developing the capacity for compassion makes us stronger and better human beings, even spiritual beings who find fulfillment in reaching out to others in love. Compassion is not easy to acquire. It comes as the result of our struggle with our suffering and our efforts to endure it. How this happens is well illustrated in the life of another biblical figure, the prophet Jonah.

Jonah is called to warn the citizens of Nineveh, the capital of Assyria, to reform in order to avoid destroying themselves through their own corruption. The Assyrians were enemies of Israel, and Jonah hated them. So when God calls Jonah to help the Assyrians, Jonah tries to run away. While trying to escape he gets shipwrecked and nearly drowns, but a "great fish" rescues him and swallows him alive. Jonah prays to God from within the belly of the fish, and this prayer describes his struggle for faith:

> *I called to the Lord out of my distress,*
> *and he answered me;*
> *out of the belly of Sheol [the grave] I cried,*

and you heard my voice.

You cast me into the deep,
into the heart of the seas,
and the flood surrounded me;
all your waves and your billows passed over me.

Then I said, "I am driven away from your sight;
how shall I look again upon your holy temple?"

The waters closed in over me;
the deep surrounded me;
weeds were wrapped around my head
at the roots of the mountains.

I went down to the land whose bars closed upon me forever;
yet you brought up my life from the pit,
O Lord my God.

(Jonah 2:2–6)

These words express profound loneliness, a fear of death, and a loss of faith. Through his experience of being rescued, Jonah's faith is renewed: "As my life was ebbing away, I remembered the Lord; and my prayer came to you, into your holy temple" (Jonah 2:7). He goes on to preach to Nineveh, and his preaching saves the city.

But resentment burns inside Jonah when he sees that the people are saved. Watching the city miss its chance to be destroyed so overwhelms him with rage that he wants to die. He presents his lament to God, but God answers only with a question: "Is it right for you to be angry?" (Jonah 4:4). Jonah appears to ignore the question, and goes out to see what will become of the city.

The Problem of Suffering

It is very hot that day, so God makes a broad leafy plant grow to provide Jonah with shade and comfort. During the night, while Jonah sleeps, a worm attacks the plant, which withers and dies.

The next day, having lost his protection and feeling faint from the hot, pounding desert sun, Jonah once again becomes angry, and expresses his wish to die. This time when God questions him ("Is it right for you to be angry about the bush?") Jonah can't hold back and he shouts: "Yes, angry enough to die!" (Jonah 4:9). But God shows Jonah no sympathy.

> *Then the Lord said, "You are concerned about the bush, for which you did not labor and which you did not grow; it came into being in a night and perished in a night. And should I not be concerned about Nineveh, that great city, in which there are more than a hundred and twenty thousand persons who do not know their right hand from their left, and also many animals?"*
> (Jonah 4:10–11)

The book ends here, with a question. How does Jonah answer it? Can he see that beyond his personal hatred there are people asking him for compassion? We are not told. We know only that Jonah hears the question, and perhaps that is enough.

God asks Jonah to learn compassion by facing his own pain and seeing it in a new way. Jonah felt pain for himself; he suffered from the heat, and he suffered from his rage. To take him beyond his self-pity God shows him a bush, whose only function in its brief life was to shelter Jonah and comfort him. At first Jonah takes this service for granted, but afterwards, looking at the plant a second time, can he see something in it that touches his heart? (The Hebrew word translated as "concern" really means kind, heartfelt love.) If Jonah can be touched by the frailty of such a humble form of life, can he not respond with compassion to a city of one hundred and twenty thousand confused souls who are struggling to find their way and who need to be healed?

God challenges Jonah to see beyond himself, to see even people whom he hates not in reference to himself but as individuals in their own right, who are seeking God in their own way, even if many of their past actions were in fact hateful. God wants to enlarge Jonah's awareness and teach him how to love.

God does not teach Jonah to love by lecturing him. God does not sit him down and patiently try to explain to him what love is. Jonah starts out so full of his own concerns and prejudices that he cannot listen to explanations. He can learn about love only through working out his own life experience, specifically his own struggles and suffering. Without having nearly died from drowning, without having almost died of the heat, Jonah could have learned nothing. Only one's own pain is powerful enough to change the heart so radically.

God probably did not speak to Jonah in words he could hear with his ears. God speaks to us through perceptions of the soul that can be given words. It is really our sense of goodness speaking to us. Jonah's blessing was his ability to see God's purpose working itself out even in all the painful experiences that befell him, and so he hears God speaking even in moments when he is most angry and lacking in faith. Jonah knows God is present with him even in his suffering, because the question he hears, which his own experience asks him, has opened something in his heart.

COMPASSION AND FAITH

Compassion's awakening is the key to transcending suffering, no matter how severe. Suffering opens us; it yanks us from safe refuges and invites us to look, to question, to become more aware of ourselves and others. It tells us we cannot simply spend our lives pursuing our own self-interest. It shows us the frailty of human life. Seeing this frailty takes us outside ourselves and opens our hearts. It enables us to respond with compassion.

Therefore suffering, which punctures our complacency and pushes us toward awareness, makes possible non-self-interested love, which is based on awareness and cannot exist without it.

THE EMERGENCE OF FAITH

We are now approaching the connection between suffering and faith. This link is love itself. "Suffering produces endurance, and endurance produces character, and character produces hope"—the basis of this hope is the knowledge that we have become stronger and better as the result of our suffering. Better: because we are more aware of our own concerns and those of others, and are more responsive to them. Stronger: because knowing what it means to confront ourselves, to endure, and to meet others with compassion makes us less likely to crumble when we are struck with hard blows. Therefore "hope does not disappoint us, because God's love has been poured into our hearts." The capacity for compassion, leading to non-self-interested love, becomes a source of hope, because this love by its very nature points toward a source of strength, wisdom, and guidance beyond the self and greater than the self.

Faith is the awareness of God's presence in spite of overwhelming testimony to God's absence. If we can respond to suffering with love, we can come to an awareness of God's presence—because God is the source of that love and God is what we find when we know the kind of love that takes us beyond the self.

The following teaching shows how this love brings the presence of God even though we may not be consciously aware of it:

> *Then the king will say to those at his right hand:*
> *"Come, you that are blessed by my Father, inherit the kingdom prepared for you from the foundation of the world; for I was hungry and you gave me food, I was thirsty and you gave me something to drink, I was a stranger and you welcomed me, I was naked and you gave me clothing, I was sick and you took care of me, I was in prison and you visited me."*
> *Then the righteous will answer him:*
> *"Lord, when was it that we saw you hungry and gave you food, or thirsty and gave you something to drink? And when was it that we saw you a stranger and welcomed you, or naked and gave you clothing? And when was it that we saw you sick or in prison and visited you?"*
> *And the king will answer them:*
> *"Truly I tell you, just as you did it to one of the least of these who are members of my family, you did it to me."*
>
> (Matthew 25:34–40)

God is present in any loving response to suffering that takes us beyond our own self-concern. This does not mean that God suffers or that God wills us to suffer—such notions are based upon thinking of God as a person, rather than as Goodness Itself. What it does mean is that the existence of suffering does not make impossible the presence of a higher order, a transcendent presence, that comforts and strengthens us, and from which we derive the energy to respond positively to a life that may not seem to deserve such a response. Suffering does not negate the love that places God's presence at the center of our being; in fact, suffering is its midwife. "The light shines in the darkness, and the darkness did not overcome it" (John 1:5).

The response to suffering that preserves our faith consists of awareness, self-honesty, and love. Of these three, love is the greatest, but to come into being it needs both awareness and self-honesty. Love leads us to faith because it gives us something beyond ourselves to live for, even if at first this is nothing more than the compassion we feel for others' pain. This alone takes us beyond ourselves and shows us something greater. If we become more aware, honest with ourselves, and compassionate, we become stronger, less afraid of pain and loss, and better able to stand up to the knowledge that life will not always fulfill our needs. If we can see this strength and love growing within ourselves we will know that life has a meaning deeper than what we find in our immediate experience, and that we are more than just accidents of nature.

The awareness and love that bring us beyond ourselves cannot be explained by any theory that denies an ultimate order to life or that sees life as merely some self-organizing chaos. Faith is the awareness and conviction of Ultimate Order; it is the sense that things finally make sense. There is no love without awareness, and no awareness without suffering. Therefore suffering does not negate faith; paradoxically, it makes faith possible.

FAITH COMES FROM LOVE

Faith is vitality. It is the energy we need to keep moving forward in spite of the obstacles we meet. This energy comes from the love that is inside faith. Love makes us aware of a universe much wider than ourselves. This is why, when God spoke to Job out of the whirlwind, God did not answer Job's question about suffering. Instead God showed him the wider universe, from the constellations in the heavens to the leviathan in the depths of the sea. God made Job aware of a creation whose scope he could hardly imagine. Thus Job, like Jonah, learned to move outside himself; he learned how to love.

When compassion touches the heart—even when the touch is excruciatingly painful—it puts our private concerns in perspective. It shows us a world wider than our doubts and fears. It helps us see others and reach out to them in love. And love's presence strengthens us when we face our own suffering. Therefore love is a source of faith, perhaps its primary source.

The love within us brings us back into the mainstream of life. If we can see others compassionately, with full awareness of their individuality, others often begin to respond to us differently, with greater warmth and affection. This helps us overcome any sense of isolation that suffering may bring. It shows us that through being loving we know that we are loved. We find that we are loved not only by others but also by God, if we can see God's presence in the capacity for compassion that visits us after we have faced our suffering.

"Many waters cannot quench love" (Song of Songs 8:7): love can thrive even in suffering. Love does not ask for a perfect life and is not afraid of life's imperfections and tragedies; it embraces life in spite of them. Love "bears all things, believes all things, hopes all things, endures all things" (1 Corinthians 13:7).

Finally, we come to the most hopeful and also the most difficult aspect of the faith that is born in love. This is trust. We have seen that confronting our suffering in great depth can lead us to a love that we know is greater than the self. The final step toward redemption comes when we can trust this "greater than" to lead us through our suffering to wherever we need to be. This trust may begin as "dark faith," but it becomes lighter as we begin to see love's results. Even if we have lost everything that gave our life meaning, if we can know the love that is born in suffering as a "greater than" and trust its power, our healing has already begun.

RECONFRONTING THE QUESTION

The problem of suffering cannot really be solved. If we view it theologically, it is a dead end; there is no way to blend God harmoniously with intractable, unmerited suffering. But if we view it existentially, then there is a way to preserve a sense of God's presence in spite of suffering. We don't need a solution, we just need a clue, something to keep us going, just enough to keep our faith from dying. Job does not find a solution. What he does find is faith in spite of not having the solution.

No true solution to the problem of suffering can be given to us on this side of the boundary of life. This is why every attempt to solve the problem of "theodicy" has failed. It is just not something we are given to know (Deuteronomy 29:29). Without certain knowledge of what lies beyond earthly life—knowledge denied to everyone, including scientists and theologians—we cannot be sure whether the question of theodicy actually has an answer. This is the real question we face: given that we cannot know the answer, can we still have faith that our lives have meaning and make sense, that God is indeed still with us, or are the atheists and naturalists correct and is life really no more than a random accident, with no value greater than its mere existence?

THE QUESTION THAT WON'T GO AWAY

We might find it easier to accept the fact of suffering once we reflect that without it there could be no compassion; there could be no love. As we have already seen, without suffering we would never develop the awareness that makes love possible.

Nevertheless, even if it is possible to respond to suffering with compassion and faith, what about those who cannot so respond, who are so crushed by their circumstances that they seem to have no chance of moving beyond it? The tired cliché that "God never gives us more than we can handle" seems empty when we consider people whose lives have been destroyed by the worst atrocities imaginable. No conceivable explanation can be of much comfort under such circumstances.

The issue, however, is not comfort but faith. We cannot always expect to be comforted in this life. God has not promised always to be comforting but always to be faithful. What can this possibly mean when dealing with extreme cruelty?

There are a few things we might consider before approaching the heart of this question. First, when we witness the suffering of others, we only see it from the outside. We cannot really know what their suffering means to them, or the nuances of their response to it. Other people deal with and overcome circumstances that to us may seem insurmountable. In my own hospice work, I have seen a lot of tragedy and marveled at how many people have still managed to respond with faith. Sometimes I think to myself, I could never muster the faith these people have if I were in their position. Yet I know that others have felt the same way about themselves when hearing of the tragedies I've faced in my own life, and I also know that I have managed to survive them. When we view suffering from the outside, we can only see its pain, not its meaning.

Another thing to consider is that no matter how extreme the pain we may suffer, it will one day come to an end. There actually is something comforting in that. We cannot fully confront the question of suffering without including the fact that we die, and for many people death comes as a welcome release. Many times I have seen people suffer unimaginable pain from cancer and other diseases, yet afterwards enter a period of profound peace as it all subsides and they wait for whatever lies ahead. The peace of those final days can be so deep, can even fill the room to affect all those who are present and whose hearts are open, that it seems to make up for every moment of pain the person previously suffered. It is truly "the peace that passes understanding," part of the mystery we must recognize when confronting the question of suffering.

If this world were intended to be our permanent home, we might indeed despair. One hospice priest I knew used to say that "We were not made to be here." One day he came to the hospice unit while I was working, and I had a chance to ask him: Then why are we here? He replied, "To build God's creation."

There is so much that needs to be built—especially when we think of the large-scale tragedies that have occurred in history and still occur, the great natural disasters, the wars and genocides, the murder of children who can hardly yet know what love really means, the extreme cruelty and torture that people inflict on each other. There are times when comfort cannot come—at least not yet. But there is never a moment when goodness cannot exist—and this can be a basis for our faith. Even under the most extreme conditions—indeed, often especially under those conditions—goodness can still be seen, and the face of God revealed.

It doesn't always happen—but when it does, it is a sign of hope. Viktor Frankl, an Austrian Jewish psychiatrist, was captured by the Nazis and spent time in several concentration camps, including Theresienstadt and Auschwitz. He lost his entire family in the camps. Though himself a victim, he spent what energy he had trying to alleviate the despair and depression of others. He gave lectures on medical and spiritual care and ministered to people individually who were overcome by their grief. One may say that Frankl was exceptional, but he bore witness to other soul-moving sparks of goodness:

> We who lived in concentration camps can remember the men who walked through the huts comforting others, giving away their last piece of bread. They may have been few in number, but they offer sufficient proof that everything can be taken from a man but one thing: the last of the human freedoms—to choose one's attitude in any given set of circumstances, to choose one's own way. (Victor Frankl, *Man's Search for Meaning* [Boston: Beacon Press 2006], 65)

People like Viktor Frankl, and no less the unnamed inmate who shared that last crust of bread even though he too surely was hungry, show us God's presence under precisely those conditions that testify to God's absence. Such people show us that there is no time when and no place where goodness cannot be detected. The awe with which we contemplate their sacrifice brings us the awareness of the eternal—and that is faith.

There are so many more of these people than we know, including many who risked their lives rescuing total strangers during this and other genocides. One we do know about was Corrie Ten Boom, author of *The Hiding Place* and *Tramp for the Lord*, who worked in the Dutch underground and hid many Jewish refugees from the Nazis. She and her family took them in and even observed the Jewish Sabbath and gave them kosher food. The Nazis arrested Corrie's family, and her father and sister Betsie perished in the camps. Just before she died, Betsie said to Corrie: "There is no pit so deep that God's love is not deeper still."

We are blessed to know of these people. We will never hear about most of them; yet each one demonstrated the survival of goodness—and thus the presence of God—just when it seemed there could be no God.

THE PERSISTENCE OF FAITH

When we reflect deeply on the presence of goodness even in the midst of evil, we can perhaps approach more closely the connection between the good and the eternal. The awe we experience gives us a hint Paul may very well be correct when he says "that the sufferings of this present time are not worth comparing with the glory about to be revealed to us" (Romans 8:18). The glory will be revealed to us—but not yet. There is a reason. If somehow we had certain knowledge—not simply faith—that we were destined for eternal bliss, or that good deeds would always be rewarded, then we would live our lives with the reward in mind. That is not what goodness wants. We are meant to value what is good because it is good, not because it will bring us a benefit or will end our suffering. We are not meant to have the complete answer to the problem of suffering now, but rather to learn to live by faith and love, and especially to love goodness even without the assurance that we will gain anything by it. The world of deep joy and intense suffering in which we live is the only kind of world in which we could learn to love goodness for its own sake.

We would love to have the assurance that everything we suffer will be compensated, that nothing we might have to suffer will exceed the limits of our tolerance, and that ultimately everything will make sense to us. But if we were able to suffer only on the terms of our own choosing, then suffering would lose its meaning; it would not offer us the same possibilities of awareness, strength, and love. A better question was asked by the Hasidic Rabbi Levi Yitzhak of Berdichev, who would cry out to God: "I do not wish to know why I suffer, but only that I suffer for your sake." Suffering cannot destroy goodness, and this can give us hope even during the worst.

THE ONLY CLUE WE NEED

The longer we live, the more quickly time passes and the shorter it seems. If we could live long enough, we would see that time is no more than a single instant. It is barely anything when compared to eternity. The suffering that, in the dimension of time, seems like our total reality, becomes the tiniest point when seen from the perspective of eternity. But right now, that is not what we see. Right now these reflections may give only small comfort, but they can keep us from making Job's mistake, which was to draw hard conclusions from limited knowledge. Within every life there are agonizing incidents of suffering that take on different meanings with the passage of time.

Given that we cannot know with certainty what our suffering ultimately becomes or whether it is ever completely redeemed, we can still explore this faith and put it to the test. With or without a belief in God, from nothing more than our own experience we can see that the world is so constructed that love in all its fullness can come only from the existence of suffering. This is not the final answer, but it is a very important clue, and is perhaps all we really need to preserve our faith. If we take this clue and follow it to the end, we may discover anew the power of love—and therefore the presence of God—in our lives.

THE SURVIVING GOD

What kind of God are we left with after we have faced the problem of suffering? Certainly not a God who wants us to suffer. If it is godlike for us to respond to suffering with love and a desire to alleviate the pain of others, then we can think no less of God. To suffer "for God's sake," as the rabbi from Berdichev put it, does not mean to suffer because God wills it but to suffer in a way that makes us better, more loving, closer to God. The God we find after struggling with this problem is a paradoxical God: this God is "in" our suffering but not "of" it.

DIFFERENT TYPES OF THEOLOGY

How can we understand this better? Most theologies fall into one of two categories: they are either anthropomorphic or metaphysical. "Anthropomorphic" theologies picture God as a person, a conscious being separate from ourselves with a will like our own, with whom we can have a relationship as if with another person. "Metaphysical" theologies view God as an abstract principle, entirely separate from our experience, without even any knowledge of our suffering. Both these types of theology are popular, and both of them are wrong.

Anthropomorphic theologies try to give us the sense that God loves us, but they cannot address convincingly the problem of how a loving God can permit the horrors of extreme suffering. Metaphysical theologies do address this problem, but at too great a cost. We have a deep spiritual need to know the presence of love in our lives, and to know that love is not denied by suffering. This need cannot really be satisfied by a God who knows nothing of our struggle and who is not involved with it. The metaphysical God is a perfect principle and can have no knowledge of imperfection or suffering. Metaphysical theologies even call suffering an illusion. In contrast, people who suffer look for a loving presence that can meet them where they are, and not merely in some abstract state of perfection they can never hope to attain. They need to know that God has not forgotten them, even if God is not a person who can literally remember or forget. If God cannot meet us on the ground of our own suffering, then the problem of suffering truly has no answer. The abstractness and detachment of the metaphysical God may be one large reason why unhealthy dependence on a guru, a human source of wisdom and love, is so epidemic in metaphysical circles. These spiritualities awaken a need they cannot fulfill.

The alternative to anthropomorphic and metaphysical theology is *existential* theology. This means God participating fully in our existence, including our suffering. This means beholding the God that survives after the God we thought we knew has died in the doubt that our suffering raises. The surviving God—the "God above God" (Tillich, *The Courage to Be*)—is a God we know much less about than the God we thought we knew in either anthropomorphic or metaphysical theology. We know of the existence of the surviving God not from the outside—from a belief in unbelievable concepts—but from the inside, from the transformation of our hearts.

DETECTING GOD'S LOVE

We find a hint of God's encompassing love through discovering the compassion that suffering awakens in us. This loving response changes us; it transforms us from separate, isolated creatures of self-interest to full participants in the community of life. We are transformed not because we suffer, but because we love. We begin our spiritual journey wanting to know that God loves us. Ironically, the only way we can know that we are loved is to become loving ourselves.

The compassionate love that grows within us is more than just our own finite response to suffering; it is a presence, abiding, enduring, and encouraging. This presence is God, or at least what we are humanly able to know of God. "God is love, and those who abide in love abide in God, and God abides in them" (John 4:16). We can live in this presence. We can know this presence directly; we need not rely on any external authority or religious belief in order to sense it as real.

This presence of love is our inner guide, directing us toward the most loving response in a difficult situation. Sometimes this response will contradict our own wishes or perceived self-interest, since love's awareness may show us deeper needs than our own. To pursue the loving response anyway, not out of a sense of duty but out of the desire for compassion that suffering awakens, may mean the temporary loss of what we want—but it also means gaining God's presence, a sense of connection to God and to the continuity of life.

Suffering is always connected with loss. We suffer when we lose something we hold to be important: our possessions, our work, our health, someone we love, perhaps even our faith. We question God; we demand to know why we have lost what we cherished. We see how foolish such questioning is when we remember that the day will come when we will indeed lose everything. We cannot prevent it. Our health, our wealth, our contact with those we love, all will be taken from us; the only question is when. Realizing this fills us either with despair or with compassion—depending on how willing we are to face it. If we can face it and live with our fears for as long as it may take, we have a chance of breaking through to a deeper, more durable faith. This faith is based on the insight that there is indeed something fulfilling in our lives that never gets lost, because it is eternal.

All material good in our lives eventually disappears; that is its nature. But there is a spiritual good that remains. It changes as the circumstances in our lives change. Sometimes the change requires us to make difficult adjustments, but the good itself does not disappear. If we have learned through suffering to become more aware, truthful, and compassionate, these changes remain; we are never the same as we were before. If we grieve over the loss of something of true value or beauty, the love we once knew is preserved even in our grief. Even if we lose those whom we most loved, we do not lose the love itself; it remains, still changing us, deepening us, and making us more responsive to life if we let it— if we do not choke it off with our anger. The material is only the temporary carrier of the spiritual. We may lose the outward form, but the love and beauty contained within continue to make their impression on our lives.

PRACTICING THE PRESENCE

Even if we are blessed to find faith, we know that our faith can be threatened. What can we do to keep it? Faith is like anything else that is spiritual: if we try to grasp it, it tends to disappear. But there is a practice we can follow to help preserve our faith in times of suffering.

We need to be willing to feel the pain that suffering brings, and especially how it opens the heart. Compassion is born in the heartfelt response to loss.

We need to focus our attention not only on what we experience but also on how others respond to their own suffering. We must maintain this focus until our heartfelt response to loss becomes a heartfelt response to their loss as well.

We need to recognize the compassion this brings as a love that is greater than ourselves. The response of another individual to his or her suffering is sacred ground. Our own response to it means we have entered that sacredness. Our compassion has pulled us outside ourselves. It has become a presence greater than we are.

Finally, we need to let ourselves live in this "greater than," to sense it as an atmosphere surrounding us, to trust it to move us, pull us forward in life, and take us to whatever our destiny intends. Our response to suffering gradually grows, from heart-rending grief, to compassion for others in pain, to sensing this compassion as something beyond us, to living in it and trusting it to reveal itself as God's presence.

Moving from our own compassion to the presence of God

may seem like a big jump. But the Bible tells us this connection is real: "Those who abide in love abide in God." God is Goodness Itself, Absolute Goodness, so there can be no question that God is good. We can know also that God has the power to transform our lives by our abiding in this love. This is the real "leap of faith": to trust this compassion as more than just a feeling but a pointer to an actual presence beyond ourselves. Trust it, surrender to it, live in it, feel its comfort, and see whether it works. That is the only way to know. Without the practice nothing, including this book, will help, and if you know the practice, you don't need the book. The verification of this faith is existential: seeing whether it works in our actual existence. It will work if the love that grows within us is spiritual love, reflecting God's nature, because God always responds to the divine qualities visible within us. This is most especially God's own love, which in human terms means the awareness of others' individuality and the respect for its sacredness.

The answer to the problem of suffering does not lie in anything we can observe from the outside. It lies within, inside our personal relationship to God. No one can judge another person's relationship to God simply from knowing that person's suffering. We cannot know from the outside what the suffering means to the person, how it has transformed that person, and what role it plays in that person's destiny. We can never say that God is absent from the life of anyone, no matter how extreme the suffering.

I have never known anyone more spiritual than Julie Swanson, an ordained Christian minister and also an American Indian spiritual guide. ("Indian" is what she called herself; she never said "Native American.") She was my teacher for several years. She devoted so much of her time serving others privately and working in hospitals without any compensation that she lived a life of poverty. She had a simple home with just her dog to keep her company, and when she could no longer afford that she lived in a trailer. Yet she never asked for or accepted donations. Because she did not have access to decent medical care, she developed a rare and painful form of cancer that went untreated for too long and that eventually killed her. After she could no longer care for herself, she spent the last weeks of her life in a nursing home.

Yet she was always—and I mean always—optimistic and in good spirits. She always had just enough energy left to support others. She was so close to the spirit that she never felt alone, even though she lived by herself in an isolated area. She was a pure embodiment of non-self-interested love.

I had the temerity one day to ask her what faith could possibly mean if innocent and loving people like her had to suffer so much. Julie reprimanded me for my presumption, telling me that she learned so much from her illness that she could never have learned without it, that she knew she was not alone, and that she would not have changed a thing about her life. There was absolutely no trace of bitterness in Julie, no "Why me?" and no sense at all of having been treated unfairly by life or by God. Julie died comforted by the presence of the love she had so freely given, knowing she fulfilled her destiny.

No suffering, however severe, can be taken as proof of God's nonexistence. That is what I learned from Julie. We can never say, no matter how hopeless someone's situation may look to us as outsiders, that God is not there. We can never exclude the possibility of God's transforming effect on someone's life, no matter how that person's experience looks to us. We can never exclude the possibility of God's transforming effect on our own lives, in the measure that we reflect God's own nature of selfless love. "The light shines in the darkness, and the darkness did not overcome it."

THE DURABILITY OF FAITH

Sifting the eternal from the temporal, recognizing what must pass away and what really endures, can change our view of earthly suffering.

> *Do not store up for yourselves treasures on earth, where moth and rust consume and where thieves break in and steal; but store up for yourselves treasures in heaven, where neither moth nor rust consumes and where thieves do not break in and steal. For where your treasure is, there your heart will be also.* (Matthew 6:19–21)

No corrupting influences can touch the changes that take place within the soul as suffering opens the heart to greater awareness and love. The heart is where our real treasure is—not in external things that decay and disappear. The changes in the soul that take place when we find a spiritual response to suffering are the treasures that do not spoil, which we are told to lay up for ourselves. These hard-won gifts of the spirit give us the presence of God. Their effects become visible even in earthly life.

Therefore Paul could say that not even all the unimaginable horrors of life—not life, death, height, depth, principalities, nor powers—can separate us from God's love. We find the answer to the problem of suffering in the compassion that suffering awakens within us, and with this comes the courage and strength to continue living until the hour arrives when we will finally see God "face to face."

Faith does not mean that we do not suffer, but that we always have God's presence to guide and uphold us. The presence of God that comes to us in suffering is real, and will take us to places we might never have imagined.

Anywhere sin, disease, pain, and destruction can go, there love too can enter.

> *By the tender mercy of our God,*
> *the dawn from on high will break upon us,*
> *to give light to those who sit in darkness*
> *and in the shadow of death,*
> *to guide our feet into the way of peace.*
> (Luke 1:78–79)

XV

FACING THE FEAR OF DEATH

Set your minds on things that are above, not on things that are on earth, for you have died, and your life is hidden with Christ in God. When Christ who is your life is revealed, then you also will be revealed with him in glory.

Colossians 3:2–4

When I was a child, people said I was more "serious" than most other kids. While other children played and had a good time, I seemed always unable to forget that the good time would somehow have to come to an end, and so it made me naturally sad. I seemed preoccupied with the temporariness of things.

As a child, what I felt most temporary was my childhood. I always knew that some day I would grow up and become an adult. So even while playing my favorite games and enjoying them thoroughly, I would experience a stab of melancholy as I thought that some day I would grow up and not be able to play them anymore. I did not yet think about death. The idea of death seemed unreal. It was something that I knew happened, but this knowledge did not mean much to me.

Nevertheless, in some way the melancholy I felt then, and still occasionally feel, must have borne within it the awareness of death. Death is something we all know about, but we have ways of protecting ourselves from this knowledge. We must protect ourselves from it if we are to function efficiently at our daily tasks. But if we have not confronted our knowledge of death and found some way of coming to terms with it, it produces a fear that always lurks in the background of our experience. It may break into the open at any moment and rob us of the joy of living. There are times when no defense against the knowledge of death will protect us from this fear, such as when a loved one dies.

The time of crisis for me came with the sudden death of my first wife. Until then I lived as though my happiness would last forever, and I would no longer have to be concerned about endings. Her death completely shattered my world and forced me to think about the meaning of life, death, and fear.

For me, the answer has always been faith. But one can never be sure about one's faith until it is tested. It is easy to utter words of faith, but words mean little if they are not connected to experience. Our experiences have ways of humbling us, showing up the prettiness of the words we may use to describe our faith. As a widower, I found a friend in C. S. Lewis's book *A Grief Observed*. Lewis, who had written so eloquently about his faith, described in that book how, after the death of his wife, his faith collapsed "like a house of cards." I was moved by the honesty of his admission.

THE FOCUS OF OUR FEARS

Death is perhaps the focus of our greatest fears. Death seems like being left alone, abandoned by those we love. Death means the end of our earthly existence, which we cherish above all else. Death is isolation, rejection, destruction, and perhaps even condemnation. Paul understood this fear when he said that "the wages of sin is death" (Romans 6:23).

If our ultimate fear is the fear of death, then the fear of death colors every other fear we may experience. The basic fear comes in many forms: a fear of good things coming to an end, a fear of abandonment, of being left behind, perhaps forever; a fear of ending one's life without the fulfillment of one's destiny. If this fear is present, it intensifies all of our suffering; every loss seems greater, every pain seems more painful. Without faith, fear is a slave master with an iron grip on our lives.

Death is a mystery, but to become liberated from the fear of it we might hope to penetrate the mystery just a little, to become able to contemplate death without experiencing it as the "wages of sin." "Even though I walk through the valley of the shadow of death, I will fear no evil" (Psalm 23:4). Bible scholars now tell us that "shadow of death" is a mistranslation, but this cannot negate the deep truth and faith that we sense in these words.

HOSPICE EXPERIENCE AND MUSIC

These reflections were far from my mind when I first began to work in a hospice. At that time all I wanted was to be with people at their most intense moments of suffering and isolation, to diminish in any way I could their feelings of aloneness. Unexpectedly, I found hospice work teaching me some important lessons about death, about fear, and about faith.

Many people believe that a hospice is a place where sick people go to die. This is a misconception. To the greatest extent possible people who enter hospice are cared for in their homes, often longer than they could be if they didn't have hospice care. The idea of hospice is to provide an environment in which the physical, emotional, and spiritual needs of terminally ill people are treated with compassionate attention.

As I gained experience using music in hospice, I became fascinated by the ability of music to communicate where words fail. I saw almost immediately the effects music can have in alleviating depression and even physical pain. What impressed me most, however, was discovering how music can be meaningful to people who cannot speak or hold a normal conversation. While patients who are relatively more alert and healthy often find the music entertaining, relaxing, or soothing, it is in working with patients who have passed beyond the realm of speech that I most discovered the capacity of music to heal. I am not speaking of healing the physical illness that brought the person into hospice, but of healing the psychological and spiritual wounds that we all bear to varying degrees.

Since working with patients who are beyond speech has brought me into contact with the frailest patients in the hospice, it often brought me to people who were close to the point of death. I have often been able to communicate even with patients in comas. It is in working with such patients that I have learned the most about death, and also about fear.

I remember one woman in her early fifties who was dying of ovarian cancer. The cancer had spread to her brain, and her doctors described her as "clearly sustaining a very poor and nearly vegetative life" and showing "no purposeful movements." These words did not describe the woman I saw when I played for her at her bedside. As I played, I would sense her breathing becoming deeper, and her eyes relaxing.

Even while in the vegetative state from which she never recovered, she would try unmistakably to make contact with me. On several occasions she reached out her hand to me. Sometimes she would touch the music on my music stand, but I was moved most of all when once she reached out and gently stroked my face. I spent much time with her, not just playing but sitting next to her, holding her hand, speaking to her, and watching her responses. I had a strong sense that many changes were taking place within her, even though she could not tell me a word about them. Her eyes and the pressure of her grasp on my fingers told me a great deal. I felt her go through a series of stages, beginning with fear, passing through grief, and finally, just before her death, reaching a state of resolution and peace. The nurses told me that they, too, felt she was hanging on until the moment when she felt ready to die.

RESPONSES TO DYING

I have had many similar experiences with patients who were close to death. I now try to involve the family in the process of caring for them and ministering to their fear. I will ask family members to hold the hand of the loved one while I play, to focus their attention and note any changes and responses. This helps family members become more active in the spiritual care of their loved one and eases their sense of futility.

Music facilitates this process, but it is only one way. Even if one is not a musician one may communicate by focusing one's attention, holding the person's hand, using one's voice to comfort and soothe, feeling the changes, and letting the person know that one is present. In such ways one may help those one loves up to the very last moment of life.

Fear is clearly not all one sees in people who are approaching the moment of death. I remember an elderly woman who had been a nurse during her life and who was now clearly on her deathbed. I had seen her in the hospital months before, when she was sick but very alert and walking around. She would look in on the other patients and take whatever care she could to see to their well-being. The love she expressed during her life did not leave her at the hour of her death. I sat with her as she was dying. She seemed surrounded by an invisible yet very discernible glow. She reached out her hand and stroked my face. She was in a deep state of peace, and I would say even of bliss. She seemed actually not to see me at all; while looking at me—or looking past me—she said she saw the face of an angel. It was difficult to avoid the sense that while she was still here on earth, she was also in another place of which I had barely the faintest notion.

To be sure, not every patient in hospice dies peacefully. I am still haunted by the image of a woman who died writhing in intense, agonizing fear, about which I could do nothing. But another woman, also experiencing great agitation and fear, became completely quiet as I played for her and held her hand. After she died, I found myself enveloped in a sense of peace deeper than anything I have ever known, and which stayed with me for days. I think that somehow we helped each other: my presence helped to ease her transition, and her trust in me allowed me to enter her world and feel just a tiny bit of the great peace I am sure she is now enjoying.

THE MASKS WE WEAR

How can I possibly express what I have learned from these experiences? I believe there is a mask we all wear, the mask of the controlling, grasping intellect, which tries to impose order on our experiences and will accept things only a certain way. In many people who are terminally ill, the mask begins to slip. Something else rises to the surface, a consciousness that when fully present is deeply peaceful. It is as though the individual, who once was completely a citizen of earth, begins to be aware of a different origin, another home. This awareness can deeply affect one who is receptive to it and who has the opportunity to be with the dying person. To be this close to death can be a profoundly comforting experience—if one is able to see behind the mask.

Another name for this mask is fear.

How ironic it is that what is for many the occasion of greatest fear—the moment when death approaches—can also become a time of great peace. I believe this is so because at that moment, when the strength of the body begins to fail, the part of us that expresses fear and that feeds on our physical strength—the controlling intellect—also begins to recede. This allows a deeper part of us—some call it soul or spirit, some even call it the Christ in us—to become more conscious, and even to take over completely at the final instant of resolution.

What may perhaps come as a surprise is that this spiritual, Christ-like part of us is always part of us, even now, even when death seems remote. This spirit, which sometimes fully reveals itself only at the moment of death, we bear within us now while we live. The author of Colossians knew about the hidden spirit within us and called it our true life, "hidden with Christ in God."

The key to overcoming the fear of death lies in recognizing that which is "hidden" behind the mask of fear, the indestructible spirit that survives even death and is revealed at death, but of which we may be totally unconscious. It is easy to speak about this but hard to realize. In the midst of a fearful experience we may not be able to adjust immediately to reflect upon our higher nature. We have to grant ourselves an allowance for that. But in the moments when our minds are clear, we can stand back from our experiences and reflect. We can enter that dark and silent place in which we listen for the voice of the spirit.

What delivers us from fear is the knowledge that we are not alone, that something actually does help us in our weakness. Thus the Psalmist can say, "Even though I walk through the valley of the shadow of death, I will fear no evil, for you are with me." The Psalmist chooses the worst fear imaginable, the fear of death, and says that even this fear is overcome by the sense that we are connected to something beyond ourselves.

Working with the dying has taught me that the Psalmist's expression of faith is no mere optimistic affirmation but is indeed based on a deeply felt reality. But it is not easy to incorporate this reality into our daily existence. The spirit beneath the mask is something for which we must search, something to which we are led by the cries of our own hearts and the hearts of others.

What is so frightening about death may well be not the event of dying itself, but our perception that it means being torn away from those we love, and thus ultimate isolation and abandonment. It is like a child's fear of being thrown into a dark closet and left there, with no chance of ever escaping. We tend to believe, in our materialistic culture, that death is the irrevocable breaking of a chain. Being close to those who are dying, however, can give one the sense that the chain of life does not break but forms a complete circle, linking our earthly and spiritual existence.

CONFRONTING FEAR

If we can actually acquire this insight, can it really conquer our fears? People who have had what are commonly called "near-death experiences" claim that it can. I must confess that I have not found such accounts helpful. Not having had such an experience myself, I have no way of evaluating someone else's report. At best it remains an intriguing curiosity, something I might hope to experience some day, but that is still not a part of my own reality. I place more trust in the unexpected, unexplainable moments of peace I have actually experienced in the presence of others who were dying. I find myself contemplating the possibility that what I experience in these people at these times, and what I experience in myself, is more real than the frantic worrier I can often become at other times.

When confronting the boundary conditions of life, particularly the experience of death, we learn the most about life, death, fear, and the spirit. We need to bring what we learn from these extreme conditions into our daily lives. The spirit within, which may become more visible as one approaches death, is still always present in each one of us. Perhaps by learning to see it in others as well as within ourselves, we can find it easier to love others as well as ourselves. By seeing this spiritual presence in ourselves and others, we can acquire the confidence of knowing we are always connected to God, a loving presence greater than ourselves that forever guides us. We do not have to wait for the imminence of death to find within ourselves a heartfelt response to the pain and joy of others.

Those who have passed through the transition of death may know more about this loving presence than we can ever know here on earth. And no matter how close to death we may have come, be it the prospect of our own death or the death of others, we cannot live as though we were already on the other side. Our business is that of living here. But if the spirit that emerges at the moment of death is truly a part of us, then it nourishes us during life as well. It may only be waiting for us to listen, when we are afraid. The presence we can offer to others, that can heal them in their own fearful moments, dwells within ourselves as well. It does not really belong to us, but to a special place that calls us back when we have strayed too far into realms of darkness.

PART 3

Approaching the Destination

XVI

SELF-ACCEPTANCE

Now after he rose early on the first day of the week, he appeared first to Mary Magdalene, from whom he had cast out seven demons.

Mark 16:9

SOME DEMONS CANNOT BE FOUGHT.

We can try to love ourselves. We can try to tell ourselves that God loves us. For many of us, it doesn't work. Reasoning ourselves into self-acceptance is futile.

THE PERSISTENCE OF HATEFUL SELF-IMAGES

There is a great industry of books and tapes on self-esteem. It exists because so many people suffer from self-rejection. It exists also because the problem has no simple solution. If it were as easy to accept ourselves as so many of these books seem to imply, there wouldn't be so many of these books. One could simply find the right book, read it, and be healed. But if we suffer from this problem, we can read dozens of books, feel better for a while, then find when the next crisis hits that our hatred of ourselves has not diminished.

How many people do we know who cannot accept good things about themselves even when friends keep trying to show them? How many of us are like this? Some people have developed a resistance against seeing anything positive in themselves, even when evidence to the contrary is abundant and obvious to others. These people may shut out not only their friends but also God, unable even to accept God's love and acceptance.

There are, of course, people who don't blame themselves for anything, who think everything bad that happens to them is somebody else's fault. I am not writing for them. For many others, hateful self-images are impervious to change, because of the time and place in which they were formed. We acquire our first images of ourselves very early in life from the perceptions that other people have of us. But most people do not see us clearly. They do not see us with the awareness that is essential for genuine love. They see us through the filter of their own experiences and desires.

Those who grow up with accurate perceptions of themselves are fortunate indeed. Many others seem to have been created in the image of people who did not love them, including not only parents but other family members, authority figures, or even their peers. The self-image one acquires from these sources may be unflattering and even abusive, creating the feeling of being trapped in a prison of self-torment from which there is no escape.

These very early images are stored in a deep part of the brain that appears to have developed before the capacity for verbal expression or rational thinking. Therefore reasoning with these bad images does not work. No matter how much one tries to talk oneself out of a hateful self-image, telling oneself how absurd and irrational it is, one may still cling to it as strongly as ever. It is as though the image were protected by some invisible, unbreakable casing that not even the sharp arrows of reason can penetrate.

No one can tolerate living in a state of such profound self-rejection. One must deal with it somehow, and most of the ways we deal with it are unhealthy. One may project it outward, becoming filled with rage toward others at even slight provocations. One may attack others to avoid facing one's own self-contempt. One may direct the rage inward, criticizing oneself for the least little thing, berating oneself, even mutilating oneself. One may retreat from rage to the safety of depression, which immobilizes and insulates and prevents one from fully living one's life. One may abuse alcohol or drugs to dull the psychic pain. None of these ways of coping provide freedom from self-rejection. They only recast it in another form.

There is a way out of self-rejection that leads to genuine healing. It is not a quick fix. It is more like a journey, a passage through fire to discover the freedom of knowing one's true spirit. There is no short-cut. But learning the way can spare many wasted hours and even years following roads that lead nowhere.

I had the privilege of accompanying someone on this journey. I will call her Alice. She was my first patient during my student internship as a music therapist.

FINDING THE HEART

The first time I saw Alice she was sitting in a wheelchair, her eyes closed, her head slumped over her chest, her expression distant and lifeless. Some invisible enemy appeared to have beaten her into submission, and she surrendered unconditionally. She was deeply depressed, withdrawn into a dead and inaccessible shell. She also suffered from a stroke that limited her movement. I was surprised to find she could actually speak and even carry on a clear conversation.

Alice was terribly homesick. The huge hospital frightened her. She missed her husband, on whom she greatly depended. At the slightest provocation she would break into tears. Matters only worsened because of the hospital's impersonality and sometimes even its cruelty. One day I approached Alice's room startled to hear the nurse's aide who was changing her screaming at her like a prison guard subduing an inmate, clubbing Alice with her loud, harsh, strident voice because she would not move fast enough or in the right direction. I reported this aide and got her transferred off the floor.

Unfortunately Alice treated herself no better than this aide did. She berated herself constantly. She hated herself for being so powerless and out of control, depending on others to move her or take her to the bathroom. If an aide failed to handle her gently when turning her over in bed Alice would scream, from fear as much as from pain. Everything that happened to her became a reason for her to attack herself. The institution's lack of love for her magnified her lack of love for herself.

Alice was so depressed that no matter what kind of song I played for her, fast of slow, or what the words expressed, hope, confidence, or joy, she would say that the song was "sad." She used to play the piano very well, but when I gave her a keyboard to play she could not enjoy it. She beat herself up every time she hit a wrong note, even during improvisations when I would tell her that there are no wrong notes. For Alice there were no right notes.

Alice was spiritually undernourished and needed simply to receive. She needed food for the heart. So I just sang for her, many different kinds of songs, folk songs, spiritual songs, popular songs.

This she loved. She always refused to sing or play with me. Just listening made her happy. When I asked her to sing, she told me with some justification: "listening is also participating."

At first I was hesitant about letting Alice remain so passive. But this was what she needed. Alice was depressed, emotionally starved, and she needed to be fed. The music was feeding her.

Alice began to pick out favorite songs, and to ask for them over and over. One song she loved was "Bridge over Troubled Water" by Paul Simon. Its last verse, which spoke about a "silver girl" who finally got to realize her dreams, made her feel hopeful. Seeing herself in that song, she began, just barely, to view herself differently from her usual way, which had always been full of self-hate. Now she could actually have a little compassion for the "silver girl," who had been through so much and still had dreams for the future.

At this point something began to change. Alice started to sing. And she no longer wanted to sing only about the "troubled waters." She wanted songs like "What a Wonderful World" and "Oh What a Beautiful Morning." Much earlier she would not even open her mouth, but now, even after the songs were finished she would keep singing the words, making us do them over again.

Not only was she willing to sing, she also ventured to write her own songs. She would improvise words over a simple melody. Here is one song she wrote, to a very simple tune that I played with her on my guitar:

> Go on as best you can,
> Go on as best you can.
> It will ease your mind,
> It will ease your mind,
> And you will feel better.

> Oh I need a family
> Right behind me
> All the time,
> All the time,
> And I will feel better.
>
> And if I need a friend,
> If I ever need a friend,
> Bill is right behind,
> Bill is right behind,
> To ease my mind.

The words "To ease your mind," "And you will feel better" were Alice's new inner voice speaking to her with love, replacing the old hated image of herself. Bill was Alice's husband, a great source of strength for her. But he comes only in the final verse. Before that, Alice must see herself in a new way and speak to herself with love.

Alice was now able to distinguish happy feelings from sad, and to tell which songs expressed which feelings. She began to appreciate uplifting, cheerful songs, since now they often expressed how she felt. When towards the end of my work with her I observed to Alice that her mood had greatly improved, she smiled and said "You bet!" The slumped, withdrawn, lifeless, and ghostly presence I had first met no longer existed.

What healed Alice? In the beginning, she hated herself because all she saw was someone sick and weak and disabled and useless. She was not truly aware of who she was. Music reached her on a deep level, a level of herself she had not previously known. Music opened her heart. Her heart was also touched when she began to see herself not as the sum of all the things she could not do, but as someone struggling to survive and make the most of the life and abilities she did have. Who would not be moved by the "silver girl" who was so beaten down, abused by herself and others, who lived in so much darkness, but who was still holding on to whatever chances for hope she had left?

THE "HEART MOMENT"

This is the way to defeat the early and lasting images of self-hatred: the heart must be touched. Facts and logic will never eradicate self-hatred. The primitive part of the brain where these images reside cares nothing about reality. Only a response of the heart can reach those deep levels of the mind impervious to reason.

Alice was transformed by being able to see herself through her heart. A "heart moment," in which one can see and feel for one's own struggle, can penetrate layers of stubborn, ancient judgmental images that otherwise seem impossible to break through. After finding such a moment, one can return to it any time one feels oneself under the attack of the old primitive judge.

Tennessee Williams dramatically portrayed such a moment in his play *The Night of the Iguana*. The protagonist, Reverend Shannon, is driven by self-hatred nearly to the point of self-destruction. He is a defrocked minister, brought down by alcoholism and other indiscretions. As the play opens he is making his living as a guide on bus tours, feeling only contempt for the rather prudish women schoolteachers in his tour group. The tour is disrupted when Shannon is caught in a sexual encounter with one of the younger teachers. Shannon goes on a drunken rampage and thoroughly humiliates himself. His self-loathing has acquired a new and dangerous edge. He goes out of control and tries to rip from his neck the last sign of his respectable past, a gold cross suspended from a chain, but he succeeds only in cutting himself. He becomes practically delirious, and the motel keeper and her assistants tie him into a hammock so that he cannot move.

Hannah, a guest at the motel where Shannon's group is staying and very troubled herself, befriends Shannon. As she talks to him, only the sound of her voice keeps in check the panic rising within him. But Shannon hates himself so much that he lashes out at her, the nearest target for the rage he cannot contain within himself.

> HANNAH: Stop it! Stop being childishly cruel! I can't stand for a person that I respect to talk and behave like a small, cruel boy, Mr. Shannon.
>
> SHANNON: What've you found to respect in me, Miss . . . Thin-Standing-Up-Female-Buddha?
>
> HANNAH: I respect a person that has had to fight and howl for his decency and his—
>
> SHANNON: What decency?
>
> HANNAH: Yes, for his decency and his bit of goodness, much more than I respect the lucky ones that just had theirs handed out to them at birth and never afterwards snatched away from them by . . . unbearable . . . torments, I. . . .
>
> SHANNON: You respect me?
>
> HANNAH: I do.

Here Hannah provides Shannon with his "heart moment," his glimpse of himself through compassionate eyes. This one encounter has the power to change him, if he will let it. It is the most electrifying moment in the play.

Love is awareness. Becoming aware of oneself through the eyes of compassion is self-love. Even if early self-hating images are lastingly engraved on our minds, compassionate seeing reaches our spiritual nature, which is stronger. The spiritual always overcomes the mental, when the spiritual enters awareness. The problem is that we are often not aware of our spiritual side.

MIND VS. SOUL

Self-rejection cannot be healed through any exercise of the mind. Analyzing the problem, doing affirmations or other mental exercises, does not produce lasting results, because the problem resides far beneath the level of the mind. It is a wound in the soul. It must be healed through the soul.

God is always speaking to the soul. But rarely do we hear the voice. It is a soft, whispering voice: a "still, small voice," or "a sound of sheer silence" (1 Kings 19:12). But our minds are often too cluttered, too filled with thoughts and words to allow anything else to enter.

> *Likewise the Spirit helps us in our weakness; for we do not know how to pray as we ought, but that very Spirit intercedes with sighs too deep for words.* (Romans 8:26)

With sighs too deep for words. The words in our minds must give way so that we can hear the voice of the Spirit. We cannot just tell it to happen—that would only be adding more words. We need to slow ourselves down, slow our minds to a crawl and eventually even to a stop, so that we become receptive to something deeper. This is the purpose of true spiritual meditation. The difference between meditation and affirmation is that affirmations fill the mind with words. Meditation helps stop the flow of words so that we become receptive to the voice of God. Meditation helps us stop talking to ourselves and become good listeners.

If meditation seems too complicated, then think of it simply as prayer. Take a moment to stop, watch your thoughts, slow down and listen. Then listen to your heart, because it is the heart, not the mind, through which the Spirit speaks to us.

It is through the heart that the soul is healed. The heart is our capacity to feel both joy and pain. If you have ever had a moment where you felt your "heart going out" to someone, then you know what heart is. If anyone's pain has ever made you feel a wound in your heart, then you know what heart is.

Self-acceptance comes when we can see ourselves through the heart. It is a breakthrough moment, in which we perceive ourselves directly, rather than through the thoughts of others. It is a moment in which we see ourselves as God sees us.

For such a moment to occur, you may need to behold yourself as if you were someone else: someone who has endured the same pain, fought the same struggle as you have. Can you see the goodness in that person? Can you see the love in that person? Can you feel how God would respond to that person? How God would accept that person? Then can you consider that such a person might be you?

The prostitute in Luke 7, who despised herself so much that she could only cry in Jesus's presence, was healed in this way. Her tears were not only of pain, but also of joy. Jesus did not see her as she saw herself. He saw her torment, he saw her pain, and he saw her loving heart. And he gave her his eyes, so that she too could see herself through the eyes of Christ. The lifting of self-hatred from her soul liberated her and ignited within her a gratitude she could hardly express.

All sincere people who are searching for the light, no matter what they may have experienced, what they have done or how they have been treated, are entitled to see themselves through the eyes of Christ. If others have hated or abused them, that hatred and abuse cannot stand in the light of Christ's vision of love. Even if they have done some terrible thing, committed some horrible sin, the remorse they feel is heard in heaven and forgiveness will come. Like the father of the prodigal, nothing pleases God more than one of God's children who is trying to return.

We need not simply affirm this. We can know it. We know it through the heart. When our hearts ache at the sight of another's pain, it is God speaking to us. And when our hearts cry for the goodness we can see in ourselves, it is God speaking to us as well. Once the Spirit engages the heart, all self-condemnation ceases.

EXORCISING SELF-HATRED

The New Testament tells a story of how Jesus healed a particularly severe case of self-hatred. It is an odd story indeed:

> *They came to the other side of the lake, to the country of the Gerasenes. And when [Jesus] had stepped out of the boat, immediately a man out of the tombs with an unclean spirit met him. He lived among the tombs; and no one could restrain him any more, even with a chain; for he had often been restrained*

with shackles and chains, but the chains he wrenched apart, and the shackles he broke in pieces; and no one had the strength to subdue him. Night and day among the tombs and on the mountains he was always howling and bruising himself with stones.

When he saw Jesus from a distance, he ran and bowed down before him; and he shouted at the top of his voice, "What have you to do with me, Jesus, Son of the Most High God? I adjure you by God, do not torment me." For he had said to him, "Come out of the man, you unclean spirit!"

Then Jesus asked him, "What is your name?" He replied, "My name is Legion; for we are many." He begged him earnestly not to send them out of the country.

Now there on the hillside a great herd of swine was feeding; and the unclean spirits begged him, "Send us into the swine; let us enter them."

So he gave them permission. And the unclean spirits came out and entered the swine; and the herd, numbering about two thousand, rushed down the steep bank into the lake, and were drowned in the lake.

The swineherds ran off and told it in the city and in the country. Then people came to see what it was that had happened. They came to Jesus and saw the demoniac sitting there, clothed and in his right mind, the very man who had had the legion; and they were afraid. (Mark 5:1–15)

"He was always howling and bruising himself with stones": what a powerful representation of what self-hatred can feel like, a bruising of the self that never stops. When Jesus talks to the poor man it is not he himself who answers but his demons, saying "we are many." They have taken over his mind.

Jesus liberates the man by sending these unclean spirits into the swine, an unclean animal. Immediately the animals drown themselves in the lake. What is this about?

Self-Acceptance

The first thing this man says to Jesus is "What have you to do with me? By God, do not torment me!" What a strange thing to say to one who would only bring you kindness—do not torment me! Kindness is a torment to those who are convinced they do not deserve it. Self-rejection so overpowers the Gerasene that he actually feels more comfortable in darkness and isolation. As it says, "he lived among the tombs." There is a safety in this darkness. To spiritual wounds, light is felt as pain.

But now we can imagine the compassion Jesus carried in his presence entering this man and holding him and filling him until there is no longer any room for those demons. They must escape, and in drowning themselves their self-destructive nature is revealed: they were no real part of this man; he did not deserve them and they did not belong to him. In their place resides the love Jesus brought, with the message that even the most wretched and demon-afflicted are included in this love.

Jesus helped the man see his demons outside of himself. Watching them from the vantage point of self-observation, the man beheld their injurious power. And seeing the demons outside of him made them no longer part of him.

We must see our own demons outside of ourselves and separate from ourselves. We can see their abuse and their violence as if we were watching them attack someone else. We need to feel compassion for the one who is attacked. Once the heart has been reached, the tricks of the mind lose their influence.

This is the key to self-acceptance: to see ourselves from a distance with compassion, as if the one we see were anyone else to whom our heart would reach out with no hesitation. It is to acquire a sense of our own struggle and above all a respect for it. It is to know through the heart that we belong to God's love.

WHO IS YOUR GOD?

All that God asks of us is to live our lives as an endeavor to become more Godlike. This sounds lofty indeed, probably unattainable, until we stop to consider who God really is. God is All Goodness, Goodness Itself. We are created in God's image. Therefore all God asks of us is to imitate and express goodness to the best of our ability. We can do no better than that.

> *He has told you, O mortal, what is good; and what does the Lord require of you but to do justice, and to love kindness, and to walk humbly with your God.* (Micah 6:8)

To love goodness and to do it: this is why we are here. If we know who our God is—All Goodness—and remember that this is the God to whom we belong and to whom we strive to be close, we will begin to see our lives differently.

All hateful images of ourselves come from one of two sources: they are either the images of ourselves we learned to see through the eyes of others, or the images we ourselves have generated by pursuing selfishness rather than goodness.

For the second source, the remedy is repentance. As the Parable of the Prodigal Son tells us, we can never stray so far away from goodness that we cannot find our way back. When we learn to value goodness itself more than self-interest, we will be conforming to the image of God in which we were created.

The first type of hateful self-image—the one we learned to see through the eyes of others—is far more difficult to eradicate. For even if we sincerely repent all of our major lapses, we may still find ourselves unable to accept forgiveness because the hateful self-image we learned is still engraved almost indelibly on our souls.

Self-Acceptance

This type of self-hate is conquered only though the power of the "heart moment."

When we become disciples of goodness, devoted to love and to living a loving life, we can view our lives from a distance and behold the love we have given and received. We must allow that love to reach our hearts. This is the critical point. If we can experience through our own hearts the love we have expressed, then we have reached the point of self-acceptance. Then the demons that have caused us to bruise ourselves relentlessly will have to flee our souls and fly into pigs in order to survive. Love is stronger than any demon, and love is known through the heart. We need only the willingness and the courage to allow our own love to be known to ourselves.

So we must always ask ourselves: Who is our God? To whom do we belong? A God who hates, punishes, and condemns? A God who looks for infractions and sends some of us to hell forever? No, this is not the God of Judeochristianity or of the Bible when considered in its totality. We belong to a God of Absolute Goodness and Infinite Love. And we know this not with the mind but with the heart. The "heart moment" is our entrance to this realization. When we live in the heart moment, we cannot hate ourselves. We love ourselves as God's loved creation. It cannot be otherwise, once the true God of All Goodness has entered our hearts and replaced all the false images humanity has invented over centuries.

May we all know these heart moments, as many times as we may need them to obtain a true sense of faith and presence of God, and may we know how deeply and truly we are loved in spite of the efforts of anyone else in our lives who may have tried to convince us otherwise.

XVII

THE MESSAGE OF THE CROSS

When I came to you, brothers and sisters, I did not come proclaiming the mystery of God to you in lofty words or wisdom. For I decided to know nothing among you except Jesus Christ, and him crucified. And I came to you in weakness and in fear and in much trembling.

1 Corinthians 2:1–3

For if we have been united with him in a death like his, we will certainly be united with him in a resurrection like his.

Romans 6:5

THE UNIVERSALITY OF THE PASSION

IF THE BOOKS OF the Bible were a family, the "black sheep" would be Ecclesiastes. One does not read it for comfort or uplift. It is not a book of "good news." Its news is in fact quite sobering. It describes life's inevitable tragedies and progression to decay, and tells us (7:1) that "the day of death is better than the day of birth." Why? Isn't life good? Shouldn't we be grateful for it? Should we instead look forward to our death?

A midrash (commentary of the rabbis, *Exodus Rabbah* 48:1) explains this verse:

> It is like two ships sailing upon the ocean. One leaves the harbor, while the other is returning home. People celebrate the first, but not the second.
>
> A wise man said: I see it differently. We should not celebrate the one leaving the harbor, because no one knows what rough seas or storms might attack it. But as to the ship that returns, we rejoice that it has come home in peace.

It is the same with us. A person who is born should be regarded as dead—and when dead, should be seen as living.

This sounds rough, pessimistic, even anti-life. But that is not the intent. This passage points to an existential truth: we greet the entrance of a new life into the world with joy, optimism, and hope, but the destiny of that creature will involve many trials, much disappointment, and almost always much suffering and a painful death. To be born is to enter a suffering world.

This is why the story of Jesus's passion is so powerful.

The greatest mystery in the New Testament is the crucifixion, its meaning, and its transcendence. We may turn to the Gospels for assurance and hope, but as the story progresses we face impending darkness as we see the tragic and painful end approaching. The signs and references that foreshadow this end, which the Gospel writers so skillfully sprinkle throughout the early chapters, create a sense of dread as we follow Jesus through his life and ministry.

The story continues to inspire so many people, Christians and non-Christians alike, because it is so much like our own story. Jesus, who is called the "son of man," experiences every emotion we do—joy, love, anger, sadness, fear—and in the hardship and suffering of our own lives we too experience something of the crucifixion.

So we read the Gospels wanting to know: How did Jesus handle the experience of being human? Was he able to overcome its terrors? Can he help us, through his example, to overcome them too?

THE MEANING OF "SALVATION"

"Salvation" is a term from the Bible that refers to this overcoming of fear through sensing one's unbreakable connection to God. Unfortunately the word has become a religious cliché, taken to mean some sort of personal lock on the afterlife. But the word is used in many contexts throughout both the Hebrew Bible and New Testament. "Surely God is my salvation; I will trust, and will not be afraid" (Isaiah 12:2). Salvation means the ultimate conquest of fear through the awareness of God's presence.

Salvation is not simply a matter of what one believes. It is the condition of finding oneself in God's care and as part of the divine plan. Finding salvation means finding a faith that allows one to move forward with confidence in spite of the fears that are inescapably part of human life. When Paul spoke of salvation he was pointing toward an existential reality, a faith that is real and has the power to lift one out of the terrors of life and into the presence of God. This salvation was meant for everyone, not just a chosen few. "For I am not ashamed of the gospel; it is the power of God for salvation to everyone who has faith, to the Jew first and also to the Greek" (Romans 1:16). What was the heart of the salvation that Paul preached?

The crucifixion! Paul understood how shocking this message was: "For Jews demand signs and Greeks desire wisdom, but we proclaim Christ crucified, a stumbling block to Jews and foolishness to Gentiles" (1 Corinthians 1:22–23). One should not read these verses as a debate between Christianity and the other religions of the world, which would impose the viewpoint of a later time on Paul's message. Paul is contrasting one way of acquiring faith with attempts people often make that do not work.

One cannot find faith by relying on miracles ("signs"), as the

Jews of Jesus's time did, or by exercising the intellect in philosophical speculation ("wisdom"), as the Greeks did. Both are attempts to locate the center of faith outside one's own personal struggle with life and the spiritual growth resulting from that struggle. The Jews sought their faith in external signs, the Greeks in external knowledge. Paul understood that the soul must be transformed from within, and that any faith based solely upon assurances from outside sources of authority is childish and fragile. So he did not come proclaiming the testimony of God "in lofty words or wisdom," in abstract concepts that might impress a theologian but that fail to touch the heart. Paul had no words of his own that could give faith to anyone else, and so he relied on the only alternative he could find: the preaching of "Jesus Christ, and him crucified."

But what does the crucifixion have to do with salvation, the conquest of fear through faith? The crucifixion stands for the last horror in life, the worst fear realized. What salvation can it possibly offer? Why doesn't Paul preach the resurrection only?

DENYING THE CROSS

Many commentators as well as some early sources, failing to understand the message of the crucifixion, have tried to deny it. Some have even said that Jesus did not actually suffer, that he chose to be crucified to demonstrate that life is really indestructible. According to the gnostic Coptic Apocalypse of Peter the crucified one was not the real Jesus. The true living Jesus stood above the cross, laughing. The account in the Qur'an also denies the cross. According to the Qur'an (4:157–8) Jesus was not crucified at all; those who believed it was Jesus on the cross were fooled by an appearance.

Many have also believed that the resurrection itself makes the crucifixion inconsequential. They prefer to jump over the suffering of the cross and go straight to redemption. Why spend any time with the cross if we know that resurrection is at hand?

The resurrection symbolizes the possibility of overcoming crucifixion. It is not given to us as a certainty. Even though Jesus predicted the resurrection, he still suffered intense anxiety and doubt. *Faith* is not *knowledge*. It is a sense of assurance, of the working of a higher goodness in our lives. But even having faith, we are still subject to the temptation to doubt. We gain faith in our journey through doubt. We cannot avoid that journey if we aspire to a faith having both depth and durability.

The resurrection was not a separate event that just chanced to happen after death on the cross. Something within the crucifixion itself made the resurrection possible. If we overlook the connection between the two, or deny the significance of the crucifixion, then the resurrection becomes irrelevant, at best merely one of the external signs Paul dismissed as having no saving power for us in our lives as we must actually live them.

The crucifixion is not just a single incident that occurred at one moment in time. It is a symbol of the suffering that is an inescapable part of being human. Paul's message intends to proclaim a faith powerful enough to take the cross into itself—a faith that does not depend on denying the hardships of human experience. This kind of faith reaches out in love to suffering people right where they are, touches them, embraces them, and gives them confidence to keep on living. This faith must take into account the certainty of the cross.

Jesus said, "Whoever does not carry the cross and follow me cannot be my disciple" (Luke 14:27). Deep faith is won only through accepting one's cross and struggling with doubt and fear. Those lucky enough to come to faith without this struggle do possess a strength, but it may not hold up when a true crisis comes, and it is likely to have limited value when called upon to offer support to others.

TWO TYPES OF COURAGE

Paul Tillich, in *The Courage to Be*, makes a puzzling statement. He says that the only real alternative to Christianity in the Western world is Stoicism. Pondering the relationship between the two, and how they are alternatives to each other, tells us something about faith.

The way of the cross and the way of the Stoic are similar in that neither one flinches from suffering in its quest for self-transcendence.

The Stoic overcomes suffering by accepting it with courageous resignation. The classical example was Socrates's courageous acceptance of his death. The society in which he lived felt threatened by the values he espoused and by his public defense of them. Fearful that he was subverting the loyalty of its youth, it condemned him to death. But the authorities offered Socrates an escape: they would spare his life if he would cease his teaching. Socrates refused. He assured them that if he were released he would behave no differently from before. On the day of his execution he drank the poison with a calmness that astonished his disciples.

While Socrates had a way out, he knew he had no honorable way out. Had he agreed to the state's terms for his release, he would have compromised the heart of his teaching. By so capitulating he would have become a coward and a hypocrite. So he accepted his fate as inevitable, and the knowledge that he was acting with honesty and honor gave him the strength to endure it.

This is the courage of Stoicism. It is a viable alternative to being enslaved by fear. But it requires much strength, more than many of us possess. It requires a self-assurance and confidence in one's convictions that few of us know.

Sometimes fear simply overwhelms us. We cannot always make the most honorable choice based solely on the strength of knowing it is right. We may lack the assurance, the freedom from self-doubt that Socrates had. Therefore we need, many of us, an alternative to Stoic courage that enables us to approach fear and suffering and to emerge with faith.

This alternative is given by the message of the cross. It is an extremely paradoxical alternative: the cross itself becomes the instrument of our salvation. To understand what this means and how it is possible, let us explore the event of the crucifixion as the Gospels record it.

We begin in Gethsemane where Jesus, alone, confronts the danger awaiting him. Jesus did not want to be alone, and it seemed he might not have to. He had, after all, twelve disciples who professed devotion to him; they were in some ways like a family. He took the three closest to him, Peter, James, and John, and asked them to watch with him. Then he moved a little farther on, and asked God to spare him, if possible, from his suffering.

His disciples had all been warned; they knew this moment was critical. Yet even these most devoted three could not face with Jesus the reality of what was about to occur. So they abandoned him. When he returned from his prayer he found them sleeping.

He tried to wake them up, three times, but without success. Still, he understood their failure of spirit. Our own situation is not very different. Even if we live with family members who love us and care for us, even if we have friends who are loyal, at some point we have to face our trials alone. Even those closest to us cannot be with us all the time.

This was definitely a trial for Jesus. He was not simply going through the motions. He really was afraid. The text tells us: he was "sorrowful and troubled"; "My soul is very sorrowful, even to death" (Matthew 26:37–38, RSV). He prayed "three times" for his suffering to be lifted: this is the Bible's symbol for the intensity of his concern. Jesus wanted neither suffering nor death. Still, during that time at Gethsemane he accepted his fate and even embraced it.

What gave him the strength to do this? Jesus did not have the Stoic courage of Socrates. In Socrates we find no anxiety, no hesitation; he knows the only right course of action to take, and he takes it because he knows it is right. In Jesus we find evidence that he experienced fear, that he doubted himself, that he doubted God, and that he was tempted to retreat. Why ask God three times to spare him from a fate he himself told his own disciples was necessary, unless at that moment his mind was full of doubt? Jesus's experience is closer by far to the experience of most of us than is the experience of Socrates. That is why Jesus and not Socrates is called "son of man."

DIFFERENT FACES OF THE CROSS

The four versions of Jesus's experience on the cross differ greatly. But taken together they tell us a lot about what it means to face one's destiny and to find strength even in one's greatest weaknesses.

In Matthew, the crucifixion is an experience of despair. Jesus's final words quote from Psalm 22: "My God, my God, why have you forsaken me?" (Matthew 27:46). The anguish in this cry is real. One trivializes the crucifixion if one tries to deny the depth of feeling Jesus expresses in these words, as, for instance, the Lamsa Bible does when it translates from a questionable reading of the Aramaic, "My God, my God, for this I was spared!" Matthew wants to show Jesus's real torment, as he describes the moment of Jesus's death: "Then Jesus cried again with a loud voice and breathed his last" (Matthew 27:50).

Mark's account closely parallels Matthew's, and may have been Matthew's main source. In Luke, however, we find something different. The despairing quote from the twenty-second psalm is missing. Instead, we find Jesus reassuring the repentant criminal crucified next to him: "Truly I tell you, today you will be with me in Paradise" (Luke 23:43). Jesus's life ends not with a cry of anguish but with an affirmation of his faith: "Then Jesus, crying with a loud voice, said, 'Father, into your hands I commend my spirit'" (Luke 23:46)—a quote not from Psalm 22 but from Psalm 31.

The original Greek text is revealing, since the English versions have Jesus, in both Matthew and Luke, "crying with a loud voice." The word translated "crying" in Luke (23:46) is *phonesas*, whose root means "to make a sound," or to speak with emphasis. The word translated "cried" in Matthew (27:50) is *kraxas*, whose root means "to scream," or "to shriek." The significance of Jesus's final cry in Matthew is very different from that in Luke. In one of Jesus's most celebrated last sayings, again found in Luke, Jesus meets his suffering with tremendous love: "Father, forgive them; for they do not know what they are doing" (Luke 23:34). Although some early sources lack this passage, the words very much fit the tone of Jesus's life and teaching, and the manner of Jesus's death as Luke portrays it.

How can we explain the apparent clash between these two accounts of the crucifixion? Can they both be describing the same experience of the same individual?

The entire message of the cross is given in the fact that these two accounts are not only consistent with one another, but that neither can really be understood without the other.

The confidence and faith of Luke's account cannot be separated from the despair and doubt in Matthew's account. True faith is possible only after confronting real fear. Fear appeared to Jacob in the form of an angel, and by wrestling with it he emerged with the confidence he needed to meet his angry and vengeful brother. Faith comes from the struggle with reality. It can never come from falsehood, from denying one's experiences and one's reactions.

Too often religion fails to respond adequately to the suffering from which the quest for faith arises. It may even deny the reality of suffering to preserve at all costs a cherished notion of God. This kind of religion confines God to a set of neat answers to simple questions that have little to do with our actual experience. True faith only grows from facing one's experiences, one's weaknesses, and one's fears. Jesus did this when he confessed his fear to God but resolved to accept his destiny.

FEAR AND FAITH

The message of the cross is the strange paradox that facing our fears is the way to faith. At first, when fear overwhelms us, this hardly seems possible. How then are fear and faith connected?

The chain connecting them has two links: truth and love. Truth and love are qualities that witness to God's presence in us.

In truth we take our painful experiences exactly as they come to us, we stay honest with ourselves, we refuse to run away from trials we know we will have to face. This, however, is only a prelude to faith.

The true source of strength in faith is a love that can reach out to the pain of the cross and embrace it with compassion. Love is at the heart of the mystery of the cross, and is what makes the way of the cross different from the way of the Stoics. Love provides the possibility of a creative response to suffering even for those who lack Stoic courage.

Jesus's acceptance of the cross was an act of love, and it was love that gave him the power to accept it. This was evident at the moment of Jesus's arrest, when he ordered Peter to sheath his sword after Peter struck the slave of the high priest. What kind of love enabled Jesus to keep moving forward in spite of the fearfulness of what awaited him?

The time in which Jesus lived was extremely difficult for the Jewish people. They lived at the mercy of the Roman occupying force. Pontius Pilate, the prefect who governed them, was known for his brutality. The tax collectors who worked for the Roman authorities were little better than highway robbers. Many of the people yearned for a messiah who would lead them to freedom in a revolt against Rome. Jesus saw their need, but knew he was not meant to establish the earthly kingdom they desired. He could not take away their suffering. He could only show them how to overcome it.

By freely choosing to accept the cross—the excruciating torture and ultimate symbol of intimidation and humiliation, the worst the Romans had to offer—Jesus expressed love for his people. He could have saved himself, he could have fled, recanted, or begged for mercy, but by doing so he would have abandoned those who placed their trust in him. Instead he chose to express a specific kind of love: the love inherent in *being present*. As an act of compassion ("suffering with") he accepted the suffering that was forced on them and that they could not escape.

Many have raised doubts about the importance of Jesus's sacrifice. After all, they remind us, the Romans also crucified tens of thousands of others. That is exactly the point! Of his own free will Jesus chose to share the worst of the suffering the Romans were inflicting on their subjects. He practiced the most literal form of compassion: being with the suffering of others.

Jesus allowed himself to be crucified between two criminals, and through his attention to them he was with them at the time of their worst pain and isolation, as well as his own. The difference between Jesus and these two others was not simply his innocence but also that he accepted his fate willingly, as he said: "the Son of man came not to be served but to serve, and to give his life a ransom for many" (Matthew 20:28). In spite of his uncertainty—faith is not a matter of certainty—he accepted his suffering based on faith that God's presence would remain with him. He could not be sure of it—we know he was not, if the words "My God, why have you forsaken me?" have any meaning—but he still had enough faith to allow him to act. And if God could, in some unforeseen way, maintain his presence with Jesus, then those who witnessed Jesus's example would be strengthened in their own faith. This was Jesus's gift to them, by his choosing not to escape his suffering.

LOVE CONFRONTS THE CROSS

This is how suffering is overcome by love. The core of love is awareness, and one part of awareness is *presence*. The love with which Jesus confronted his own suffering consisted of *maintaining a compassionate presence* with a suffering people who needed to witness the spiritual conquest of the pain and humiliation by which they themselves felt threatened. Jesus demonstrated this presence by *choosing* the suffering with which they were already afflicted.

If we are indeed healed through Jesus's death, as Christianity claims, it cannot be because his dying somehow magically erased our sins, as the ancient killing of the scapegoat was believed to have done. It is because Jesus's compassionate acceptance of the cross shows us that God's love overpowers the deepest threats to physical and spiritual existence. It shows us we can meet suffering without losing our faith, and that God's presence continues to act as a discernible reality in our lives.

But here is the paradox: how can accepting the cross conquer anything? The people were hoping for a show of strength; they wanted a gallant leader who would stand up to the power of Rome. Instead Jesus demonstrated what appeared to be weakness: he chose to suffer, to bear his own cross. When they arrested him he said nothing; when they tried him and whipped him he said nothing; when they crucified him he did not resist. The meek do not inherit the earth, they are crucified: this has always been the criticism of Jesus's message. Choosing to suffer when he could have escaped? What kind of spiritual triumph is this?

The triumph came not from weakness itself but from the willingness to see and to accept weakness, which is actually a great strength. That Jesus could see his own weaknesses, face them squarely, yet maintain his full awareness and presence in spite of them, led him to find strength. He knew he could not stand up to the Romans, and he was afraid of what they could do to him.

Though tempted to escape, he never considered escaping his full awareness of the event. He did not pretend a courage he could not feel. He confessed to God his doubts and anxieties. Then fully conscious of them, and willing to live with his fear, he went ahead anyway.

OUR GETHSEMANE

Fear is the great enemy of faith, the testimony our experience gives us that there is no God. Fear undermines our faith in many ways. It shakes our trust in the essential goodness of life. It causes us to resent those who make us afraid. It also makes us hate ourselves.

Fear, resentment, and self-hate are closely linked. Resentment is a natural reaction to fear: nobody likes to be intimidated. The underside of resentment is self-hate: we hate the image of ourselves as being afraid, meek, lacking courage, being a victim of others or of circumstances we cannot control. We may try to compensate for this sense of weakness with an insensitive, hostile aggressiveness, but the anger behind it is evidence that the self-hate still exists.

The self-hate inside resentment is what makes resentment so unbearable; it gnaws at our insides, placing us under tremendous tension and threatening our health. Resentment always expresses self-hate because it is always a physical and emotional attack on the self; this is clear once we become aware of the stress that it produces.

Sometimes we can overcome resentment by facing the contribution we have made to our own suffering, letting other people "off the hook" and healing our sense of powerlessness. Yet there are times in our lives when we really are powerless, when we have little control over our suffering, and seemingly little escape from resentment. Such moments attack our faith at its core.

I am writing this shortly after having seen one of my cancer patients at the hospice, whom I will call Susan. When I entered her room this evening I saw her angrily slapping her paralyzed leg because it would not move. She made a tremendous effort to move it, managed to budge it just an inch or two, but the effort took so much out of her that she lost her voice and could not speak above a raspy whisper.

Susan is full of contradictions. She loves the company of others, but can be quite nasty to people who are trying to help. No false move goes unpunished. If I play a wrong note on my guitar, she lets me know it. To a nurse who suggested she could be a little nicer, Susan snapped that she, Susan, is the patient, and it is the nurse's job to be nice, not hers. Susan has alienated a number of staff members whose help she really needs.

One day I found Susan on the floor, upset and practically in tears. She had made a bowel movement and could not get to the bathroom in time. Because she could not walk, she fell as she tried to get out of bed. Fortunately she was wearing a diaper, but she did not trust it. It was too humiliating.

I wet some paper towels, put soap on them, and helped her clean up. I told her she could trust the diaper, that's what it's for. She understood, but still clung hard to her determination to walk. Susan is a deeply religious Christian, and for her the effort to regain her ability to walk is a test of her faith.

But what if she never does walk again?

I decided to put the question to her. Can she accept herself and her condition, no matter what happens? No, she answered, she cannot.

And so we talked, about her disability, her loss of control, her paralysis, her frustration, the simple humiliation of not being able to go to the bathroom by herself.

And we talked about her anger. She was surprised when I told her that her anger came from self-rejection. But once it was identified, she could see it clearly. She hated herself for being what she now was: helpless, unable to care for her most basic needs.

I reminded her of what Jesus said: that if we are to be his disciple, we must be willing to take up our cross. The cross takes a different form for each individual. This is the form it is taking for her.

I also reminded her of how Jesus said we must become like children if we are to enter into the Kingdom. What is it about a child? A child trusts. A child has faith in the direction of its parents. And if a child is young enough, sometimes a child uses a diaper.

When Susan heard this she took my head into her arms and kissed me. She didn't have to hate herself now. She is being called to realize this teaching of Jesus in the most radical way. She is being asked, by her own personal cross, to drop her insistence on control and her resentment of her weakness to discover the childlike faith of which Jesus spoke—and through this faith, to learn to love herself. Or perhaps more to the point, to learn that she is loved.

Susan remembered a verse she had quoted to me just the week before: "The Lord will fight for you; and you have only to keep still" (Exodus 14:14). To this I added the words of St. Paul: "Whenever I am weak, then I am strong" (2 Corinthians 12:10). Susan's physical condition did not change. The difference was that now she became conscious of God's presence. Something beyond her carried her in spite of her helplessness.

This was Susan's Gethsemane. Her struggle recalled that of Jesus: when faced with suffering one cannot control or avoid, one does not flee, one remains present. And then one discovers that being present is a deep form of love. It can even be an entrance to the knowledge of a love that is beyond any human capacity.

LOVE DEFEATS THE CROSS

Love is presence. Children know they are loved if they know their parents are present. They feel secure knowing that as they sleep, their parents sleep in the room next door. In the Bible God's love is often described in terms of being a watchful presence: "He who keeps Israel will neither slumber nor sleep" (Psalm 121:4), "I will be with you; I will not fail you or forsake you" (Joshua 1:5), "You know him, because he abides with you, and he will be in you" (John 14:17).

The simplest act of love is to maintain a presence with one who needs to be loved. This presence must not be merely physical, but psychological and spiritual.

To be psychologically present means to maintain an awareness of the situation at hand, the individual and what he or she needs. It means not to shut ourselves off from whatever may be frightening us, not to allow panic to drive us into a frantic search for escape routes.

To be spiritually present means to maintain a sense of clarity, to stay grounded in the moment, not to abandon ourselves; it means to find an objective, observing inner presence that accompanies us through the difficulty. Even while remaining physically present in a tough situation we can still run away from it in spirit if fear sets our thoughts racing. Fear makes it difficult to be courageous, but even if we hardly feel capable of courage we can still respond positively to fear by maintaining a presence within it.

And so to accept the cross means to take the burden of fear upon ourselves. When overpowered by fear, the only response immediately available may be to choose to stay aware of it. We accept fear's presence until something in our perception of it changes. We may not know when the change will come or what form it will take, but a turbulent situation never remains static.

The beginning of inner strength is facing our own fears. Paul understood this: "For the sake of Christ, then, I am content with weaknesses, insults, hardships, persecutions, and calamities; for when I am weak, then I am strong" (2 Corinthians 12:10, RSV). It is not weakness itself that makes us strong, but the willingness to accept our awareness of it and to remain present in spite of it.

We now come back to those two links in the chain of faith. When we maintain a presence with our fear we realize two divine qualities: truth and love. Truth is evident in our resolve to be honest with ourselves, not to escape the awareness of our difficulty, not to trivialize the problem but to face it directly. Love is evident in our resolve to stay present with ourselves, not to fly into fantasy or panic, but to accept ourselves as we are and watch over ourselves in time of trial. From truth and love comes the strength to endure and persevere. Thus even in our weakness we know that we are strong.

The compassionate presence we maintain within ourselves even when we are afraid is the seed of faith in the midst of suffering. We may experience this presence as a way of loving ourselves. But we are not the source of this love. We cannot decide to love ourselves. The love we experience toward ourselves results from the strength we develop as we continue to persevere in fear's presence. To know this love for ourselves while we so strongly feel our weaknesses is really to know a love that comes from beyond ourselves.

We know this love is indeed greater than ourselves because it gives us the strength to reach out to others when they too are weak, even while we are still broken. The presence we maintain within ourselves becomes a presence we maintain with others. The gift of love we offer to those who are suffering has nothing to do with worrying about them, sharing their fear, trying to change them, or trying to interfere with their problems. Often simply being present, perhaps not even physically but certainly spiritually, with someone in distress can have a healing, calming effect, even if we do not utter a single word. At some level others will know that we are with them, even if they cannot respond to our presence.

Love that takes us beyond ourselves is evidence of God's presence. It is therefore a basis for faith. Jesus exemplified this by choosing to live with his fear until it became faith. Paradoxically, his outcry to God against God's having abandoned him was itself an act of faith.

Jesus's refusal to break his dialogue with God transformed the cross. No longer dreading it, he chose it as an act of love. From the compassionate presence he established within himself he could reach out to comfort the one crucified next to him.

Love embraces the cross and overcomes it. Love can begin in the willingness to live with fear, through which we discover our inner strength. We become a compassionate presence, which may even touch others. Through this compassionate presence we gain God's presence. It gives us faith. It protects us from spiritual death, which is a loss of vitality due to the destruction of our faith. This conquering of spiritual death is the meaning of resurrection. The changes that make resurrection possible, however, must take place while we are still on the cross. Not every crucified is resurrected, but only those who find a way to overcome the cross through inner strength and love.

The despairing Jesus of Matthew, who honestly confesses to God his sense of abandonment, makes the confident, faithful Jesus of Luke possible. By confessing his weaknesses and remaining spiritually present in spite of them, Jesus finds the strength necessary to offer faith to others. This conquest of suffering through love is the fulfillment of the crucified Jesus in the Gospel of John, who while still on the cross, just before his death, can say with confidence that "It is finished." This Jesus dies not with a loud outcry but with a simple bow of the head (John 19:30).

WE TOO ARE RESURRECTED

The love through which Jesus transformed the cross is available also to us. Paul captures it in a single sentence: "And I came to you in weakness and in fear and in much trembling." Experiencing weakness, fear, and trembling, I nevertheless remain present. I call my weaknesses by their names, I know that I have them, but I am here, I am with you, I am aware of myself, and I am aware of you.

Compassionate, "suffering-with" love conquers fear in a most ironic way: it meets fear right where it lives. It overcomes fear by being aware of it, by reaching out to it, holding it, and being present with it. Compassion is the true source of our power to accept the cross. Even when we are gripped by fear, through maintaining our compassion we become instruments of divine love, a love that breaks through our self-interest to witness to something greater than the self.

Compassionate, all-embracing love is the condition for resurrection from spiritual death. "For if we have been united with him in a death like his, we shall certainly be united with him in a resurrection like his." We can be revived, but first we must die a death like his. A death "like his" death is a death we embrace through the power of compassion.

Above all, a death "like his" death is a death accepted as the natural and inevitable end of life. This was Jesus's great gift: that by accepting even the most painful death, and by transforming it into an act of love through his compassionate presence, he gives us hope that we too can overcome our own painful death. For Jesus was not the only one who died on a cross. My patient Susan died on a cross of linen, whose pain and the fear it created lasted far more than a single night.

Many of us will know similar pain and fear. However long it may last, Jesus's gift of choosing to experience it with us tells us it is one of the many brief moments of our lives, which will disappear as quickly as it came. If life is "a mist that appears for a little while and then vanishes" (James 4:14), then how much more transitory is death. Though it may seem like eternity while we are passing through it, it is as swift as any other time in life, which quickly becomes a memory we can barely grasp. When we know this, and feel the persistent reality of compassion, we can join Paul in affirming that "the sufferings of this present time are not worth comparing with the glory about to be revealed to us" (Romans 8:18).

When we resolve to meet suffering with compassion, we really will be able to choose our suffering, in the sense that we would no longer exchange the lessons we have learned for the ease of not having experienced the pain we needed to learn them. If we can become capable of choosing our suffering, we acquire a taste of the resurrection. There is new life within us in spite of the pain and death that may surround us.

Therefore Paul could say that suffering for God leads to a salvation that erases all regret: "For godly grief produces a repentance that leads to salvation and brings no regret, but worldly grief produces death" (2 Corinthians 7:10). The Bible does not promise that faith will bring an end to suffering. It says only that when we do suffer, we can still know that a higher, guiding and loving presence accompanies us.

> *Do not fear, for I have redeemed you;*
> *I have called you by name, you are mine.*
> *When you pass through the waters I will be with you;*
> *and through the rivers, they shall not overwhelm you;*
> *when you walk through fire you shall not be burned,*
> *and the flame shall not consume you.*
> *For I am the Lord your God,*
> *the Holy One of Israel, your Savior.*
> (Isaiah 43:1–3)

You may still have to pass through the waters; you may still have to walk through the fire. The difference is that this time you will sense a loving presence beside you.

If we know how to meet suffering in a way that increases our inner strength and deepens our capacity for love, then whatever the specific outcome of our difficulty, it will leave us in a better place than we were before: more self-aware, more loving, more available to others, and closer to God. Therefore "All things work together for good for those who love God" (Romans 8:28): *all things*, even the unknown suffering still waiting for us. Problems cease to be threats of destruction and become instead the means of the building of our character. Instead of fearing that the crisis we are facing will be the end of us, we will ask: How will God also transform this one, and where will God take me as I pass through it?

When we can suffer with this much awareness we will have received the message of the cross: that by embracing it with love, we need never have to fear it again.

XVIII

FAITH

Do not store up for yourselves treasures on earth, where moth and rust consume and where thieves break in and steal; but store up for yourselves treasures in heaven, where neither moth nor rust consumes and where thieves do not break in and steal. For where your treasure is, there your heart will be also.
Matthew 6:19–21

 STORY WAS TOLD, BY the Brothers Grimm, about a fisherman and his wife.

They lived together in a dirty old shack. One day the fisherman caught a big one. The biggest flounder he had ever seen. But that was not the most remarkable thing about this fish. It also talked.

"Master," it said to the fisherman, "I am not what I seem. I am an enchanted prince. You would not like to eat me. Please let me go."

Well, what was the fisherman to do? He could not disobey a talking flounder. So he let him go.

When the fisherman's wife heard what happened, she was not pleased. "A talking flounder? And you let him go? Certainly this was a magic flounder. You fish head, you should have asked him for something!"

"But what would I ask for?" queried the startled fisherman.

"A nice cottage instead of this ramshackle shack!" barked his wife.

So reluctantly the fisherman went back to the sea. Very apologetically, he asked the flounder if one favor might be granted, a new cottage to make his wife happy.

The flounder prince was only too happy to oblige. "It is the least I can do," he said, "for a kind fisherman who spared my life."

So the fisherman returned to his home, which was now a lovely cottage. His wife was standing by the door, a frown on her face. The cottage was too small. She wanted a palace. So she sent him back to the fish.

The fisherman, embarrassed about imposing on the flounder's generosity, nevertheless obeyed his wife. He went back to the sea and asked for a palace. Again the flounder obliged.

And again, the palace was not enough for the fisherman's wife. Now that she had a palace, she wanted to be queen. Her wish was granted, but being queen was not enough for her. She wanted to be emperor. Her wish was granted. But even being emperor did not suffice. She wanted to be the Pope. So her wish was granted, and she became the Pope.

This time the fisherman was sure his wife would be happy. She was the Pope. How much higher could she go? But his wife, very discontented, insisted that Pope was no longer enough. Now she wanted to be God.

So the fisherman returned to the sea for the last time, and sheepishly told the flounder of his wife's latest request.

And when he came back home, he found his wife once again clad in her dirty old rags and standing by the old shack they had known from the very beginning.

THE ELUSIVE STATE OF FAITH

There is a reason this story has endured. It describes a very common condition: what we are like when we lack faith.

There is something missing in the life of the fisherman's wife. Nothing satisfies her. She fixates on one thing after another to give her happiness, but nothing does.

When we don't have faith, this is what our lives are like. For what is faith? Faith is the sense that there is more to life than the apparent randomness of the material world. A sense that indeed, "our Father's house has many rooms," and one of those rooms belongs to us and is our dwelling place. A sense that we are known to a greater reality, are given our destiny by that reality, and will return to that reality. A sense that, in the words of the old hymn, "*Sea que muramos o que vivamos, somos del Señor*": "Whether we live or whether we die, we belong to God." The God who is All Goodness.

When we are aware of this, we may say we are in the state of faith. When we are not in the state of faith, we feel alone and adrift without an anchor. So we cast about for one. The anchor could be another person, or a possession, or the status that comes from a job. Whatever it is, we hold onto it with tenacity, and part with it in great anxiety. Losing that anchor throws us into turmoil. And since any anchor we grasp is impermanent, suffering is unavoidable.

The great insight of the Eastern religions is the recognition of the impermanence of all temporal anchors. They tell us that to find happiness we must recognize and accept the impermanence of everything in this world, including even the self, and detach ourselves from it. This is the path to enlightenment.

There is one very serious problem with this approach. It is

not humanly possible. We cannot, through our own resolve, stop clinging to impermanent things. When we grasp hard at things that pass, we are not in the state of faith. Lacking the one true anchor, the awareness of the eternal, we are driven to cling to substitutes. When we are aware of the eternal and our place in it, "it is well with our souls," and we feel no lack. This is why the Psalmist says, "The Lord is my shepherd, I shall not want." When we are aware of our participation in Absolute Goodness, we feel no need to cling to anything else.

Non-attachment by itself can never be a goal. I have seen many who became so attached to pursuing non-attachment that they never overcame their frustration. We were designed to be attached, attached specifically to the eternal and to God as Absolute Goodness. Lacking this awareness, we will seek attachment elsewhere. We cannot eliminate our need to attach. But we can understand our attachment to temporal things as a symptom of spiritual need, and seek to fulfill that need.

When non-attachment becomes the goal, we may begin to abandon the world. To Eastern religion the world appears as *saṃsāra*, a place of suffering to which we endlessly return, and from which we yearn to escape. This view is pessimistic. In the vision of Judeochristianity, developed throughout the Bible, the world indeed is a place of suffering, but still touched by eternity. Heaven and earth, the eternal and the temporal, are not separate realms. On earth the eternal is mostly hidden from us, but we still have contact with it. We can still know it and feel it and draw from this contact confidence and strength.

THE NEED FOR FAITH

Everyone needs faith in something. We all need to make some kind of sense out of the world in which we live. We also long for presence, to know we are not alone in the universe, to overcome the threat of cosmic isolation.

There are many kinds of faith. There is religious faith: a sense of the world's coherence based on received religious teachings. This is the most obvious kind of faith. It has great advantages and great disadvantages. Its advantage is that it really can inspire confidence and assurance in the face of adversity. Its disadvantage is that, since it has been received rather than discovered, questioning or doubting it can elicit deep fear. It therefore has a tendency to become rigid and intolerant. Most world religions claim exclusivity and discourage questioning, and countless wars have been fought in the name of one exclusive religion asserting its dominance over others.

Not all faith is religious. In some scientific communities disparaging religion has become popular, but scientists themselves are hardly without faith, if one thinks of faith as "the evidence of things not seen." The principles of science order the world and provide a sense of coherence, relieving many of the need for a God to explain things. Yet science too has its irrational but scientifically acceptable forms of faith. Many scientists believe the theory of evolution makes God irrelevant, even though that theory cannot explain the most important fact of creation: why does anything exist at all, especially anything with the power to give rise to life? Many also advance the conviction that life must exist on other planets, even though they have no more evidence for it than religious people have for the existence of God. Indeed, some are prepared to spend billions on this tenuous quest in spite of the great need for these resources here on earth. The belief in extraterrestrial life has become a socially acceptable faith for many scientists who would not go near any traditional religion. Nobody wants to be alone in the cold, black darkness.

Finally, there is one genuine kind of faith, which Judeochristianity defines as the *awareness of the power of eternity*. Genuine faith can be present in both religious faith and scientific faith, or it can be absent from both. Neither is a guarantee of genuine faith, although neither excludes it. However, the discouragement of free inquiry in much religious faith can impede the search for genuine faith.

Genuine faith grows from points of contact between the temporal and the eternal, between ourselves and the divine reality that touches us. We may become aware of such contacts in many different ways: for example, through the experience of beauty. Aesthetic experience and spiritual experience are not identical. But some expressions of beauty may convey an awareness of the spiritual if, even for just a moment, they bring us the sense of a reality beyond our experience that is unifying and redemptive. Any form of goodness that gives us a sense of this unifying and redemptive reality can bring us to the awareness of the eternal and therefore to faith.

Genuine faith can be hard to come by, if we cannot say we have any conscious awareness of such contacts. Religious faith tries—with varying degrees of success—to play the role of genuine faith. Religious faith is a symbolic approximation—and distortion—of genuine faith. Those who have a strong religious faith may feel no need for anything more. Those for whom religious faith is not the answer—either because they have not received it, or because they cannot help questioning it—are thrown into the struggle for genuine faith. So much in our experience testifies against faith: natural disasters, human cruelty, catastrophic things that happen to any of us without any apparent reason. Genuine faith is not easy to come by.

LOSING FAITH—AND FINDING IT

Those who are satisfied with received faith have no need for this book, and I expect they won't be reading this. Received faith has value, and can aid and comfort many. But received faith has limits, and even dangers. It may fail, and once it does, one may experience a crisis if no other faith appears to take its place.

The world has long been a battleground for the armies of conflicting received faiths. The mere fact of having received one's faith seems enough to convince many of its truth. But the accident of receiving is certainly no criterion of truth. At some deep layer of the soul we realize this. So we can feel threatened by others who, through the accident of having received a different faith, are as convinced as we are that their own faith is the true one. The rational response would be to question all faiths, to wonder at the oddity of thinking one's own faith is true and all others false simply because it is the faith in which one happened to be raised. But people are not rational. Questioning one's faith in that way opens one to the anxiety of losing faith and not having any faith. Therefore the more common response is to protect one's own faith from the claims of other faiths by denying or eliminating the other faiths.

This act of elimination can be performed in the mind—by becoming dogmatic, rigid, refusing to consider any truth other than one's own. It can be performed politically, through establishing one faith and suppressing all others. It can be performed violently, eliminating rival faiths by eliminating their members. The dynamic is the same: self-protection accomplished by negating the other. This is always the danger of received faith—that it separates people and sets groups against each other, thus acting contrary to love and therefore contrary to genuine faith itself.

But what if one dares to venture beyond the safety of received faith? One indeed courts trouble, for there is a real risk of ending up with nothing. Thus not many undertake this journey of their own volition. Sometimes, however, we are thrown into it—when we experience a catastrophe for which our faith has left us unprepared. Our foundation may crumble, and we look for some new ground on which to stand protected from the fear that inevitably comes from the experience of chaos.

We have already considered one great story about the shattering of received faith. It is the Book of Job. Job was a religious man "who feared God and turned from evil." Nevertheless he lost everything, his possessions, his family, his health. He also lost the faith he had been raised with. When friends came to console him with words of this faith, he found them anything but comforting; indeed they were oppressive. Job suffered the wrenching loss of the faith that he knew—but still found himself talking to God! Job found the deeper God who can appear when the God of our received faith is destroyed by our experience.

Paul Tillich's book *The Courage to Be* describes the same transition from a very different perspective. Tillich covers the question of confidence and faith in the history of Western theology. He ends with a discussion of our present time, in which received faith has been undermined by doubt as old teachings are no longer always taken for granted. Yet even when this faith is lost, one is still seized by the question of faith. One is still involved in the struggle, like Job continuing his argument with God. In the absence of faith one is still captured by the eternal and still involved with faith.

Those who have the courage to face this will experience something awesome. They will come into full contact with the power of something greater, the radically negative side of faith, felt as a deep void, but nevertheless grasping them and propelling them forward towards the boundary of this life beyond which lies the eternal.

This is a paradoxical faith, the power of the eternal experienced through the absence of received faith. It is faith experienced through the loss of faith, God experienced through the loss of God. In his book's conclusion Tillich sums it up in this haunting phrase: *The courage to be is rooted in the God who appears when God has disappeared in the anxiety of doubt.*

When one has lost everything connected to faith and nothing makes sense anymore, there is still something left. It is a void that cries out to be filled. And in that cry is an energy that impels one toward the search for faith. We are driven to fill the void.

Outworn theologies will not fill it. Every theology has a lifespan. Theologies are born and theologies die when they no longer speak to their times. Even the greatest theologians of the past tend to sound dated when one reads them now. Old theologies have been preserved by rigidifying them, like mummies impervious to change. But these do not speak to the heart that has lost received faith and is yearning for something to replace it.

Everyone has a way of filling the void, of finding something that makes sense of the world and of life and so becomes a basis for faith. Like the fisherman's wife, if we lack genuine faith then we repair the emptiness with something temporal, but it never satisfies and there is always something more that we want. The anxiety of our attachment is the sign that we're grasping the wrong thing. If we use an object, some prized possession, to fill the void, then when we lose that object we feel like we've lost ourselves. If we fill the void with our status, a job or position in some social organization, then when we lose that our sense of identity crumbles. If we are attached to our health and physical fitness, it is certain we will lose that too. We want to base our faith on permanence, but nothing temporal is permanent. We can attempt an escape into nonattachment, using nothing to fill the void, but such efforts violate human nature. Everyone is attached to something, even sometimes the idea of nonattachment.

We cannot not be attached, for good reason. We were designed to be attached, not to a temporal good that inevitably fades away, but to the goodness that is grounded in eternity. "For where your treasure is, there your heart will be also." If your treasure is in this world, your heart and your entire sense of being will be there too, and the existence of both you and your treasure will be constantly threatened. If your treasure is in the eternal, you will have something that never dies.

A Samaritan woman came to draw water from a well. Jesus told her: I can give you "living water." This is a play on words, for in both Hebrew and Greek the phrase "living water" actually means "running water." The woman takes it in this pedestrian sense and asks, "Sir, you have no bucket, and the well is deep. Where do you get that living water?" (John 4:11). But Jesus means it literally. He replies: "Everyone who drinks of this water will be thirsty again, but those who drink of the water that I will give them will never be thirsty. The water that I will give will become in them a spring of water gushing up to eternal life" (John 4:13–14).

Those who grasp onto anything temporal for their faith will not be satisfied. They will continue to thirst. But we cannot not be attached. We must grasp onto something, and Jesus offers us the water that becomes a "spring gushing up to eternal life."

But what is this exactly? Just what is this "treasure in heaven" that cannot be consumed? It must be more than a theological abstraction, or else it would be useless. It must, in fact, be something very simple.

THE BASIS OF GENUINE FAITH

It is most amazing that even if we feel we have no faith to which we can point, we still possess a sense of goodness. We may feel there is no God, there is no redemption, there is no meaning to life, there no sense to anything, but still be able to recognize goodness and to conceive that some things are good and others not.

"Goodness" can have different senses. We may call something good if it serves its intended purpose well: a good hammer drives in a nail with minimal effort and won't fall apart in your hand. We may call something good if we benefit from it in some way, if it is good for us, like winning the lottery. Or we may call something good because it has intrinsic value. Kindness is good. Compassion is good. Beauty, truth, and justice are good. And these remain good even if we have no faith, even if nothing makes sense and things threaten to fall apart.

It is only this latter sense of good, of having intrinsic value, that concerns us here and that is relevant to faith.

Our ability to perceive this value in goodness, even if we feel completely without faith, is a light cutting through the void. It tells us there is still meaning in spite of meaninglessness, sense in spite of senselessness. It is a sign of the eternal. Therefore it is a source of faith.

If we need an attachment to something, we can attach ourselves to goodness, to seeking it and knowing it and practicing it, which is the pursuit of a lifetime. Goodness is still good, even if our God has vanished and we are left alone in the void. What makes goodness good? It can be nothing else but God. Through the persistence of goodness—even if it exists only as a hope not yet realized—God appears even after the God of received faith has disappeared. This is the seed of genuine faith.

Knowing goodness even just enough to feel and grieve its absence means that goodness is still real for us. In truth there is no place or moment where goodness cannot be. If deprivation, emptiness, and suffering can be met with compassion, even where there is no hope, then there is still love, and if there is love, then there is still God. Even in grief we still experience goodness; otherwise we would feel only indifference. Grief is our conviction that goodness is real, but unreachable. It is still an experience of goodness, in a paradoxical way. And God, being Goodness Itself, is present in this experience. The "abyss," the "void," the "dark night of the soul" are all ways of pointing towards the experience of God in what we think is the loss of God but is really our sense of goodness remaining with us and driving us towards God. "The light shines in the darkness, and the darkness did not overcome it" (John 1:5).

RELATIVE AND ABSOLUTE GOOD

Expressions of goodness are intrinsically valuable, but they are not absolute. Truth is not good if telling the truth exposes an innocent person to danger. Justice when not tempered with mercy is not always good. Compassion is not good if applied in a way that encourages an attitude that anything goes, that having hurt others is inconsequential, and that forgiveness erases all responsibility. Beauty too is not absolute: art, music, and literature, even when truly beautiful, can still be used contrary to love or even to attack others (an example would be some early passion plays, or much nationalistic music expressing the superiority of one race or nation).

Even the holy grail of goodness in much of psychology and religion—unconditional love—is not always good. It is not good to receive others with the same love and acceptance no matter what they do to each other. Sometimes mercy must be tempered with justice. Even if our response is tough love, it is still modified by conditions. The Jewish sage Maimonides stated (*Guide to the Perplexed* 3:39) that "Compassion for the wicked is cruelty to all creatures."

Yet in all these ambiguous cases good is not negated; it is only modified by another good. Concealing the truth to protect the innocent is a modification of truth by both love and justice. Relaxation of a harsh judgment, even if deserved, if it encourages repentance and rehabilitation, is a modification of justice by compassion. Holding people responsible for their hurtful actions, even when we would rather simply release the offender, is a modification of compassion by justice. How do we know which good should prevail in a given situation? Is there some unconditioned good that stands over and above all these relative goods, guiding us to make the decision?

There is but one Absolute Good and that is God, and is beyond human understanding. We don't have the wisdom to make judgments of goodness with absolute certainty. Our sense of goodness is fallible and tinged with ambiguity. But there is one good accessible to human beings, which appears free of any conditions. It is not unconditional love but *non-self-interested love*.

As we have already defined it, non-self-interested love is *the awareness of the individuality of others*. On the deepest level this awareness leads to respect and reverence for each person's individuality, and engenders the desire for the other's well-being that we associate with love. Non-self-interested love is the standard by which all other goods are judged. It helps us to see what combination of justice and mercy will most benefit both the offender and the victim, or what other good should be applied to any situation for the greatest benefit. We have not yet evolved to where we can apply this standard consistently on a societal level, but we can practice it in our individual lives, and it can inform the judgments we are constantly called upon to make in our dealings with others.

And so the fact that some goods are relative does not mean that genuine faith is relative. All goods are unified in the one Absolute Good, beyond understanding yet still approachable in the greatest good that human beings can know, which is non-self-interested love.

ATTAINING GENUINE FAITH

Genuine faith is the awareness of the power of eternity. The existence of goodness in spite of all the threats to our well-being—indeed, the existence of goodness at all—is a sign of the eternal. We find genuine faith through our relation to goodness.

This awareness needs to be cultivated. Jesus gave us a striking image, meant to shake us into this awareness:

> *The land of a rich man produced abundantly. And he thought to himself "What should I do, for I have no place to store my crops?" Then he said, "I will do this: I will pull down my barns and build larger ones, and there I will store all my grain and my goods. And I will say to my soul, Soul, you have ample goods laid up for many years; relax, eat, drink, be merry." But God said to him, "You fool! This very night your life is being demanded of you. And the things you have prepared, whose will*

> *they be?" So it is with those who store up treasures for themselves but are not rich toward God.* (Luke 12:16–21)

In this parable Jesus is telling us where to seek the foundation of faith. The foundation of faith is very much like the foundation of a house. It is invisible, yet supports the entire structure, and if it is faulty the house cannot stand.

> *Everyone then who hears these words of mine and acts on them will be like a wise man who built his house on rock. The rain fell, the floods came, and the winds blew and beat on that house, but it did not fall, because it had been founded on rock. And everyone who hears these words of mine and does not act on them will be like a foolish man who built his house on sand. The rain fell, and the floods came, and the winds blew and beat against that house, and it fell—and great was its fall!* (Matthew 7:24–27)

The sand in this parable is the temporal good that perishes, the drink that leaves one still thirsty, the earthly wealth, power, and glory of the fisherman's wife. The rock is the good that endures because it originates in the eternal and brings us back to it.

To sense the difference more vividly, here is a mental exercise, or meditation: Imagine yourself standing at the gates of eternity, after the brief instant of this earthly life is over. What good will you still have with you? And what will have vanished like the wind? Job said: "Naked I came from my mother's womb, and naked shall I return there" (Job 1:21), but this is not the whole truth. The spiritual good that we have known and shared does not disappear and is with us always, "where neither moth nor rust consumes and where thieves do not break in and steal."

Earlier we mentioned the Eastern view, exemplified in Buddhism, that we suffer because we do not realize the impermanence of things. We can now take the discussion a little further. We cling to impermanent things for security and fulfillment, and they always disappoint because they always change and disappear. Everything around us is impermanent. We cannot reach enlightenment before we understand this. In the Buddhist view, wisdom consists in realizing the inherent emptiness of everything we touch, see, and experience, which we have taken to be substantial, mind-independent realities.

There is much real insight in this view. We suffer from seeking permanence in what is transitory and fleeting. But from Judeochristianity's perspective there is something more. We cannot not cling to something. What we really seek is eternal. Not aware of this, however, we believe we are seeking permanence. *The permanent becomes a substitute for the eternal*, actually a counterfeit of it. We look for security in permanence, in the hope of something that will last, in "happily ever after." But nothing in the temporal world lasts. Our possessions, our relationships, our health, all come and go—just as Job discovered as he lost each of these one by one.

So while the Eastern answer to this dilemma is enlightened wisdom, penetrating to the emptiness of all things, the Western answer is faith. The Eastern approach seeks liberation from attachment through the realization of emptiness. This may take years, even a lifetime of discipline, and even then it may not come, requiring many, many more lifetimes to attain. The Western approach seeks redemption from suffering through faith. This faith is grounded in conscious connection to the eternal, seeing the goodness that endures rather than relying on temporal substitutes.

To find this faith we don't need a system of esoteric practices. What we need most is to make one basic decision: to commit our lives to the knowledge and practice of the greatest good of all that is possible for human beings to know, which is non-self-interested love. Non-self-interested love is the only unconditional good that is humanly knowable; therefore knowing, expressing, and being this love is the closest we can come to knowing God, as God is Absolute Goodness. The closer we come to non-self-interested love, the closer we come to awareness of the eternal, which is faith.

We build faith through the appreciation and practice of goodness. Appreciation of good in any form contributes to faith, but by far the good that strengthens faith most is non-self-interested love. As a direct expression of God it brings us to the eternal, and hence to faith. For this reason the Bible states that "perfect love casts out fear" (1 John 4:18). It does so by bringing us the awareness of the eternal, and the sense that something beyond our experience knows us and redeems us and has a direct effect on our lives. We are on the path towards genuine faith.

FAITH'S TRANSFORMING POWER

Continuing our comparison of Eastern and Western views, here is another point of contrast: In both religious traditions we are accountable for how we have lived our lives. The Eastern view is more specific than the Western concerning exactly how this works. In that view the consequences of our actions, which take shape as our karma, are visited upon us in successive earthly incarnations. Everything that happens to us that cannot be explained by present conditions is explainable by what we did in a past life. The past determines the present. It is cause-and-effect: what happens in our present life, both good and bad, has been fixed by what we did in the past. There is no room for divine guidance, or for eternity breaking into temporal existence in a redemptive way.

In the Western view, or at least the view taken by Judeochristianity, there is always the possibility—and hope—of the redemptive action of eternity in the midst of time. People often think of "miracles," but no dramatic supernatural occurrence is necessarily involved. Most often we see God's presence in the course and timing of events in our lives in a way that brings us to fulfillment. A great biblical example of this is the story of Joseph.

When Joseph was growing up his father thought he was pretty special, but no one else would have thought so. In fact Joseph seemed quite ordinary. Like most kids he was quite self-centered, and not very mature. He was his father's favorite, and we may imagine this went to his head, since the Bible tells us Joseph tattled on his brothers every chance he got. Joseph certainly suffered for his indiscretions. He was cast into a pit by his brothers, then into a prison in Egypt, and came close to losing his life. Finally he recovered through distinguished service to Pharaoh during a time of widespread famine. Through this long struggle he matured and eventually developed compassion towards his father, his younger brother Benjamin, and even his older brothers who betrayed him.

Joseph did not believe that all these events of his life were coincidences. He had been left for dead, yet he attained a position of influence and renown, and became able to help his family through the crisis. When he is finally united with his brothers in Egypt, and after he reveals his true identity, he makes this important statement: "Do not be afraid! Am I in the place of God? Even though you intended to do harm to me, God intended it for good, in order to preserve a numerous people, as he is doing today" (Genesis 50:19-20).

There is always the possibility of the unexpected, of some unseen guiding power helping to shape the course of our life's events, through perfectly natural means. Events that seem meaningless or even tragic at the time they occur may, later on, reveal a deeper and even redemptive significance. There is never any guarantee, but there is hope. What are the best conditions for this hope? Paul says, "We know that all things work together for good for those who love God" (Romans 8:28). To love God means to cherish goodness, the highest form of which is devotion to the realization of non-self-interested love. If we make this commitment, we have the greatest hope of witnessing God's redemptive action in our lives. This is a matter of faith.

We can explain this by saying that since God is Absolute Goodness and the highest good is love, when this love—specifically divine-like, non-self-interested love—is present in our hearts, God sees that aspect of divinity within us and responds to it. It is God's own nature recognizing itself. "God is love, and those who abide in love abide in God, and God abides in them" (1 John 4:16).

Ultimately this is what is meant by "covenant." The biblical Covenant is a promise, a reciprocal relationship between God and human beings: "They shall be my people, and I will be their God" (Ezekiel 14:11, 37:23). The reciprocity is expressed by God's becoming more visible in our lives as God becomes more present in our hearts. As we cultivate the kind of love that is like God, we have the hope of experiencing God's redeeming presence.

Knowing this, however, can fill us with dread rather than hope. Who can possibly come close to non-self-interested love? Can one even conceive of any human action without self-interest? Nobody can perfectly realize non-self-interested love. To do so would mean we had no human nature but only a divine one. If we already had to be perfect, there would be no point in a spiritual path. Scripture acknowledges this: "All have sinned and fall short of the glory of God" (Romans 3:23). But the divine response to this existential fact is not judgment but compassion:

> *As a father has compassion for his children,*
> *so the Lord has compassion for those who fear him.*
> *For he knows how we were made;*
> *he remembers that we are dust.*
> (Psalm 103:13–14)

We are not expected to realize this love perfectly, but only to make it a priority and to follow it as best we can. In *Sayings of the Fathers* (2:16) Rabbi Tarfon states: "You are not obligated to complete the task, but neither are you free to desist from it." We are not realized saints; we are pilgrims on the path, which is all that God requires of us.

Nor does falling under the divine Covenant guarantee we will have an easy time. That is not what we are promised. Joseph certainly didn't know where he was going for a long time before he got there. Even Jesus suffered terribly before his destiny was fulfilled. We cannot expect a life without pain, but only that (ultimately) "all things work together for good."

> *When you pass through the waters, I will be with you; and through the rivers, they shall not overwhelm you; when you walk through fire you shall not be burned, and the flame shall not consume you.* (Isaiah 43:2)

We may still have to pass through the waters, or walk through the fire, but it all becomes part of our destiny. The suffering of Jesus is again the prototype: he knew he would have to suffer, he spoke of it in advance; yet for a while he too was afraid and feared that God had left him. But in the end he saw it all was necessary to bring him to his final transformation. We will never know, in this earthly life, why all the terrible things happen, and there is much for which we may never be compensated. But we will have a sense—maybe not immediately, maybe only much later, but it does come—that God has always been present in our lives, even during our most traumatic experiences. That sense of presence remains with us, "and we will be changed" (1 Corinthians 15:52).

Often we do not see God's action in our lives except in hindsight. After we've gone a certain distance, we can look back and sense an unseen guiding presence that has accompanied us along the way; we can see patterns in the seemingly disconnected events in our lives, and perceive that each one of those events has contributed in some way to the person we were meant to be. That is the fruit faith can bear. Before we reach that point we may have to travel a long time seemingly without direction, or as the Bible puts it, to "wander in the desert." But the moment comes when we feel that God has known us all along.

> *Thus says the Lord:*
> *I remember the devotion of your youth,*
> *your love as a bride,*
> *how you followed me in the wilderness,*
> *in a land not sown.*
> (Jeremiah 2:2)

This is "dark faith": committing ourselves to God's goodness before we know that we too participate in it.

THE LIFE OF FAITH

A life of faith may be full of doubt and fear. But such a life will also know moments of spiritual presence, a growing sense that even in the most desolate times one has never really been alone. Faith—the awareness of eternity's power—tells us of a reality beyond the one in which we suffer, but not totally separate from it. We don't have to wait until the end of this life to know it. It is here already, a part of this life. "The kingdom of God is not coming with things that can be observed; nor will they say, 'Look, here it is!' or 'There it is!' For, in fact, the kingdom of God is among you" (Luke 17:20-21). Time and eternity intersect. Were it not so, there would be no hope except to wait for death. That's why Jesus spoke so much about sowers and harvesters—we begin to harvest the treasures of eternity even within time.

The temporal world is not the only world. The eternal is already present in the temporal.

This is always true, but we suffer because we do not know it. The gift of faith is the grace to know it. Therefore faith is the strongest spiritual resource we can acquire. Awareness of the eternal heals our clinging to temporal substitutes, our attachment to the things of this world that is our greatest source of fear. The more we become blessed with this expanded awareness of reality, the more our lives make sense, even the tragic events, and we come to feel surrounded by God's love.

The Bible has metaphors to describe this. The Kingdom of God is the biblical symbol for eternity, not only as we will eventually know it "face to face" (1 Corinthians 13:12) but also as we can come to know it here on earth. The "new creation" (2 Corinthians 5:17) is the being we become to the extent that we know the Kingdom of God here and now. May we all know the blessing of becoming this new creation!

Just as every tragedy contains a hint of the cross, every good contains a hint of eternity. We build faith by realizing fragments of goodness. The ultimate act of faith is commitment to non-self-interested love in spite of one's present circumstances and as far as one's limited abilities will allow. This basic act is all that is asked of us: "I give you a new commandment, that you love one another, just as I have loved you" (John 13:34). In it are included all the duties we owe to one another—and more, the ability to see others as fellow children of God. We may still have difficulties with others, we may still have enemies, but we strive to perceive their individuality, and even just this inner shift has the power to change our relationship to them. It is the task of a lifetime, but since it is God's will, "the Spirit helps us in our weakness" (Romans 8:26).

The life of faith is mirrored by the cycle of the year: Christmas is the recognition that eternity enters time. Easter is the recognition that eternity transforms time. Advent prepares us for the coming of the divine light with joyful anticipation. Lent prepares us for the transforming of our lives by this divine light, through all our struggles and sorrows. Through faith we come to know what really endures, and this becomes a refuge in times of stress.

> *God*—Absolute Goodness and Steadfast Love—*is our refuge and strength, a very present help in trouble.*
> *Therefore we will not fear, though the earth should change, though the mountains shake in the heart of the sea.*
> (Psalm 46:1–2)

A faith even of this great magnitude is not inconceivable.

The life of faith is the life God intended for us and the life God wants for us. Faith cannot be proven. None of this can be demonstrated through any scientific principle. If it could, we would not have to find it through living, and we could simply know about it instead of growing to become it. But we are invited to live it, to try it, to test it out, and see how it changes our lives. Each individual life must discover it anew; it cannot be given in a pre-wrapped package. It is not an easy path to which we are called, but it is a simple one. Too much theology only complicates it. Jesus gave it all in a single commandment, which is the foundation of spiritual life and of faith.

This world, with all its inescapable suffering and grief, feels like an exile. This journey "to a far country" teaches us what we must learn about love, and therefore about God. But we are all meant to return. God wants to reclaim every single one of us. The way back has been shown. We don't need to see its end. We only need to walk it, and we will find that indeed, God's love is real.

XIX

A NEW CREATION

Blessed are the poor in spirit, for theirs is the kingdom of heaven.
Matthew 5:7

"I AM SO GRATEFUL TO be here in this hospital sitting in this wheelchair. And do you want to know why? Because right here in this chair is where God is."

So said Muriel, 83 years old and dying of cancer, a patient in my hospice. She seemed especially blessed. "I have no pain," she often said. And perhaps more remarkably, she had no fear.

Muriel did know moments of deep discomfort. Not infrequently I would see her holding a plastic basin in front of her mouth. She was prone to fits of vomiting. Still, it never affected her spirit. She always had a "So what?" attitude about it. When you feel God present with you, what's a little thing like vomiting?

Muriel loved music, especially Gospel hymns. She must have known every hymn that ever graced the lips of a worshiper. She would test me: Did I know this one? Did I know that one? And when she succeeded in stumping me she wouldn't let me go until I found the hymn she wanted. My hymnals got a real workout while I was visiting her.

Muriel loved hymns that told stories of persevering faith, and her favorite was one thanking Jesus for having brought her "a mighty long way." Things had not always been easy. Muriel really had come "a mighty long way" to acquire her faith. I wanted to know where her faith came from. She could not easily tell me herself, but her daughter filled in many of the details.

Muriel first learned about faith from her mother. The faith her mother taught her was genuine, rooted in love and expressed in acts of love. When Muriel was a child they had a neighbor, Miss Jane, who was old and frail and who could not feed herself. Muriel's mother prepared meals for Miss Jane and sent Muriel to feed her.

Muriel never forgot Miss Jane. After she grew up and became active in her church, Muriel cooked Thanksgiving turkeys for the homeless people in one of the city's worst neighborhoods. She brought them the dinners herself. And when others came to this country from her native Trinidad and had no place to stay, she would open her own home to them for as long as they needed.

Muriel's final hours were among the most peaceful I have witnessed in my two decades of hospice work. She showed no signs of distress, nor the agony that can afflict people with end stage pancreatic cancer. It was as though God, who was always present with her, had rocked her to sleep.

I have seen this before. Surprisingly often, those who face sickness and death with the most faith and confidence have lived lives of love and service, and the love they shared with others comes back to support them when they need it most.

Muriel was extremely fortunate not only because her faith was genuine and based on love, but also because she learned this faith as a child. Her mother had been a good teacher, imparting the most precious of all resources to help her daughter at critical moments. This is something else I've noticed in my years of hospice work: those patients whose faith was strongest, who were best prepared spiritually and emotionally to deal with their illness, usually learned that faith when they were children.

This poses a dilemma for the rest of us. If we have not learned this faith during our childhood, when we could have absorbed it most easily, how can we learn it now? Even for the most prepared, faith can be a challenge. Accidents and tragedies may leave us feeling there is really nothing beyond ourselves that we can trust and that faith is an illusion. It can certainly seem that way when we observe other people's lives from the outside: we witness their suffering but cannot go inside it to know if they had a chance to find a redemptive meaning. Even if we have faith we may not easily succeed in finding the meaning of our own suffering, and may experience strong doubt and fear. Muriel told me that sometimes when her spirits were low she might feel discouraged, but music always reconnected her to her faith.

Doubt and fear are very much part of the life of faith, and must not be mistaken for signs that a person has no faith. The question is not whether doubt and fear are present, but whether they are victorious. Faith can sometimes be dormant but nevertheless constant, returning to awareness at unexpected moments.

When something shocks us we have a tendency to regress, to go back to the familiar and react in ways that may or may not be the best but that offer the security of what we know. For this reason most people never change their religion. They may strongly believe that the religion of their upbringing just happens to be the only true one—the association with childhood is powerful and hard to break, and the need for the security such certainty provides is strong. When we are under extreme pressure we tend to regress—we take refuge in our roots and fall back into response patterns we learned early, which by now may have become automatic. If we were blessed to have been brought up in faith, then when we return to the past, faith is what we find. If upon revisiting the past we find trauma and fear, then that is what comes back with us to the present.

Jesus saw one man struggling with this, Nicodemus, a Pharisee who wanted to know about faith and who wanted the faith Jesus had.

> Now there was a Pharisee named Nicodemus, a leader of the Jews. He came to Jesus by night and said to him, "Rabbi, we know that you are a teacher who has come from God; for no one can do these signs that you do apart from the presence of God." Jesus answered him, "Very truly, I tell you, no one can see the kingdom of God without being born anew." Nicodemus said to him, "How can anyone be born after having grown old? Can one enter a second time into the mother's womb and be born?" (John 3:1–4)

It is as if Jesus were telling Nicodemus, "If you want real faith, you can't rely on what you've already learned. The circumstances of your birth may not have prepared you for faith. You need to experience a new, spiritual birth." And Nicodemus answers: "But we only have one birth, one childhood. If I've emerged from that childhood without faith, how can I go back?"

Jesus answers, but his answer is a riddle:

> "Very truly, I tell you, no one can enter the kingdom of God without being born of water and Spirit. What is born of the flesh is flesh, and what is born of the Spirit is spirit. Do not be astonished that I said to you, 'You must be born anew.' The wind blows where it chooses, and you hear the sound of it, but you do not know where it comes from or where it goes. So it is with

everyone who is born of the Spirit." (John 3:5–8)

Jesus tells us there is hope, that we need not remain limited by the circumstances of our human birth and childhood. We were intended for faith, and even if we did not learn faith when we were young, it need not be denied to us. But what can it possibly mean to be "born of water and Spirit"?

In the Bible water is a symbol of life. In both Hebrew and Greek, the term for running water is "living water." Water is also a symbol of purification. A rebirth through the Spirit purifies us and gives us life. When a traumatic event jolts us and shakes us but we return to that new birth in place of our human birth, then instead of our childhood fears we find the Spirit of God.

Clearly it will take more than belief to accomplish this. Simply adopting a certain creed will not make us "born again," a term that has unfortunately become a terrible cliché. We require a complete inner transformation—something Paul understood well. He had his own language for it. He called it the "new creation":

> *So if anyone is in Christ, there is a new creation: everything old has passed away; see, everything has become new!* (2 Corinthians 5:17–18)

And elsewhere we read:

> *You have stripped off the old self with its practices and have clothed yourselves with the new self, which is being renewed in knowledge according to the image of its creator.* (Colossians 3:9–10)

We can become a "new self" or a "new creation." How does this seemingly impossible transition take place?

To answer this question we need to return to the meaning of genuine faith, which we defined earlier. Genuine faith is the awareness of the power of eternity. It is conscious contact with a reality beyond the sensible world, which becomes a source of meaning and hope. We find this reality through the awareness and practice of goodness, in all its forms. Each of us must discover it in our own individual life. If we are exposed to others who have genuine faith, we are greatly helped. By the way they live their lives, by their acts of kindness and goodness, and by their response of love to fearful situations, such people show us the face of God. If those people happen to be our parents, or others who raised us and took care of us when we were young, then we are remarkably blessed. We still have to do the work, but we have a tremendous head start. Muriel learned faith from her mother, but she strengthened that faith and made it her own by the love she practiced throughout her whole life.

Many of us are not so blessed. Many of us begin life trained not in faith but in fear. Our primary caregivers may not only have lacked faith, they may have been actively abusive, or our earliest years may have been marked by some other kind of trauma. If this is our experience, finding faith can be extremely difficult. Faith can seem an unattainable ideal once trust has been shattered.

Once again Paul gives us a clue: "... nor height, nor depth, nor anything else in all creation, will be able to separate us from the love of God." (Romans 8:39). And there is also this:

> *I pray that, according to the riches of his glory, he may grant that you may be strengthened in your inner being with power through his Spirit, and that Christ may dwell in your hearts through faith, as you are being rooted and grounded in love. I pray that you may have the power to comprehend, with all the*

saints, what is the breadth and length and height and depth. (Ephesians 3:16–18)

In both places Paul speaks of height *and* depth. Faith is not simply a "peak experience," always accompanied by feelings of spiritual elevation. We can find faith when we are at the lowest, most desperate points of our lives. At precisely those moments we can become most open to faith. As one reads through the Gospels, one discovers a truth that applies today as much as in Jesus's time: Those whose lives were comfortable, who thought they already had faith, were not the ones open to the real message Jesus brought. They may even have thought they knew everything Jesus had to teach—and so they felt no need to change. They may have rejected Jesus, been indifferent to him, or even called him "Lord" (Matthew 7:21, Luke 6:46): all of them tuned him out. No, it was those who felt desperate, who knew they had no faith, who felt rejected by both God and their community: it was those who turned to Jesus in true open-heartedness and poverty of spirit.

We have already met the woman in Luke 7 so despised by others and who despised herself because of her life as a prostitute. Yet Jesus accepted her and loved her without wanting anything from her. This unexpected acceptance shook her so deeply that she could not speak, but could express herself only by washing Jesus's feet with her tears. Faith is born in moments like this.

There is no soul so tormented that faith with its attendant peace cannot enter. Mary was 64 and came to our hospice dying of ovarian cancer. She was suffering from severe dementia and could not speak a coherent word. Some private terror so tortured her that she could only scream. The chaplain entered the room to greet Mary and tapped her lightly on the shoulder. As soon as Mary felt that touch she broke into an ear-piercing shriek, and continued without stopping for several minutes. The chaplain fled the room.

I felt the tension around Mary like an electrified fence forcing me away. I soon discovered exactly what a safe distance was, and I kept it. I just sat in a corner and played my guitar and sang to her screams until they began to subside.

Mary's daughter arrived from out of town. She was heartbroken to see her mother in that condition. I felt her tender love for her mother, and told her I was confident that together we could help her mother find peace. Not surprisingly, Mary's daughter greeted this prediction with skepticism.

We worked together. I lent the daughter a guitar, and she sang sweetly to her mother about surrendering herself to love. When I was alone with Mary I continued using music to create a safe atmosphere around her, a place she could trust. Mary still did not speak a word to me. But one day she was resting her hand against the bed rail, and I placed my own hand close to hers but not touching. Mary took off her watch and placed it gently in my hand. She had finally begun to trust me.

We continued our work, Mary's daughter and I, surrounding Mary with love. Peaceful moments increased, but Mary's demons returned to take revenge. They made their presence known as Mary became agitated and started screaming. I offered her my hand, and this time she reached out and grabbed it and squeezed it hard. She was no longer afraid of me.

Mary's daughter could feel the changes in her mother and spoke to her, telling her she was finally allowing God's love to touch her and God's light to enter her heart. I could now count on the music to bridge the distance between Mary and me. While at first contact she still resisted my approach, after I sat with her for a while in music she would squeeze my hand and even allow me to stroke her forehead. Mary's daughter cried softly as she watched these changes.

The day Mary died her daughter said she felt "a profound sense of peace and beauty in the room." I felt it too. It was the same deep tranquility I have felt at other times when someone has been blessed to make a peaceful transition. This peacefulness came to us, it held us, then invited us to become part of it. In it all else, including time, disappeared. It was the trace of eternity.

This peace is the deepest experience of faith that one can have. In moments like this the eternal enters our experience and we are held by its power. Sometimes it comes only after our last defenses have broken. We may hold fast to such moments to keep them from fading, but as soon as we do so they vanish. Still, we know we have been present in them and we belong to them; we belong to the eternal.

When the boundary between time and eternity breaks, even for just an instant, then we are in faith. It may not be the end of our fears and sorrows; nevertheless, it changes us forever.

What the experiences of Mary and of the woman in Luke 7 have in common is exposure to a different consciousness, a different way of knowing and being. It is the consciousness of Absolute Goodness in the form of infinite love. We know we are in the presence of all-encompassing love, and we are changed. We may call it the "Christ consciousness," since those who came to Jesus for help felt this love transmitted through his presence. Experiencing this consciousness is our key to finding faith if we have lacked faith.

If we have not experienced this consciousness, how can we come to know it? We can look for examples of it, like the above, and meditate on them until we understand them not just with the mind but with the heart. We can wonder what that woman must have felt in Jesus's presence, and perhaps catch some of the mystery of the infinite love people felt when they came to him for healing. And, perhaps most importantly, we can imitate this love ourselves.

The Bible tells us we can do it: "Let the same mind be in you that was in Christ Jesus" (Philippians 2:5). We too can be channels for the Christ consciousness. We may not do it perfectly, but that is not expected of us. "The Imitation of Christ," not "The Duplication of Christ," is the title of a great spiritual classic. We can imitate, however imperfectly, the love we sense through the consciousness of Christ, until it starts to become real to us.

Whenever we are kind and loving in act or in deed, with no expectation of a return but only with awareness of the other's individual circumstances and needs, we are bringing to that person the Christ consciousness. In so doing we contribute not only to that person's healing but also to our own. Note the emphasis on *awareness*: this is not an exercise for do-gooders. Many people do good for selfish reasons, but if our true motivation is the awareness of the individuality of others, we cannot be selfish. Without this awareness, even good intentions can have harmful consequences.

As our awareness grows, we will see people everywhere searching for this love—even if they seem to reject it. I did my internship in music therapy at a hospital for people with neurological disabilities. One patient in my group, Lucille, age 60, was recovering from a stroke. She was angry, and antagonized the other members of the group. "There is not enough love in this hospital!" she would announce, with audible bitterness. She lectured others about their lack of love, which did not inspire them to become more loving. She attacked me too, letting me know quite clearly that she did not trust me and did not like the way I ran the group.

One day on my way to the group I heard a loud crash. I rushed into the meeting room and found Lucille sprawled on the floor. She did not like the position of her chair, but did not trust others enough to ask for help in moving it. So she tried to move the chair herself, even though she could hardly walk. She slipped and banged her head hard on the floor. Fortunately the nurses were able to revive her. She had to be taken to another hospital for treatment, and returned to our group two weeks later.

Even though Lucille was still as ornery as ever, the group members welcomed her back warmly. One of them faced her and said, "You know, there's a lot of love in this group." This time Lucille heard it. She allowed the Christ consciousness to enter her.

On the last day of my internship Lucille was too sick to come to group. I went to her bedside to say goodbye and gave her a copy of the group songbook, in which I had written a personal note. She looked up at me and said, "You really do love me."

That was all she really wanted.

The Christ consciousness is always present, but may seem invisible. We can learn to detect openings for it. Whenever it is asked for, it has an opening. And it is asked for much more often than we realize. Anger often masks a plea for the Christ consciousness, as in the case of Lucille. Learning to see the need, to respond not in kind but with this special consciousness, which is loving awareness, can transform not only the situation but ourselves as well.

When we are in need of faith, when our experience seems to tell us there is no God, this will be our greatest resource. As we contemplate examples of the Christ consciousness—in the Gospels, in our own experience, in the experiences of others—it becomes increasingly a part of us. Then when stress and suffering threaten to break us down, instead of regressing back to the fears of childhood we can fall into the Christ consciousness, which replaces those memories as our refuge in times of crisis.

We can approach this consciousness by always asking, What would it feel like to be in the presence of Christ? What did those people feel, who actually were in Christ's presence? When else have we known such moments? If we are assaulted by self-doubt or self-hatred, we can reverse our position by asking, How does Christ consciousness see us? How would we see someone who has been through what we've been through, if we practiced this consciousness ourselves? Our responses to these questions must come not just from the mind but from the heart. Only then can genuine faith take root in us.

The Christ consciousness, infinite loving awareness, is Jesus's answer to Nicodemus. Through the presence of this consciousness we can become a new creation. We can be born anew. We can discover faith.

XX

A HINT OF A GREATER LOVE

I am with you always, even to the end of the world.
Matthew 28:20

I KNOW OF NO MORE reassuring passage in scripture. We all need to know we are not alone. Being left completely alone, abandoned, is perhaps a child's greatest fear, and one that most of us never outgrow completely.

Sometimes this fear is reawakened by the thought of death. It may be the fear of our own death, or the death of someone we love. After the sudden, violent death of my first wife my childhood fears of abandonment revisited me. The presence of family and friends comforting me was a great resource, but still I needed something more. I would go into open, empty churches and meditate for long periods of time. There is something about the energy inside a church or a synagogue that is healing, that hints of a higher Presence. I needed this kind of comfort too.

One night, about six months after she died, I sensed her presence. I did not literally see or hear anything, but I had an unmistakable sense that she was in the room with me, speaking to me. She told me, at my lowest point, that I need not fear, that my life would be fulfilled. This comforted me greatly, and I carried the moment with me for some time. I would speak to her often in prayer, but in the years since her death I never had such a sense of her presence again.

I have often wondered since about finding a spiritual presence that overcomes even the fear of death. Perhaps it was this desire that led me to work in hospice. For a while I worked in two hospices not far from each other. They were only a few blocks apart, and when I finished my work in one, I would take a short walk to the other.

Patients who cannot speak still often respond to music. There is a facial expression I sometimes see when I first enter the room of a coma patient. The eyes are widely dilated, and the face looks frozen in an expression of fear. The patient, seemingly unconscious, appears to express a fear of being isolated and abandoned. Many times as I have played at the bedside of such patients or just held their hands, I have seen their faces relax and their eyes close slowly to an expression of peace. All I have done is let them feel my presence, letting them know they are not alone.

One day I met a patient whom I will call Fern. She was reading a book, and put it aside to greet me as I entered her room. I played for her a little while, some soft flute music, and she enjoyed it. She made me promise to see her on my next visit.

A week later I went to see her again. Her condition had deteriorated drastically. She was comatose now and moaning, almost screaming in fear. She flailed her arms in movements that seemed uncontrollable. The nurses told me she had been that way all morning. Nothing could calm her down.

I took out my wooden flute and played for her a long, slow, and plaintive Irish folk tune, over and over. I would play for a few minutes, then sit and hold her hand or stroke her face, then play again. After a while she became completely quiet. I stayed with her a few more minutes, making sure she was rested and would continue to rest.

A volunteer came into the room to tell me a patient wanted me to see her. I left Fern to visit the other patient. When I was finished I heard one of the nurses say that Fern had just died. I knew that my music had helped Fern to let go, and I needed to complete my contact with her.

I went back into Fern's room, where she still lay, and I sat by her bed, took her hand, and held it for several minutes. I felt a calm quietness in the room. Finally I left to go to the second hospice.

I walked the few blocks to the hospital where the second hospice was, and entered the lobby. I made my way toward the elevator, and took it to the hospice floor. Just as I was about to step off the elevator, I stopped. I was not ready to resume my work. Something was pulling me: a strong urge to find a quiet place, just to sit and listen. I took the elevator back to the lobby. I went to the meditation chapel, but a service was in progress; it was too noisy. I quickly left and returned to the lobby. An empty chair was waiting in one of the corners, not far from the admitting office.

I felt a deep peace covering me like a blanket, deeper than any peace I have ever known. The room began to look different. I saw as if through a cloud. I heard children next to me, running and talking loudly, and I saw them not as children but as fragmentary expressions of pure love. A wonderfully sweet feeling came: I was not alone; a presence much greater than my own was right there with me. I stayed for a long time.

This feeling of deep peace remained with me for three whole days. During those three days, I took a vacation from time. In everything I did, I felt a loving presence beside me. It was with me, watching over me, assuring me. I could almost hear a voice telling me not to fear, that everything will be all right, that in the end not one of us will be forgotten. I cannot remember experiencing greater joy and reassurance.

I do not know quite what to make of this. I sense, somehow, that Fern and I were helping each other. I helped her prepare to leave her present form of existence, to enter a different world where she would have a new and better home. And I think she was helping me come to terms with my own existence in this world.

I wish I could say this experience transformed me forever. When those three days were over, I missed them greatly. But I know there are moments when one feels an accompanying presence dispelling one's sense of aloneness, and this knowledge endures. We are not always given such moments, but we can pray for them when we need them most.

I used to think that going through a long, protracted terminal illness was the worst fate a human being could suffer. I now know that if such people are surrounded by others who care about them, it can be a time of great resolution and healing. Some of the hospice nurses see death as a different kind of birth, and compare their role to that of a midwife. In being present at the preparation for this rebirth, whether of a stranger or someone close to us, even through our grief we are also affected. We may be just slightly pulled toward the world that the dying person is beginning to enter, just slightly absorbed into an aura of peace. In such moments we can sense the smile of heaven, a hint of a greater love.

XXI

THE HOPE OF RESURRECTION

Since, therefore, the children share flesh and blood, he himself likewise shared the same things, so that through death he might destroy the one who has the power of death, that is, the devil, and free those who all their lives were held in slavery by the fear of death. For it is clear that he did not come to help angels, but the descendants of Abraham.

Hebrews 2:14–16

I went in the wilderness one day to pray,
The angel's watchin' over me, my Lord.
My soul got happy, an' I stayed all day,
The angel's watchin' over me.

Let me tell you, it's all day, all night,
The angel's watchin' over me my Lord,
All day, all night,
The angel's watchin' over me.

As Alqueen sang the old spiritual I listened to the words on their sliding pitches, hitting the "blue" notes, making them cry. This song was a part of her soul.

It is now six months since Alqueen entered the hospital where I was on staff as music therapist. She is in her seventies, but the smoothness of her face belies her age. Alqueen lost her leg due to poor circulation and atrophy, and is slowly learning to walk again with the aid of a prosthesis. The one she has now is too heavy for her, and even though she uses a walker to support herself, her physical therapy sessions end with her in total exhaustion. Still, she beams with pride every time she sets a new personal record for steps taken.

In our music therapy group, Alqueen's voice is always the loudest. She is usually not quite on pitch, but her harmonies still add spice to the singing. Her voice is a picture of her: an expansive person who always has a kind, supportive word when somebody needs one. I wanted very much to know what enabled her to get through her experience of being hospitalized and disabled. I wanted to know the source of her courage. Her answer was distressingly simple: It is God's love.

Knowing that God's love is real, she says, "One can live out one's days without a leg, or without an arm, or whatever one must go through."

From anyone else's mouth, such words might sound like platitudes. But from the simple honesty that Alqueen's presence expressed, I knew that her words were real. In fact it was her presence, more than her words, that answered my question.

It puzzled me how faith enables Alqueen to face what many people would consider the loss of something necessary for them to function, something that forms a part of their identity, even a part of their purpose in living. It has been said that life is a succession of losses. I have worked a lot with people who are elderly, which has made me acutely aware of losses that are commonplace if one just lives long enough: the loss of one's health, the loss of friends, the loss of loved ones.

THE RISK OF OPENING OURSELVES

Working with people who are suffering great losses can be

dangerous. Depression is a contagious disease, especially to those who have a capacity for empathy. One can protect oneself by remaining emotionally distant from such people: this may explain much of the casual cruelty I have often witnessed in hospitals and nursing homes, the cruelty not of outright abuse but of cold neglect and the failure to pay attention. One can hear a certain heartlessness in the voice of the emotionally distant caregiver: the abruptness, the quickness, the reluctance to meet and engage the other person. One can sense the unintentional but often brutal contribution this makes to the loneliness of those who are already isolated.

To join the world of people who are isolated involves risk. It means opening oneself to another's pain. Distance affords protection, but it is the protection of insulation. If we remain beyond the reach of others' pain, they remain beyond the reach of our love.

Becoming witnesses to others' frailty makes us more aware of our own—this is the price of reaching out. To see the losses others have suffered reminds us of the losses we have known or may yet be called upon to face. To be with others in a truly compassionate spirit, we need a way to meet these fearful images that does not isolate us in cold self-protection.

FACING THE POWER OF DEATH

Helping others deal with their losses is a perilous path if we have not learned how to deal with our own. Many people are drawn to a helping vocation because they are acutely sensitive to the fact of loss. This sensitivity, which all of us have in varying degrees, makes us vulnerable to fear. "And free those who all their lives were held in slavery by the fear of death"—this is the greatest fear of all, what the Bible calls fear of the "power of death." This power is the tendency within life itself to undo that which life creates, to bring life's motion to a halt.

We experience this power not only in physical death but in life's more limited losses: the way the passage of time seems to accelerate as we grow older, the physical problems we encounter with greater frequency, the increasing frailty we observe in friends and relatives. And there are other losses that threaten us: the loss of opportunities, the loss of relationships, the loss of familiar surroundings. There is even the potential loss of our destiny, the unique purpose for which each of us was created, whose threatened loss we experience as a sense of emptiness and meaninglessness. A good friend and teacher used to tell me often: Prepare yourself, because everything you now have, you will one day lose.

As we have observed, Eastern religion, and most especially Buddhism, recognizes that suffering originates in attachment to that which is impermanent, which we cannot escape losing. Victory over suffering comes through liberation from desire. Through commitment and self-discipline one can wean oneself away from clinging to what is material and therefore transitory. The resulting state of enlightenment is called *nirvana*. The associated ideal is detached compassion: feeling for the suffering of those still holding on to things that do not last, still enmeshed in the cycle of life and death that seems never to end. This compassion is the product of a wisdom that sees through the illusion of the cycle, and that has learned the true proportion of things.

The Western mind has difficulty comprehending this solution. It thinks not in terms of cycles but of a linear history, an ongoing record of human action in which our involvement is inescapable. The Bible itself uses history as a backdrop for divine revelation. From this perspective, "detached compassion" is a self-contradiction: compassion means "suffering with," becoming actively involved with others' pain, with all its attendant risks. To love is to expose oneself to danger.

In the Western worldview we cannot become unattached; while we might hope to overcome our anxiousness about the things we need (Matthew 6:25), we cannot stop wanting them. To require the cessation of desire is to ask for what is not humanly possible, as well as to snuff out the energy that empowers love. The Western response to the problem of suffering and loss is to embrace the world, not to renounce it. It is not nirvana. It is *resurrection*.

RESURRECTION AS PROCESS

Resurrection with a capital "R" is the climactic event of the New Testament, but the theme of resurrection runs through the Hebrew Bible as well. It is present in the numerous stories of childless women giving birth late in life, in an enslaved people finding a home and the presence of God, in the renewal of hope and confidence after the exile. It is present in Isaiah's great words of comfort during that exile, in Ezekiel's vision of the dry bones gathering and coming to life, and in his vision of the future Temple. It is evident in Job's regaining his health and well-being. The power of resurrection runs throughout biblical history; in fact, it governs that history. It was made evident in the individual life of Jesus and its effect on his disciples, but it was known long before.

Resurrection is not an event, it is a *process*. To understand resurrection only as one single event in history imprisons it in time and makes it remote from us today. Resurrection is an aspect of reality, as real as the power of death, which it balances and ultimately transcends and transforms. Resurrection is not the opposite of death. It is not birth, it is rebirth. It is life *beyond* death, creation *beyond* destruction. It is *the revivifying power* of God.

The term "resurrection" is symbolic. It is borrowed from Jewish apocalyptic literature, writings and speculations that flourished after the prophetic period, claiming to reveal what would happen at the end of time. It therefore does not refer to something whose time is fixed, but to an aspect of reality not visible in ordinary time. The Bible speaks of the "power of death." This power can be observed in time: the progressive weakness of the body and the event of death itself are accessible to the physical senses. Processes associated with "resurrection," the progress of the soul after death, and even the healing and renewal that very often follow grief, are not directly accessible to the senses. Once healing has taken place, we know it, but we do not observe it in the same way that we observe death. For this reason, we may not trust it the way we trust the inevitability of death.

The Bible portrays the timeless aspect of resurrection. The four Gospels agree on the broad outline of Jesus's life and career up to the moment of his death. In fact, three of the Gospels are called "synoptic," meaning they can be "seen together" in parallel columns showing roughly the same sequence of events. However, after Jesus is resurrected, the four Gospels diverge in four totally different directions, even hopelessly contradicting each other if one takes them literally. This is because once we speak of resurrection we are no longer in time. Temporal elements become symbols pointing to that which has meaning only in eternity. The Gospel resurrection accounts are real, but they are not real in time. They are real beyond time, and can be grasped only with the senses of the soul.

Like any symbol, resurrection has a literal meaning that hides a deeper meaning. Resurrection in the deeper sense is not something that happens to the body. It is a transformational process that brings new life out of the worldly process of decay. The Shroud of Turin, for example, has no bearing on the reality of resurrection. Likewise, theologies of resurrection in both Judaism and Christianity that take literally the raising of the physical body are in error and fail to understand the use of temporal symbols to describe eternal reality.

The "ultimate" resurrection is what we conceive may happen "after" death. But the meaning of resurrection is much more than this. The power of resurrection is evident in any renewal following a crisis. It may be seen in any recovery after loss in which we feel assisted by a power greater than ourselves, whether it be the loss of a job, a coveted opportunity, a relationship, or the loss of a loved one through death itself. Jesus was unique because he possessed a prophetic gift through which he knew, almost beyond any possible doubt, that the power of death had no hold over him. "For the ruler of this world is coming. He has no power over me" (John 14:30).

While death is inevitable, resurrection is not. We need to open ourselves to it. In hospice I met a man whose mother was a patient very near death. This man must have been at least in his forties, but he asked all who would listen, "Who will take care of me now?" I was touched when he asked the head nurse to give him a hug. All his life he lived as a loner, depending only on his mother. I suggested that her death may be a challenge to him to begin forming connections with the outside world. I told him not to be ashamed to rely on the support of others, perhaps beginning with his A A group, which he joined long ago but seldom attended. His fate will depend on whether he can live with the uncertainty of radical change.

RESURRECTION AND FAITH

When is despair the end of the road, and when is it a prelude to resurrection? If we need to open ourselves to rebirth before it happens to us, how is this accomplished?

My wife Karen, who is totally blind, told me a story. One night it was raining heavily, and she was waiting to cross the street. Cars were competing impatiently with each other to traverse the intersection, maneuvering for position, paying scant attention to traffic signals. How could she safely weave between those oblivious autos to find the distant curb? The thought entered her mind like a voice that spoke: "Follow your dog." After that her passage was automatic; she needed to do nothing but simply allow herself to be carried by a guiding force beyond herself.

I am legally blind; I have some usable vision, but travel with a cane. Sometimes when I am with Karen I hold her arm and let the dog guide both of us. The difference in sensation is immediate: a cane gives me a sense of control; the dog forces me to give up control. Cane travel is slow and deliberate; with a dog, movement is swift, and a little frightening if one is not used to it. A dog does not lead you in a straight line; it bobs and weaves, avoiding obstacles and people who might be in the way. And yet when it reaches the block's end and stops at the curb you can almost see it. A guide dog user knows what it is like to trust a force one cannot see, a movement that follows a circuitous and sometimes tortured path but that still reaches the destination.

The Bible speaks of trust as the door to deliverance; this is why Jesus so often uses the image of children to illustrate receptivity (Matthew 18:3-4). Noah trusted: he heeded a warning about "events as yet unseen" (Hebrews 11:7). Abraham trusted: he obeyed the instruction to leave all that was familiar behind him, "and he set out, not knowing where he was going" (Hebrews 11:8). Faith is "the conviction of things not seen" (Hebrews 11:1). These acts of trust marked the beginning of a saving and transforming pattern of events.

It would be easy to stop right here—except that life teaches us not to trust. Trouble often comes unexpected; the things we trust so often betray us. As often as not, experience teaches us that simply waiting does not mean things will turn out for the better. If one has trust, one may keep fear at the door. Those for whom trust is difficult are precisely the ones for whom the struggle for faith is so important.

Resurrection means that in giving up even what is vitally important in a spirit of trust, one may witness a transformation. But this cannot happen without the preceding dry period. It does not happen without first experiencing deep uncertainty. If we cannot trust, if we cannot look to the future with confidence and hope, we can still cooperate with the power of resurrection by becoming willing to live with this uncertainty. The willingness to live with uncertainty does not mean one relies on anything or hopes for anything. It only means that one suspends judgment.

To be willing to live with uncertainty may seem difficult if we find trusting difficult. But when trusting, even trusting in God, seems like relying on what is not even there, the willingness to live with uncertainty relies on nothing. It is what we have called "dark faith": faith in its most radical form. Many images in the Bible symbolize trust—the rock, the shield, the good shepherd—but there is one particular symbol of the willingness to live with uncertainty.

HOLY SATURDAY

To be willing to live with uncertainty means living through the dry time, even if it is a long time, as if it were Holy Saturday. The first Holy Saturday must have been a terrible time for Jesus's followers, a time of hopelessness. But at one point Jesus himself used a strange and intriguing image to describe it: "For just as Jonah was three days and three nights in the belly of the sea monster, so for three days and three nights the Son of Man will be in the heart of the earth" (Matthew 12:40). On the first day the destruction occurred; the third day was Easter. The middle day was rest "in the belly of the sea monster": Jonah's refuge, and also an image suggesting impending birth. The middle day was a day of lost hope, but it was also a day of rest; it was the Sabbath. In Jewish apocalyptic the end of time is described as a day that is "completely Sabbath," a paradoxical time when time stops. It is a point of contact with the eternal.

The first Holy Saturday was a time before there had ever been an Easter. The memory of this day is Easter's prelude. As a day in ordinary time, Holy Saturday is a day of fear, or a day of having already given up, a day of darkness. Willingness to be in this day, not to move, to stop with the stoppage of time, can bring the day out of ordinary time. It then becomes a moment of anticipation, though in real time it may last for years. The five young maidens (Matthew 25) observed this Sabbath by watching, waiting, even sleeping, before the delayed appearance of the bridegroom.

Paul also uses the image of impending birth to describe both the pain and the waiting that come with Holy Saturday:

> *We know that the whole creation has been groaning in labor pains until now; and not only the creation, but we ourselves,*

> *who have the first fruits of the Spirit, groan inwardly while we wait for adoption, the redemption of our bodies.* (Romans 8:22–23)

Paul, who spoke about the frailty of living in "earthen vessels," was acutely sensitive to the fragility of existence as flesh and blood. "Who will rescue me from this body of death?" (Romans 7:24) is not just a question but a cry of anguish. For Paul the body is a symbol of human weakness: the needs, the limitations, and the pain that make us utterly dependent on a power greater than ourselves (2 Corinthians 4:7). The position of faith is that this dependence, which is not psychological but existential, has a focal point, a place where it finds a response.

There is nothing we can do that will guarantee our witnessing the power of resurrection. Faith in the form of "believe and you will receive" makes God a servant of our wishes. Can we truly say "Your will be done" without knowing in advance what God's will is? If so, that is faith. It is being open to that which we do not know, even that which might cause us pain. The presence of God—but not the absence of pain—is promised to all those who ask for it.

"For now we see in a mirror, dimly, but then we will see face to face" (1 Corinthians 13:12). This is Holy Saturday: it is waiting in obscurity.

EMBRACING OUR DESTINY

How can we distinguish the pain of labor from the pain of death? Or the darkness that precedes light from the darkness that precedes only more darkness? There is no certain way to know. Perhaps it all begins with the ability to ask a simple but awesome question: What is my path?

At its deepest, this question expresses more than a desire to know something. It communicates a willingness to accept and to encounter one's destiny. The turbulence that engulfs you may not just be an obstacle in your path—it may be your path. Can you see how this might be true? Can you accept it?

The position of faith is that this path can be found. The Lord "makes a way in the sea, a path in the mighty waters" (Isaiah 43:16). Asking for our path means being willing to enter those waters. The path must be there, if it makes sense to ask at all.

> *Are not two sparrows sold for a penny? Yet not one of them will fall to the ground apart from your Father. And even the hairs of your head are all counted. So do not be afraid; you are of more value than many sparrows.* (Matthew 10:29–31)

Either these words make sense, or they don't. And if they do make sense, they do so in the presence of any event that attacks our human frailty. At such moments the only way to make sense of this promise may be to wait.

But it will not be a passive waiting. Waiting in anticipation of the response for which we were created is active faith. It is working with our destiny. And waiting through pain for the sake of a higher value is an act of love.

The enemy is doubt in the existence of that higher value. This doubt is always potentially present, a powerful destroyer of confidence. But doubt belongs to uncertainty. The willingness to live with uncertainty, in its deepest existential sense, looks at this doubt and accepts it without protest. By joining this doubt, it joins the world. It becomes an act of love, and so while the uncertainty remains, it does not become emptiness.

THE CROSS REDEEMED

Understanding resurrection in purely physical terms runs the risk of diminishing its significance. Resurrection is more, not less, than a physical event. It might take expression in the physical world, but it does not belong to this world. Resurrection is the power of eternity breaking into this world, surprising us, healing us, redeeming us. It is God's presence having become perceptible to us. It is the evidence of salvation.

Once faith becomes love, we are on the path toward resurrection. A faith that waits on Holy Saturday, that willingly lives with uncertainty, that imposes no demands, and that does not flee the cross—can we not say such faith "hopes all things, endures all things"? So does love (1 Corinthians 13:7). When we reach love, we realize God's image. And God always responds to this image, by giving us a sense that God is present, that we are not alone. The way to prepare for resurrection is to prepare our hearts to love.

To ask with open-hearted sincerity for our path, for God's will, means it will be shown to us—this is the Bible's promise. It might not be what we would choose for ourselves. Faith is the hope that what is destined for us is ultimately better than our own choices, because a wisdom greater than our own never lets us alone and is constantly challenging and shaping us. This hope becomes knowledge only at the moment of resurrection, when we can look back at time and begin to understand what our experiences have meant. Until that moment, it is still hope, and hope can exist only in the presence of uncertainty.

But in this hope we can still find rest, if we can allow ourselves to consider whatever may happen to us as part of our destined path. No danger is so total as to preclude absolutely the hope of resurrection, a resurrection that may occur at any moment, even as late as the moment of death itself. And then we witness a shift in the meaning of time. It is no longer the inexorable measure of decline. It is the bringer of restoration.

All the different hints of resurrection we may know in this life, if we are attentive to them and are grateful for them, prepare us for the final Resurrection with a capital "R": the moment beyond time when eternity reclaims us. Then faith, "the conviction of things not seen," passes away, as goodness itself becomes our reality and we finally see "face to face." The goodness we sense now speaks to us of the home to which we will return. This is our hope.

About the Author

Charles "Carlos" Gourgey, PhD, LCAT, MT-BC, is a board certified and New York State licensed music therapist. He has over 20 years of experience working in hospices and nursing homes, and for 10 years was Music Therapist for Cabrini Hospice in New York City. He has published articles on psychology and religion in various journals, notably *Modern Psychotherapy, Hospice Magazine, Spiritual Life, Clergy Journal, Pulpit Digest, Fellowship in Prayer*, and *Journal of Religion, Disability, and Health*.

His wife Karen directs the Computer Center for Visually Impaired People at Baruch College in New York City. Together they perform together under the name FolkSpirit and have offered seminars on disability and religion at Stony Point, Ghost Ranch, and Montreat Conference Centers.

You may contact the author at carlos@judeochristianity.org.

www.ingramcontent.com/pod-product-compliance
Lightning Source LLC
Chambersburg PA
CBHW020346170426
43200CB00005B/66